Happiness is...

Morning Must-Have Breakfast Bars p.141

Dedicated to you Dear Readers,
May you learn to live a life of absolute
wellness and bliss by learning to cook,
eat and feel healthy and vibrant!
To my Master, Angels and Spirit Guides
who have guided my creative and
cooking efforts with their infinite
gentleness and wisdom and
to my Earth Angels, Bharat & David

Contents

Introduction

Dear Reader, allow me to introduce myself so that you can get a feel for who I am and why I wrote this book.

Let me start by saying that I am a self-proclaimed nutritionist. I have had no formal training in nutrition. You see I am so passionate about health and eating right that I find that sometimes when I attend lectures by certified holistic nutritionists, I actually end up knowing more about what they're teaching than they themselves. This is probably due to the fact that I have been self-studying nutrition and health for over 20 years. I first started speaking about the dangers of aspartame and fluoride in 1999! This was way before this information was in the common media.

In fact, in 2013 I was tossing the idea of enrolling in a nutrition certification course, and I decided to take their entrance exam. I am proud to say that I made an 89/100, needless to say I didn't even study!

So you may ask why am I telling you all this? Well because you will find in this cookbook lots of information on health and nutrition, so I wanted to be upfront with you and let you know that I am no trained professional, but I definitely know how to lead a "healthy life"!

As far as my culinary skills go, I have had some formal training in Thailand in the Spa Resorts Raw Food Centre. Most of my cooking skills, however, have come from spending time in restaurant kitchens with great chefs in Hong Kong who also happened to be close friends of mine. Then there was a very dear chef who prepared meals for my family, she was our family housekeeper – a demure little lady called Atoi Ho – who happened to be a dynamo in the kitchen! I spent many hours watching her as she prepared our daily meals. Food was always gourmet with Atoi! And of course growing up I watched my mother cook – and she was an oh-so-fabulous cook too – so many of my skills come from my awesome mother.

In America you only seem to be recognized if you are certified this and certified that, but I think real world experience speaks volumes. So for whatever it's worth, here I am with decades of world experience and self-study, writing this cookbook and health manual to help you dear reader to live a better, more vibrant lifestyle.

I love cooking and everything it symbolizes – a time for bringing friends and family together. I love seeing people's mouths water when they prepare to feast on my new culinary creations. But best of all, when one cooks, and if that meal can make everyone happy – herbivore, omnivore, carnivore – then all the better! This is why in 2009 I started to teach vegan cooking classes.

> The kitchen is my playground, my own laboratory. I have several experiments bubbling and brewing all the time, which end up becoming delicacies that I teach to my students.
> Each recipe is truly tried and tested.

I take pleasure in re-vamping popular international dishes or creating some new renditions from all over the world, that are easy to make and truly delectable. Each recipe is truly tried and tested in my vegan cooking classes. A lot of people approach vegan food with hesitation thinking it's only going to be salads or some bland dishes, but after eating my food, they definitely change their mind! At my vegan cooking classes I get students that are vegan, vegetarian, and my all-time favorite, veggie-curious. At every class the vegan dishes have left them awestruck, smacking and licking their lips, as they savor the food samples at the end of the class and come back for seconds and thirds! Even the veggie-curious people have gone home with "happy tummies" having their own worlds open up to a great new journey of veganism!

I follow a different food theme at every class. Some previous themes have been: "Singapore See-Food Creations", "Fantastique French Fare", "Breakfast of the Champions", "Awesome Rawsome" etc., and my students inspire me to continue to develop new and exciting world recipes. In every class my husband and I also conduct a mini-health seminar, as we stir and prep the dishes. We cover the health benefits of the key ingredients and teach people how to make healthy swaps. So this cookbook and health guide is like an extended manual of our many cooking classes.

I love it when students tell us how much healthier and better they feel after making the healthy swaps that we have introduced in our classes. We feel especially happy when students share how their non-vegan family enjoyed the dishes that they prepared from the recipes we taught. At moments like that I am so grateful that I have been given the opportunity to teach people how to cook especially because this is "compassionate cooking" and helping save the animals, save the planet, and save ourselves.

Throughout the book you will notice several icons.

After most recipes, you may see 🐷😊 where I have included health and beauty benefits of the key ingredients in each dish. Then you might see 🐷 where I give you interesting facts about something. Sometimes when you see 🐷 I have given you some helpful hints which will make the cooking process easier and more fun. Then there's 🐷 which is my recommendations of how to enjoy the dish in its best capacity. If a recipe is raw, you will see 🌿 and if a dish can be made gluten-free you will see **GF** . If you are looking for metric conversions to any of the measurements, go to tables on page 19.

Many recipes in this book call for store-bought ingredients e.g. puff pastry sheets, seitan etc, I do this because I like to keep my cooking experience quick and easy for those who feel overwhelmed by making everything from scratch.

In every recipe I also give you a "Suggested Shopping List", please note that these are mere suggestions and I don't work for these companies and am not promoting one product over another – you are always free to choose your own favorite brands if you prefer.

Also since a lot of vegan food seems to be comprised of soy, where I can help it, I like to use non-soy versions of certain pre-fab products e.g. the non-soy versions of vegan mayonnaise and vegan buttery spread. Additionally, where I can help it I like to use organic and certified non-GMO verified 🦋NON GMO Project VERIFIED ingredients unless I absolutely cannot find organic versions of them.

I have also shared with you information on home remedies and recipes on beauty treatments that have been in my family for generations. I hope you can benefit from these as much as all those I have shared them with have.

Lastly, I have added a section called "Let's talk a little about Ayurveda". I love this Healing Tradition, and so the little information that I know on this very vast topic, I have shared with you. I hope you will find it both interesting and enlightening!

Use this book to have fun, heal yourself, and enjoy the kitchen to the fullest! My recipes are designed to help you build confidence to allow you to prepare tasty, gourmet, restaurant-quality meals. I teach recipes from all over the world because in Hong Kong, I learned to cook that way. Plus I want to show people how flavorful and diverse vegan food can be.

For every recipe I try my best to give you an option for a gluten-free version of the dish – just see the substitution after the symbol **GF** . Many of the recipes are completely gluten-free too! I personally lost 5 pounds right off the bat just by adopting a gluten-free diet.

I hope this book appeals to many tastes. I have tried to include a little bit for everyone, from day to day staples to more exotic dishes. I have included many vegan versions of popular meat favorites as well e.g. Beef Stroganoff, Rendang, Reuben, Spaghetti Bolognese, and many more. So if you have been searching far and wide for a vegan version of your favorite dish to no avail, then hopefully this cookbook will give you the boost you need to veganize it on your own – ending up with a meal that's healthier and friendlier to animals and the planet than the non-vegan equivalent.

Thank you for taking the time to enjoy Veganize and Heal Your Life – All the best to you in Your Culinary World!

Love, Light & Laughter
Chef Neeta Sanders

Here's what our students are saying about us:

"Hello, Neeta. My 12 year old son and I were in the veggie-curious group. We traveled 2½ hours through the rain and were not disappointed at all. You and your family made a wonderful team to show that cooking healthy is a family affair. Although my son prefers Meat Lover's Pizza, he did taste all the dishes without making the "I'm going to die from veggie overload" face I usually get. Thanks again. Many blessings on your new book offering."

~Carolyn H.
Perry, GA – Dec 16, 2013

"Neeta, I was inspired by you and your family. I would like to learn more ways to make raw food choices. I stared at you the whole time, because your skin is beautiful. I can't believe that you and your husband have a college bound student. I was glad that I made it to this meeting. Great insights and great tasting desert. I am a chocolate lover, and am glad to have a new recipe for dessert – Avocados chocolate mousse. I also enjoyed the coconut cookies. Thank you!"

~S.B
Duluth, GA – May 20, 2013

"I love the Vegan cooking classes offered!! Each recipe is easy, understandable, and modifiable. Most importantly, it is much more than just a Vegan cooking class, but also an educational class where the discussing covers what to look for when purchasing an ingredient. It is a real eye-opener when ingredients we think are safe are generally not the safest option."

~Vanessa L.
Atlanta, GA – May 20, 2013

"I specially wanted to attend this class because I did not know what to do with Tempeh. I could not make it palatable any which way I tried. It was delicious the way you prepared it. Thanks to you, now I have recipes I like for Tempeh."

~S. Stewart
Tucker, GA – February 13, 2012

"I really enjoyed your presentation and look forward to future demonstrations. The information you shared related to utensils, ingredients, retailers, etc. was very informative. I also like the way you had your video set up so the audience could see the detailed preparation and cooking. Very professional. Keep up the good work!!"

~Felicia
Atlanta, GA – December 13, 2011

"This class was a lot of fun. The instruction was informative and inspiring--I'll definitely be trying out the recipes. The final dishes were delicious."

~Leslie B.
Atlanta, GA – August 16, 2010

SIPS AND SLURPS

SMOOTHIES & SHAKES
APPLE PIE SMOOTHIE   148
PUMPKIN PIE SMOOTHIE   148
ORANGE & KALE CREAMSICLE   148
STRAWBERRY DREAM SHAKE   149
CARIBBEAN COOLER   149
CURE A COLD CHARM   149
HAWAIIAN FUN IN THE SUN   150
MANGO MAGIC   150
PBJ SANDWICH DRINK   150
POM-CHERRY BLAST   150

JUICES & ELIXIRS   151
KOMBUCHA
CARROT GINGER APPLE
APPLE CUCUMBER CELERY
TOMATO CARROT APPLE
BITTER GOURD APPLE & NON-DAIRY MILK
ORANGE GINGER CUCUMBER
PINEAPPLE APPLE WATERMELON
PEAR AND BANANA
CARROT APPLE PEAR MANGO
HONEYDEW GRAPES WATERMELON NON-DAIRY MILK
PAPAYA PINEAPPLE & NON-DAIRY MILK
BANANA PINEAPPLE & NON-DAIRY MILK

SOUPS

CREAM OF BROCCOLI   22
FRENCH ONION   23
IRISH POTATO LEEK   24
MINESTRONE SOUP   25
PERSIAN RED LENTIL SOUP   26
RAW TOMATO   27
RAW VEGETABLE ENERGY   27
QUICK RUSSIAN BEET BORSCHT   28
TOM YUM SOUP   29

APPETIZERS

BABA GANOUSH   32
Fire-roasted eggplant dip blended with creamy tahini,
garlic and aromatic herbs and spices

BASIL ROLLS   33
Delicate fresh rice spring roll skins filled with chunks of
spicy seitan, fresh basil, sautéed tangy mixture of
cabbage and carrots, and rice noodles

BARBECUED TOFU   35
Succulent slabs of marinated tofu bursting with flavor
grilled to sizzling perfection

WHAT WOULD YOU LIKE TO COOK TODAY?
MENU

BEAN DIP 36
Savory refried beans with southwest seasonings and melted vegan cheese

FALAFELS 37
Fried golden crispy lentil balls served in pita bread and topped with Tzatziki sauce

FRIED "MOCK" CHIK'N 38
Compassionate version of southern fried chicken. Chunks of crispy seitan strips that pack a big crunch in every bite

GUACAMOLE 39
Creamy chunky irresistible ripe avocado dip

HUMMUS + SUN-DRIED TOMATO HUMMUS 40
Two versions of a hearty dip made with a blend of garbanzo beans, sesame seeds, lemon juice, garlic, and aromatic spices with a hint of olive oil and a variation with sun-dried tomatoes and basil

KALE CHIPS – CURRY & SOY SESAME 41-42
Raw crispy hot curry and Oriental soy sesame kale chips – munch on some healthy crunch

KATI ROLLS/FRANKIES 43
Intoxicatingly flavorful soy protein granules seasoned with Indian spices and stuffed into a roti paratha (puffed bread)

MEATLESS MEATBALLS 44
Succulent, spicy, sweet and sour meat-less balls of absolute delight which can be eaten as they are, in a submarine sandwich on hoagie bread or with a bed of spaghetti

MILLET BURGERS 45
Shallow fried patties of cooked millet and mixed vegetables seasoned with Indian spices and herbs served with or without a bun

ONION PAKODAS 46
Crunchy, crispy golden brown onion fritters

POTATO BURGER PATTIES 47
A great alternative to soy burgers – try these hearty mashed potato patties delicately flavored with fragrant herbs and spices

SALSA-FRESH 48
Fresh Salsa made with delicious red ripe tomatoes, peppers and fresh cilantro

SAMOSAS 49
Flaky puff pastry stuffed with savory potatoes and green peas seasoned with pungent Indian herbs and spices

SPANAKOPITA 50
Flaky Pastry Triangles filled with a savory spinach mixture baked to perfection

SPANAKOPITA WITH VEGAN FETA 51
Whole wheat flaky phyllo pastry loaded with savory spinach, tomatoes, pine nuts, tofu, and fragrant herbs

SPRING ROLLS 52
Spicy savory cabbage and carrot mix wrapped in a thin crackly crisp shell

SUSHI 54
Five Bite-sized morsels of Japanese bundles of Joy
   a. "Piinatsu maki" – Peanut roll
   b. "Abokado Creamchīzu maki" – Avocado and soy cream cheese roll
   c. "Kariforunia maki" – Vegan California roll (with spinach, carrots, seaweed seitan)
   d. "Kappa maki" – Cucumber roll
   e. "Vegan Hamu maki" – Vegan ham and dollops of vegan mayonnaise roll

SALADS

BEET & CARROT 58
A pretty in pink raw medley of two roots – a combination of sweet, sour and salty

GREEK MILLET 59
A spicy and tangy Mediterranean salad made with healthy millet

PINEAPPLE CHIK 60
A creamy pasta salad with diced celery, chunks of sweet pineapple and savory seitan tossed with raisins and blanched almonds

POTATO 61
Creamy classic potato salad made with vegan mayonnaise and tossed with mustard, peppers, scallions, celery, seasoned with parsley and dill

PROBIOTIC COUSCOUS/QUINOA 62

Cooked couscous or quinoa (your choice) tossed with a medley of vegetables and nuts flavored with garlic and curry and mixed with the probiotic goodness of raw sauerkraut and fermented cucumbers

SEAWEED 63

Wakame seaweed, tossed with garlic, sesame oil, scallions and soy sauce topped with raw sesame seeds, cashews and cranberries

SANDWICHES

BEEF-LESS SOFT TACOS 65

Marinated "TVP" – textured vegetable protein sautéed with onions and bell peppers simmered in a zesty sauce infused with tomatoes, cilantro, cumin and melted vegan cheese served on flour tortillas

BREAKFAST BURRITOS 66

Zesty southwest tofu scramble sautéed with peppers and onions, hash brown potatoes and a touch of salsa, dollops of vegan sour cream wrapped in flour tortillas.

CHIK'N SALAD SANDWICH 67

A mixture of celery and onions sautéed in vegan butter tossed with faux chik'n (made of seitan) topped with granny smith apples and raisins and a touch of vegan mayonnaise seasoned with exotic spices like caraway, cumin and anise on Irish soda bread or sourdough bread

CHIK'N TANDOORI WRAPS 68

A wholesome wrap filled with seitan, veggies, fruit, nuts seasoned with Tandoori and Tulsi (Holy Basil)

COLLARD GREEN WRAPS WITH NUT PÂTÉ 69

Fresh collard green leaves smeared with a tangy lemon nut pâté or a sundried tomato and macadamia nut pâté wrapped around the goodness of avocados, tomatoes, carrots and other nuggets of raw happiness

DULSE POTATO ROLLS 70

Fluffy flour tortillas rolled and filled with a palatable potato, cilantro and dulse mixture simmered in fragrant Indian spices topped with vegan cheese

EGGLESS EGG SALAD SANDWICH 71

A creamy delectable faux egg preparation (made with tofu and aromatic herbs and spices), topped with chunks of avocado, tomatoes, lettuce and sprouts on a crispy baguette

FISH-LESS SPICY SOFT TACOS 72

Pan fried vegan fish strips with a mildly spicy cabbage and scallions relish infused with a chili garlic sauce and topped with creamy avocados and fragrant cilantro on flour tortillas

QUICK QUESADILLAS 73

Spinach, bell peppers, salsa and melted vegan cheese stuffed in flour tortillas and then skillet fried

ROASTED EGGPLANT & TOFU PITA-WICH 74

Roasted eggplant seasoned with zesty sauces topped with pan-fried tofu and melted vegan cheese stuffed into pita pockets

TANDOORI FAUX CHICKEN PITA POCKETS 75

Faux Chicken (Seitan) marinated in a mouth watering cultured coconut mixture blended with tandoori spices, then sautéed with peppers and onions served in pita pockets drizzled with a Vegan Tzatziki dressing.

TEMPEH REUBEN 76

Slabs of marinated tempeh on a bed of raw sauerkraut slathered with Russian dressing grilled to perfection on foccacia bread with melted vegan cheese.

UN-TUNA SANDWICH 78

A mixture of celery and onions sautéed in vegan butter tossed with faux tuna (made of seaweed flavored seitan) or a chickpea gluten-free version and a touch of vegan mayonnaise topped with fresh sweet basil leaves on Italian bread

ENTREES

ADZUKI BEANS AND KALE MEDLEY 80

A deeply satisfying macrobiotic dish with adorable adzuki beans, curly kale leaves and tempting tempeh all mixed in a blend of savory spices and herbs

ASPERGES À LA BÉCHAMEL 81

Tender asparagus spears smothered in a cheesy béchamel sauce infused with aromatic dill and garlic and garnished with capers

BAKED BEAN BURRITOS 82

Sautéed onions, tomatoes and the bold flavor of baked beans garnished with my own version of mole sauce, sprinkled with vegan cheese, rolled in flour tortillas and baked until warm and bubbly

BEEF-LESS RENDANG 83

An Indonesian specialty made vegan – Chunks of vegan beef slices (or tempeh) and broccoli simmered in a sumptuous sauce with coconut cream and a rich blend of lemongrass, coriander and ginger

BEEF-LESS STROGANOFF 84

From Russia with Love we bring chunks of tender seasoned seitan soy protein and spinach stewed in a creamy vegan sauce served over a bed of fettuccine brown rice noodles

BLACK-EYED PEAS STEW 85

Precious little black-eyed peas simmered in a tomato and onion gravy and the most fragrant of Indian spices served with Indian breads

CHOW FAAN – ORIENTAL FRIED RICE 86

Fragrant jasmine rice stir-fried with cubes of marinated eggplant, mixed vegetables, scallions and seasoned with soy sauce, liquid amino acids, rice vinegar, garlic and ginger

CREAMY CELERY RISOTTO 87

An Italian savory celery flavored "soy-creamy" rice dish garnished with Italian herbs

CROCKPOT SPINACH LASAGNA 88

Layers of lasagna noodles smothered in a savory tomato sauce with oregano, spinach and oodles of melted vegan cheese baked to savory crockpot perfection

CURRIED SINGAPORE NOODLES 89

Intoxicatingly flavorful curried rice noodles stir fried with juicy tomatoes and green peppers

CURRIED VEGETABLE POT PIE 90

Bold flavor of curry and mixed vegetables stewed and cooked, sprinkled with vegan cheese, and then filled in savory pie shells and baked in a hot oven

EGGPLANT VEGASAN 91

Thin slices of broiled eggplant and tomatoes, fried tofu, fresh basil, sautéed peppers and onions smothered with marinara sauce and vegan cheese baked to perfection.

EGGPLANT IN SZECHUAN SAUCE 92

Braised Eggplant and Zucchini sautéed in a "mildly spicy" garlic sauce served over a bed of intoxicatingly fragrant jasmine rice

FAUX CHIK'N MAKHANWALA / CHIK'N TIKKA MASALA 93

Chunks of seitan simmered in a tasty tandoori, tomato and vegan buttery sauce blended with an array of spices and thickened with a rich coconut cashew cream served with Indian breads or rice

FAUX TURKEY AND VEGAN STUFFING 94

Puff pastry cleverly fashioned as a faux turkey stuffed with a celery, onion and a bread stuffing garnished with slices of Tofurky® deli slices served with vegan gravy and cranberry sauce

FETTUCCINE ALFREDO & RAW VERSION 96

A raw Alfredo sauce made with succulent sun-dried tomatoes and creamy avocado, tofu & coconut milk on a bed of tender brown rice fettuccine noodles or raw zucchini noodles topped with capers and vegan parmesan

GARBANZO BEAN CURRY/CHANA MASALA 98

Protein rich garbanzo beans simmered in a savory mixture of onions, tomatoes, ginger and garlic, garnished with cilantro and chole masala spices making a rich fragrant gravy

HALLOWEEN TAMALE PIE 99

A medley of southwest flavors coming together in a tamale layered pie of refried black beans, corn, tomatoes, vegan ground beef, grits, and vegan cheese – this tamale pie takes Tex-Mex to a whole new level

3-LENTIL STEW 101

Three different lentils, and mixed vegetables simmered in a tomato and red wine sauce seasoned with aromatic herbs and spices slow cooked to perfection

MA PO TOFU 102

Minced tofu stewed with a blend of tomatoes, green peppers, and TVP (textured vegetable protein) in a succulent "mildly spicy" cilantro & scallion sauce

MACARONI & CHEESE 103

A creamy melted vegan cheese sauce made with caramelized onions and coconut milk, tossed with elbow macaroni

MASSAMAN CURRY 104

Malaysian yellow curry sauce simmered in coconut milk and spices cooked with a medley of mixed veggies and tofu served either with rice or mashed potatoes

NASI GORENG – INDONESIAN FRIED RICE 105

Pan-fried rice with chunks of tofu, carrots, tomatoes, and cucumbers flavored with a thick aromatic sauce blended with garlic, scallions and flavorful Indonesian spices

PAD THAI 106

Flat rice noodles stir fried with seasoned tempeh, mung bean sprouts, and scallions in a tasty tamarind sauce simmered with tempting Thai spices and garnished with crushed peanuts

PALAK TOFU PANEER 108

Golden cubes of lightly fried tofu simmered in a creamy spinach and coconut cashew cream gravy flavored with aromatic cilantro, ginger and garlic

PESTO PASTA – 2 TYPES 109-110

a. Pesto made with fresh basil, pine nuts, vegan parmesan, green peas and fresh garlic tossed with brown rice pasta
b. Raw pesto made with fresh basil, parsley, raw cashew nuts and fresh garlic tossed with zucchini noodles

PINEAPPLE FRIED RICE 111

Intoxicatingly fragrant jasmine rice stir fried with chunks of pineapple, tofu, cashew nuts, raisins, and a medley of mixed vegetables bursting with a rich curry flavor

POMMES DE TERRE AU GRATIN 112

Scalloped potatoes covered in a rich white mornay sauce topped with melted vegan cheese, and baked to excellence

POTATO HEARTY CASSEROLE 113

Chunks of mashed potatoes and garden green peas smothered and baked in a vegan creamy mixture

RATATOUILLE WITH A CURRIED TWIST 114

Traditional French vegetable stew with eggplant, tomatoes, zucchini, peppers, and onions, but untraditionally seasoned with Indian spices and herbs

RAW MARINARA ZUCCHINI PASTA 115

Zucchini Pasta mixed with a tangy and tasty raw marinara sauce, a classic Italian blend – quick, raw and absolutely delightful

SHEPHERD'S PIE 116

Layers of tenderly cooked mixed vegetables, followed by seasoned vegan ground beef, and topped with vegan mashed potatoes and crunchy breadcrumbs, baked to perfection

SINGAPORE VEGAN FISH CURRY 117

Chunks of succulent seaweed soy protein, broccoli and potatoes simmered in a mild yellow coconut curry sauce served over fragrant jasmine rice

SPAGHETTI BOLOGNESE 118

Heartwarming spaghetti tossed in a rich tomato vegan-meaty sauce full of zest, flavor and aroma

SPINACH & CORN IN CREAM SAUCE 119

A creamy preparation with the wholesome sweetness of corn and the vitality of spinach tempered with delicate herbs

SPINACH STUFFED SHELLS 120

Jumbo brown rice pasta shells filled with a blend of tofu ricotta, spinach & Italian herbs smothered and baked in a creamy sauce

STUFFED BELL PEPPERS – 2 TYPES 121

a. Tex-Mex – whole peppers stuffed with grits, onions, peppers, salsa and taco seasoning topped with a rich tomato sauce and melted cheese
b. Indian – whole peppers stuffed with a curried preparation of quinoa, onions, peppers, fruit and nuts smothered with a rich tomato sauce and melted cheese

SWEET & SOUR TOFU 123

Pan seared slabs of tofu drenched and simmered slowly in a sweet and sour sauce with pineapple chunks, bell peppers and onions

SZECHUAN SHREDDED FAUX PORK 124

Strips of marinated soy protein, tossed with bell peppers and onions, cooked in an aromatic garlic and scallions Szechuan sauce served over fluffy jasmine rice

TANDOORI TOFU BIRYANI RICE 125

Tasty Indian version of fried rice – white rice cooked with cubes of tofu and fresh vegetables mixed in a creamy sauce infused with aromatic Indian spices and garnished with cashew nuts and raisins

THAI BASIL NOT-CHIK'N 126

Pan-seared chili peppers stir-fried with bell peppers, onions and sliced spicy bits (seitan), aromatized with basil leaves and sautéed in a hot chili garlic sauce

THAI TEMPEH WITH QUINOA 127

A medley of marinated tempeh with sweet smelling cilantro, quinoa, broccoli, cabbage & carrots sautéed in a savory peanut sauce

TOFU & SPINACH QUICHE 128

Eggless quiche made with protein-packing tofu and vitamin-rich spinach great for breakfast, lunch or brunch

TOFU LOAF 129

Vegan meatloaf made with spiced TVP (textured vegetable protein), spinach, and onions baked with a strawberry balsamic glaze

DESSERT

ALMOND & PECAN CHOCO RAW COOKIES   132
Nutty, chewy, chocolaty morsels of delight rolled in decadent coconut and sweetened with maple syrup

APPLE PIE   133
Raw apples mixed in a sugary, buttery blend dusted with cinnamon , filled and baked in whole wheat vegan pie crusts

AVOCADO CHOCOLATE MOUSSE   133
Moderately sweet creamy chocolaty smooth indulgence topped with fresh organic strawberries & bananas

BANANA & CASHEW CREAM PUDDING   134
Creamy banana & cashew nuts with a tinge of orange – a tasty combination blended to smooth delight

BANANA NUT BREAD   134
A moist and delicious treat with loads of banana flavor and the crunch of pecans and walnuts – Enjoy toasted with a dab of melted vegan butter

BROWNIES – FUDGY AND GLUTEN-FREE   135
Fudgy dense chocolate chip brownies with walnuts – moist and rich with a crispy crust

BUTTERSCOTCH PECAN BARS   136
Melt in your mouth bars made with vegan butter, flour, sugar, vanilla and chocolate – little morsels of delight

CHOCOLATE CHIP COOKIES   137
Moist and delicious cookies with just the right amount of sweetness and loaded with chocolate chips

CHOCOLATE MOUSSE CAKE   138
Light, fluffy, delicious moist cake with chunks of pecans and chocolate chips covered in a rich peanut butter chocolate vegan cream cheese icing

FRENCH TOAST – MADE VEGAN   139
Thick slices of bread dipped in a tropically flavored batter made of bananas, coconut milk with a touch of sweetness and a hint of cinnamon and nutmeg, then pan-fried to perfection – completely egg-free, low in calories and cholesterol

MANGO VERY BERRY CRUMBLE   140
Layers of sweet mangoes, strawberries and blueberries covered in a crumbly, crunchy oat mixture – low calorie, anti-oxidant-filled, tropical delight

MORNING MUST-HAVE BARS – 2 KINDS   141-142
a. Cereal bars made with granola, puffed rice and millet, seeds, nuts, dried fruit, dulse, psyllium husk, chia, flax, coconut oil, nut butter, maple syrup – loads of healthy goodness
b. Cereal bars made with puffed rice and millet, peanuts, chocolate chips, dulse, nuts, maple syrup, nut butter, dried coconut and sesame seeds – tastes like a candy bar

ORANGE GLAZED MUFFINS   143
Mildly sweet light and fluffy mini citrusy muffins covered in orange glaze

SCONES   144
English bread-like treats with a lovely crisp crust and a rich buttery flavor, light and mildly sweet cut in half and served with vegan butter and jam perfect for high tea

TRIFLE O'CHOCOLATE FANTASY   145
Cup of pure fantasy with a layer of chocolate orange cake, rice whipped cream, topped with creamy chocolate mousse, garnished with crushed roasted peanuts

SAUCES & SIDES

DIPS, SAUCES & CHUTNEYS
Coconut Chutney   154
Chili Garlic Sauce   154
Green Goddess Chutney   156
Tasty Tomato Chutney   159
Vegan Mayonnaise   162

SIDES & MISCELLANEOUS
Easy Peasy Homemade Bread   155
Garam Masala   156
Raw Sauerkraut   157
Vegan Ground Beef   161

Things you will need before you start cooking

I have given you below a list of appliances, pots and pans, and other gizmos and gadgets you might need before you start embarking on a cooking adventure with this book. Here are my suggestions:

Note: these are mere suggestions. I do not represent any of these companies and am not trying to sell you any particular product – these are just the ones I use, but feel free to use the brands you prefer

Food Processor – I use a Cuisinart® 14 Cup Food Processor	Blender – I use a Vitamix®
Rice Cooker – I use a Vitaclay® (aluminum-free, Teflon free – clay pot rice cooker)	Pressure Cooker – I use Fagor® (stainless steel) I have two sizes for different sized meals
Pots & Pans – I use Tools of the Trade® or Belgique® Stainless steel cookware	Non-Stick skillet I use Zwilling J.A. Henckels® 12 inch ceramic frying pan / Non-Stick skillet (PFOA-free) Mainly for frying tofu (for everything else the ceramic one works) Ecolution®
Dehydrator – I use Excalibur® 9 tray dehydrator	Julienne Peeler – I use OXO® / Oil Sprayer – I use Misto® (Stainless Steel)
Mandolin Slicer – I use Farberware®	Mini Food Chopper – I use Proctor & Silex®

Items To Stock Your Refrigerator And Pantry With Before You Start Cooking

Here's a list of ingredients you might want to stock your fridge and pantry with before you begin your fun in the kitchen!

Note: Again these are mere suggestions. I do not represent any of these companies and am not trying to sell you any particular product – these are just the ones I use, but feel free to use the brands you prefer

For your Pantry:

Miscellaneous
Canned Organic Coconut Milk – Native Forest®
Himalayan Pink Salt – Saltworks® – available at www.saltworks.us
Organic Vanilla Extract – Simply Organic® or Flavorganics®
Raw Sugar – Sucanat® or Organic Whole Cane Sugar

Flours, Rice, Pasta, Grains
Brown Rice Pasta – different kinds – Tinkyada®
Chickpea Flour
Egg Replacer – Ener-G®
Ground Flax Seeds
Chia Seeds
Jasmine Rice
Organic Brown Rice
Organic Millet Flour
Organic Puffed Millet

Organic Puffed Rice
Organic Quinoa – Earthly Delight® or Ancient Harvest®
Psyllium Husk
Textured Vegetable Protein – Bob's Red Mill® TVP Granules or VegeUSA® vege soy chunks
Unbromated Unbleached Organic Flour – Bob's Red Mill®
Gluten-free flour (if you are gluten-free)

Oils & Vinegars
Grapeseed Oil – San Giuliano Alghero®
Organic Cold Pressed Extra Virgin Olive Oil – Napa Valley®
Organic Fresh Pressed Virgin Coconut Oil – Dr. Bronner's®
Organic Raw Apple Cider Vinegar – Bragg®
Organic Sunflower or Organic Canola oil – Spectrum®

Sea Vegetables
Dulse Flakes, Wakame, Nori Wrappers, Kelp – Maine Cost Sea Vegetable®

For Your Spice Drawer:

Cayenne Pepper
Cinnamon
Coriander Powder
Cumin (ground)
Cumin Seeds
Curry Powder (Mild Madras) – Kim Thu Thap®
Dill, dried
Garam Masala
Italian Seasoning

Oregano
Paprika
Pepper Grinder with Organic black peppercorns
Taco Seasoning – Bearitos® or Simply Organic®
Tandoori Powder
Turmeric (ground)
Vegetarian Bouillon Cubes – Edward & Sons® Not Chick'N Natural Bouillon Cubes

For Your Refrigerator:

Miscellaneous
Aluminum-Free Baking Soda – Bob's Red Mill®
Nutritional Yeast Seasoning – Bragg®
Organic Maple Syrup (Grade B or higher – not Grade A – Grade D is best, if available) – Coombs®
Organic Peanut Butter – Tree of Life®
Organic Almond Butter – Tree of Life®
Organic Raw Cocoa Powder
Organic Tahini – Tree of Life®

Herbs & Spices
Organic Minced Garlic – (make it in your mini food chopper or store-bought)
Organic Minced Ginger – (make it in your mini food chopper or store-bought)

 Freeze your ginger root so that peeling and grating it becomes a breeze!

Condiments
Black Sesame Oil – Wei-Chuan®
Chili Garlic Sauce – Sriracha® or Lee Kum Kee®
Liquid Amino Acids – Bragg®
Mirin – Eden®
Organic Brown Rice Vinegar – Eden®
Organic Barley Miso (or for gluten-free Chickpea Miso) – Miso Master®
Organic Ketchup – Tree of Life®
Organic Shoyu – San-J®
Organic Tamari (if you are gluten-free) – San-J®
Organic Yellow Mustard – Eden®
Vegan Mayonnaise – Follow Your Heart®

Raw Nuts, Seeds & Dried Fruit
Almonds
Cashews
Macadamia Nuts
Pecans
Pine Nuts
Walnuts
Pumpkin Seeds
Sunflower Seeds
Cranberries
Dried Dates
Raisins
Sundried Tomatoes

Most of the products should be available at your local health food store or the Natural Food section of your local grocery store, but if you are in an area where you don't have access to all these products, then you can buy them online at www.vitacost.com, www.veganessentials.com or www.amazon.com

Vegan Dairy Products
Organic Coconut Milk – So Delicious®
Organic Vegan Cream Cheese – Follow Your Heart®
Organic Vegan Sour Cream – Follow Your Heart®
Organic Vegan Sour Cream – Follow Your Heart®
Vegan Buttery Spread – Earth Balance® (Non-Soy version)
Vegan Cheese Shreds – Daiya®

Vegan Protein
Organic Sprouted Tofu – Extra Firm or Super Firm – Wildwood®
Organic Tempeh – Lightlife®
Seasoned Seitan Strips (Wheat protein) – WestSoy® or Trader Joe's®

Your Health is in Your Hands
Healthy Food Swaps and More

Part of the reason for my writing this book was to inform my readers on how to live a healthy life and how to make positive lifestyle changes. A lot of times I get asked by my students "What sugar should I be eating?" or "What oil should I use?" Hence in this part of the book, I list some healthy swaps that you can make for everyday foods. Here I have also taken the opportunity to cover what common foods to avoid and how to detect common "food baddies". Lastly, I have gone into some detail on why it is important to stay away from GMOs (genetically modified organisms)

What **Sugar** Should I Eat?

Organic Whole Cane Sugar (panela) is a raw sugar product made by extracting pure sugar cane juice (using a press). This juice is then evaporated over low heat, then sifted and ground to produce a rich grainy sugar. Its organic quality comes from the fact that it is not processed over high heat, nor spun to change it into fine crystals, and the molasses has not been separated from the sugar. It contains no chemicals or anti-caking agents. Each batch of sugar varies – some lighter, some darker, based on sugar cane variety, soil type and weather.

Because its molasses are not separated, it contains more nutrients, vitamins and minerals. Plus also due to the fact that it is dehydrated at very low temperatures, the vitamins and minerals are preserved. It still has the natural balance of sucrose, glucose, and fructose, and contains components essential for its digestion. It is metabolized more slowly than white sugar, and therefore will not spike your blood sugar levels as much as refined sugars will. The more refined a sugar is, the more it will raise your blood sugar.

Sucanat is a *similar* product to Organic Whole Cane Sugar. SU-CA-NAT stands for sugar cane natural. The only difference between Sucanat and Organic Whole Cane Sugar is that the sugar stream and the molasses stream are separated from each other during processing of Sucanat, and then the molasses are added back in. I personally like the flavor of Sucanat better than Organic Whole Cane Sugar, but both products are superior to refined white sugar.

What **Salt** Should I Eat?

Himalayan Pink Salt
Did you know that commonly sold table salt is composed of 97.5% sodium chloride and 2.5% chemicals? Common salt is also dehydrated at more than 1,200° F, a process which zaps many of the natural chemical structures of naturally-occurring salt.

The table and cooking salt found in most homes, restaurants, and all processed foods, is empty of any nutritional value. It is missing the precious trace minerals that make salt good for us. After processing, salt is basically sodium chloride, an unnatural chemical type of salt that our body actually sees as a foreign toxic invader!

When we ingest this type of salt, our body cannot dispose of it in a natural, healthy way. This can lead to inflammation of the tissues, water retention and high blood pressure over time. In order for our body to metabolize chemical table salt, it must waste tremendous amounts of energy to try to keep the body at its optimum fluid balance. This creates an unnecessary burdening of the elimination systems in the body. Water is also removed from other cells in the system in an attempt to neutralize the unnatural sodium chloride.

Studies show that for each gram of table salt that your system cannot process, the body will use over twenty times the amount of cellular water to neutralize the sodium chloride in chemically-treated salt.

This can lead to water retention, cellulite, rheumatism, arthritis, gout, as well as kidney and gallbladder stones.

Choosing to use Himalayan Salt as an alternative can have a big impact on total health and well-being. Biophysical research on this pink salt has identified crystals that contain 84 essential minerals required to sustain human life. Himalayan salt has no additives and can alleviate the symptoms of a variety of conditions.

A study conducted at the University of Graz in Austria found that people who drank water containing Himalayan pink salt daily experienced improvement in respiratory conditions, organ functions, and connective tissues. Participants also reported sleeping better and having more energy. The study also noted a boost in the ability to achieve higher concentration levels. Some of the study participants stated they lost unwanted weight while others involved in the study showed enhanced hair and nail growth.

What Oil Should I Cook With?

Grapeseed Oil
Grapeseed oil is as versatile as olive oil, but is often preferred because it has a higher smoke point and is able to withstand higher cooking temperatures than its olive-based counterpart since olive oil can turn toxic when heated at high temperatures.

Benefits of Grapeseed Oil:
• High in vitamin E and omega-6 fatty acids
• Contains natural antioxidants
• Has been shown to raise good cholesterol (HDL) and lower bad cholesterol (LDL)

Note: May cause allergic reactions in people who have known allergies to grapes

Coconut Oil
If you don't mind all your food tasting like coconut, then this is really the superior oil to use. Coconut oil like grapeseed oil also has a high heat index and does not turn rancid when cooking food at high temperatures.

Benefits of Coconut Oil:
• Contains many vitamins, minerals and electrolytes such as potassium, calcium and chloride
• Helps with weight loss – the saturated fat in coconut is made up of fatty acids that the body quickly turns into energy instead of storing as fat, plus it helps restore normal thyroid function
• Fights diseases – the lauric acid in coconut oil is anti-viral, anti-bacterial, anti-microbial and anti-fungal – thus it boosts the immune system
• Natural remedy – helps relieve the symptoms of sore throats and ulcers
• Great for skin and hair and helps relieve dry skin, rashes and blemishes, and inhibits aging
• Reduces the risk of heart disease, stroke, cancer, osteoporosis, diabetes, digestive problems, and skin cancer
• Good for your brain – prevents and reverses Alzheimer's, Parkinson's and other forms of dementia

Why should I pay attention to what kind of Flour I Consume?

Flour should be Unbleached, Unbromated Flour

Enriched or refined also called bleached flour should totally be avoided. Refined flour is very high in carbohydrates and increases blood sugar very quickly within half an hour of eating. Hence consuming large amounts of refined flour can increase the risk of diabetes.

First you need to understand what "bleached flour" is. As you might expect, it is whiter than the unbleached version, but have you wondered how it got that way? Do they put the flour through a "Clorox®" rinse? Well sort of. Let's examine the steps in making "Bleached, Enriched or Refined Flour":

- After the flour is milled, it is put through a chlorine gas bath, which whitens it, reduces the gluten content and provides a finer grain.
- The chlorine combines with proteins in the flour to produce a by-product called "Alloxan", a known carcinogen. Note: Alloxan is used in laboratory tests to induce diabetes in rats and mice because it destroys beta cells in the pancreas.
- Since the gluten content is reduced, they have to "bromate the flour". Bromated flour is treated with potassium bromate to improve dough elasticity which allows it to stand up to commercial baking practices, and produce a higher rising bread. "Potassium bromate" is also a potential carcinogen that has been banned in the U.K. It has been associated with thyroid dysfunction. Some states but not all require that "potassium bromate" be disclosed on food labels.

So when you use flour or when you buy pre-packaged bread, make sure the label reads: "Unbleached, Unbromated Flour"

What Non-Dairy Milk Should I Drink?

Coconut Milk (unsweetened)

A lot of vegans turn to soy-milk when they give up dairy. Since the vegan diet does consist of a lot of soy, it is probably better to not consume soy milk. Soy tends to increase the estrogen in the body and creates some imbalances which can lead to health problems. Hence when on a vegan diet, too much soy should be avoided. Thus a better substitute is coconut milk. A lot of people ask if almond milk is a good choice. Well unless it is organic, almond milk is devoid of nutrition since all almonds are pasteurized. Plus almonds should be blanched before they are consumed to allow our body to absorb the nutrients from them. I'm not sure if this is a regular practice in commercially bought almond milk where they remove the skins to make the milk.

Coconut milk contains all the benefits that were listed above for coconut oil. In all my recipes that require a non-dairy beverage, I have listed coconut milk. But if you prefer you can substitute the coconut milk with any non-dairy beverage you choose e.g. almond, soy etc. Just make sure any non-dairy beverage you use is unsweetened.

Why is it important to eat Seaweed when on a vegan diet?

When you buy sea vegetables or seaweed make sure it comes from a good source. Maine Coast Sea Vegetables® makes good quality products.

Did you know that iodine deficiency is rampant in the US? This can result in ailments like thyroid problems, goiter and dementia. Studies have shown that iodized sea salt does not provide enough iodine. Sea vegetables are not only excellent sources of iodine but they are super foods and contain lots of protein, vitamins, and minerals which are sometimes hard to obtain from non-animal sources. Here I have mentioned 2 of my favorite ones. I have used these in my recipes in this book.

Dulse

Dulse, also known as Palmaria palmata, dillisk, dilsk, red dulse, sea lettuce flakes or creathnach, is a red algae. It grows on the northern coasts of the Atlantic and Pacific oceans. It is a well-known snack food. In Iceland, where it is known as söl, it has been an important source of fiber throughout the centuries.

It is popular in many countries including Northern Europe, not just in Asia and Japan. In Ireland, many people use dulse to make sandwiches. Its savory quality can enhance flavor without the need to add salt.

Health Benefits:
- Filled with lots of protein
- Contains many vitamins e.g. Vitamins B6, B12, C, E, A
- Contains important minerals e.g. potassium, iron, calcium
- Is a natural source of fiber

Kelp

Kelp is large seaweed (algae) belonging to the brown algae. Kelp grows in underwater "forests" (kelp forests) in shallow oceans. The organisms require nutrient-rich water with temperatures between 6 and 14 °C (43 and 57 °F).

Health Benefits:

- Provides a natural source of iodine which protects against radiation poisoning
- Helps with the immune system, and female hormone regulation
- Helps with thyroid health – the rich iodine content regulates thyroid hormones
- Prevents estrogen-related cancer – It has long been known that Japanese women, whose diets are rich in kelp, have lower rates of ovarian, breast, and endometrial cancer. A study at UC Berkeley found that a diet containing kelp lowered serum estradiol levels in women and had phytoestrogenic properties
- Prevents other forms of cancer – the fucoidan in kelp has been shown in studies to have the ability to induce apoptosis (cell death) in cancer cells
- Reduces the pain of endometriosis – a condition in women when cells from the lining of the uterus grow in other areas of the body. This can lead to pain, irregular bleeding, and problems getting pregnant (infertility). One research shows that women with endometriosis who supplemented 700 mg of kelp capsules per day had a significant reduction in pain
- Anti-Inflammatory – with its fucoidan content, a complex carbohydrate that is a powerful anti-inflammatory
- Unique Antioxidants – Sea vegetables contain antioxidants not found in other vegetables
- High in Iron – preventing anemia and low energy

What is the difference between all the Soy Sauces out there?

In my cooking classes I get asked this question a lot so I decided to convey this information to you dear reader in case you were wondering too.

Shoyu

"Shoyu" is the Japanese word for soy sauce made of soybeans, roasted wheat (hence not gluten-free), sea salt, and koji (Aspergillus oryzae), mold spores that when exposed to moisture begin growing giving rise to unique enzymes that create the fermentation process. Always buy "Organic Shoyu".

Fermentation is the process of koji enzymes breaking proteins down into amino acids and carbohydrates into simple sugars, so it's an easily assimilated food requiring little energy for us to digest. Shoyu harmonizes and enhances food.

Tamari

"Tamari" in Japanese literally means liquid pressed from soybeans. Tamari is brewed from whole soybeans, sea salt, water, and koji (Aspergillus hacho). Tamari is wheat-free and popular with those who have wheat allergies and choose a gluten-free diet. Tamari has a stronger flavor and implants its flavor in foods. Always buy "Organic Tamari".

Liquid Amino Acids

Liquid Amino Acids (Bragg®) – is a certified non-GMO liquid protein concentrate. It is not fermented or heated and is gluten-free. It is derived from healthy soybeans and purified water. It contains the following essential and non-essential Amino Acids in naturally occurring amounts: 16 Amino Acids; Alanine, Arginine, Aspartic Acid, Glutamic Acid, Glycine, Histidine, Isoleucine, Leucine, Methionine, Phenylalanine, Proline, Serine, Threonine, Tyrosine, Valine, and Lysine.

Soy Sauce

Commercial soy sauces (even some labeled as Shoyu or Tamari) are usually made from soybeans that have been defatted with hexane, a petroleum derivative. Common shortcuts are artificial fermentation methods including genetically engineered enzymes. In fact most soy sauces are actually caramel colored water with lots of salt, (some of them fermented with alcohol), hydrochloric acid treated soy isolate, and sugar added. Look for the words traditionally brewed and organic when buying commercial soy sauce.

Is it really important to pay attention to what Water I Drink?

According to Ayurveda the oldest form of medicine, having iced or cold water especially with or right after a meal will hamper effective digestion. It's like pouring cold water over hot coals.
When you drink cold water with your meals, it solidifies the oils that you have consumed with the food in your body, which in turn slows down the digestive process. This causes weight gain.
The best practice is to drink a glass of lukewarm or hot water 30 minutes before or 30 minutes after your meal.
You may have noticed the Japanese & Chinese never drink cold water with their meals – only hot tea. This is probably a major factor why obesity is very low in China & Japan, whereas Americans frequently consume glasses of ice water, iced tea, and sodas filled with ice.

The water you drink should be filtered. We personally have a whole house filter, a system called the "Rhino Whole House Filter" by Aquasana®. This way everything that comes out of all our taps is filtered water – so the water in our shower, kitchen, laundry etc. is all filtered. There are some great filtration systems out there. Find one that you like, and use it. It really makes a difference in your skin, hair and health.

A good resource for understanding common water filter technologies is
http://www.foodmatters.tv/articles-1/what-water-filter-should-I-be-using

Why should I buy Organic?

- Avoiding Pesticides – In the first State of the Science review, a report entitled "Minimizing Pesticide Dietary Exposure through the Consumption of Organic Food", the findings showed that In the US alone more than 1 billion pounds of pesticides are used daily in the food we eat and the environment. Children, especially unborn fetuses and babies, are more vulnerable to exposure to pesticides.

- A new Harvard study has linked pesticide exposure to a 70% increase in Parkinson's disease. The study which is the largest ever conducted was released in July 2006 issue of the Annals of Neurology.

- Saving our Planet – Did you know that converting 10,000 medium sized farms to organic production reduces carbon dioxide (which accounts for 80% of global warming). This is as much as taking 1,174,400 cars off the road. Every time you buy an organic product, you're helping to save the earth.

- Reducing your exposure to the dangers of GMOs (Genetically Modified Organisms) – see next section for information on GMOs.

Organic Facts

- Did you know that the only way to remove conventional pesticides (not GMOs) completely from produce is to wash them in apple cider vinegar – otherwise traces of pesticides still remain even when you wash thoroughly with water?

- You can tell produce is "organic" by its sticker – organic produce have 5 numbers always starting with a 9 (9xxxx).

- When you see a non-organic shiny apple that sheen comes from glazing the apples with shellac, a brittle or flaky secretion of the lac insect *Coccus lacca or Laccifer Lacca*, found in the forests of Assam and Thailand or they are made shiny with paraffin wax.

What are GMOs and why should I avoid them?

The following information is condensed from the book *Genetic Roulette: The Documented Health Risks of Genetically Engineered Foods* and *Seeds of Deception*, both written by Jeffrey Smith.

- GMOs are genetically modified organisms, where genes are taken from one species, like bacteria or viruses, and forced into the DNA of other species, like soybeans and corn plants. Irrespective of what particular gene you insert, the very process of creating a GMO results in massive collateral damage in the plant, which can increase toxins, allergens, carcinogens, and anti-nutrients.

- The only published human feeding study revealed what may be the most dangerous problem from GM foods. The gene inserted into GM soy, transfers into the DNA of bacteria living inside our intestines and continues to function. This means that long after we stop eating GMOs, we may still have potentially harmful GM proteins produced continuously inside of us. To put it more plainly, eating a corn chip produced from BT corn might transform our intestinal bacteria into living pesticide factories, possibly for the rest of our lives. This study was conducted by Dr. Arpad Pusztai, the world's leading expert in his field, working at a top nutritional research institute in the UK.

- Dr. Pusztai's team of scientists created a GM potato that produced its own insecticide. They fed the GM potato to rats. They also fed another group of rats a potato spiked with the same pesticide that the GM potato was engineered to produce, and the third group got regular potatoes. And all groups received a balanced diet. The group that ate the GM potatoes was seriously damaged. The potato spiked with the insecticides did not show problems. What then was the cause for the health damage? It was not the insecticide. It is most likely the process of genetic engineering.

- The rats developed potentially precancerous cell growth in the digestive tract, smaller brains, livers and testicles, partial atrophy of the liver and damaged immune systems.

- GMOs have been eradicated in Europe.

So How Can We Stop GMOs in our Food?

In the US, if only 5 percent of the U.S. population rejected GMO brands, it should be more than enough to reach a *Tipping Point*. Whatever the magic percentage is, there are certainly far more people in the US who would buy non-GMO products if given a choice. In fact, 53 percent of Americans say they would avoid GMOs if they were labeled. This is how they got rid of GMOs in Europe. Stop buying GMO foods – buy only foods that say "Non-GMO verified" on them. Here's the icon to look for   on pre-packaged foods.

Metric Conversion

We in the US tend to do things a little differently from the rest of the world. So if you are in a part of the world where you use the metric system, here's a table you can use to convert the measurements in this book.

VOLUME MEASUREMENT CONVERSIONS

U.S.	METRIC
1/4 Teaspoon	1.25 ml
1/2 Teaspoon	2.5 ml
3/4 Teaspoon	3.75 ml
1 Teaspoon	5 ml
1 Tablespoon	15 ml
1/4 Cup	62.5 ml
1/2 Cup	125 ml
3/4 Cup	187.5 ml
1 Cup	250 ml

WEIGHT MEASUREMENT CONVERSIONS

U.S.	METRIC
1 Ounce	28.4 g
8 Ounces	227.5 g
16 Ounces (1 pound)	455 g

OVEN COOKING TEMPERATURE CONVERSIONS

FAHRENHEIT	CELSIUS	GAS MARK	HEAT OF OVEN
225°	110°	1/4	Very Cool
250°	120°	1/2	Very Cool
275°	140°	1	Cool
300°	150°	2	Cool
325°	160°	3	Moderate
350°	180°	4	Moderate
375°	190°	5	Moderately hot
400°	200°	6	Moderately hot
425°	220°	7	Hot
450°	230°	8	Hot
475°	240°	9	Very Hot

Abbreviations, Symbols & Icons Used In The Book

TSP	Teaspoon
TB	Tablespoon
OZ	Ounce

Neat Idea	Did you Know?	Health & Beauty Benefits
Chef Neeta's Tip	Raw Food Recipe	GF Gluten-free Option
Soups	Appetizers	Salads

Entrees	Dessert	Sips & Slurps	Bits & Bobs
American Food	British Food	Chinese Food	French Food
German Food	Indian Food	Indonesian Food	Irish Food
Italian Food	Japanese Food	Malaysian Food	Mediterranean Food
Mexican Food	Russian Food	Singaporean Food	Thai Food

Soups

Cream of Broccoli

This creamy delicious soup is easy and makes a substantial meal by itself with half the calories of regular broccoli soup

Serves 4

What You Will Need:

2 Cups Fresh Organic Broccoli florets
_or_ 1 of 10 ounce bag Frozen Organic Broccoli
1½ Cups Organic Coconut Milk
2 Vegetable Bouillon Cubes
4 Cups Filtered Water
3 TB Organic Vegan Buttery Spread
3 TB Unbleached Organic Flour

 Use gluten-free flour or Arrowroot

1 TSP Garlic – minced
1 Cup Organic Onions – diced
Himalayan Pink Salt to taste
Pepper to taste
1 Cup Organic Cashew Nuts
– soaked in filtered water for at least 30 minutes

Suggested Shopping List:
- Earth Balance® Natural Buttery Spread (non-Soy version)
- Edward & Sons® Not Chick'n Natural Bouillon Cubes
- So Delicious® Organic Coconut Milk (unsweetened)
- Bob's Red Mill® Organically Grown Unbromated Unbleached White Flour

To Make The Soup:

1. Steam the broccoli and set aside to cool.
2. In a large pot, melt 3 tablespoons of vegan buttery spread.
3. Once the vegan buttery spread melts, add garlic and onions.
4. Lower the burner, sauté onions and garlic until onions are softened.
5. Add 3 tablespoons flour to the onion mixture. Mix thoroughly until it forms a large lump.
6. Add the coconut milk, increase your burner to high, and keep stirring the mixture until there are no more lumps and the mixture thickens.
7. Add 4 cups of water and 2 vegetable bouillon cubes. Keep stirring until the cubes dissolve.
8. Process the cooled broccoli with the soaked cashew nuts (drain water from nuts) in a food processor or blender until completed puréed.
9. Add the processed broccoli and cashew nuts to the soup mixture.
10. Season with salt and pepper.
11. Let the soup simmer for another 5-7 minutes on low heat.
12. Serve with homemade bread (see page 155 for recipe).

Health: Broccoli is good for your eyes and full of calcium and protein helping build strong bones
Beauty: Vitamin E in Broccoli is a natural defense for your skin against UV radiation damage. Eat broccoli before you go out in the sun!

 Melt some vegan cheese into this soup before serving for a burst of extra flavor!

 You can use this soup as a casserole starter by adding cooked vegetables, rice and smothering the top with vegan cheese!

French Onion Soup

This gourmet soup is so hard to find in restaurants without the beef broth so make it yourself and enjoy its bold flavors and rich aroma

Serves 6

What You Will Need:

6 Red Organic Onions – julienned
1 TSP Organic Garlic – minced
2 TB Organic Vegan Buttery Spread
2 Cups Non-Alcoholic Red Wine
4 TSP Raw Sugar
4 Vegetable Bouillon Cubes
8 Cups Filtered Water
1 Cup Organic Carrots – finely diced
1 Cup Organic Celery – finely diced
1 TSP Dried Thyme
1/2 TSP Dried Rosemary
1 TSP Dried Dill
1/3 Cup Organic Miso
1/4 TSP Ground Pepper
1 Cup Vegan Cheese Shreds
French bread, sliced to 1/2 inch thick slices

 Use gluten-free bread

Vegan buttery spread to spread on the bread

Suggested Shopping List:
- Earth Balance® Natural Buttery Spread (non-Soy version)
- Edward & Sons® Not Chick'n Natural Bouillon Cubes
- Miso Master® Chickpea Miso
- Daiya® Vegan Cheese Shreds – Mozzarella

To Make The Soup:

1. In a large pot, sauté the garlic and onions in the vegan buttery spread until the onions are softened.
2. Add the red wine and sugar, and let the onions and garlic cook in this mixture on a medium burner for about 7-10 minutes until the wine is almost evaporated.
3. Pour in 8 cups of water.
4. Toss in the bouillon cubes, and increase the burner to high so the bouillon cubes can dissolve.
5. Stir in the thyme, dill, rosemary and ground pepper.
6. Add the carrots and celery and lower heat to low, cover the pot, and allow the vegetables to cook for about 10-15 minutes.
7. Once vegetables are tender, turn off the heat.
8. Place miso in a small separate bowl. Take a few tablespoons of broth from the pot, and mix in with the miso to make a thick paste. Once miso is well whisked, add to the soup.
9. Spread both sides of the French bread rounds with vegan buttery spread.
10. Sprinkle one side of the French bread round with vegan cheese shreds.
11. Arrange bread rounds on a baking tray.
12. Bake bread rounds in a preheated oven for 10 minutes or until the bread is crisp and the cheese has melted.
13. Serve soup by first placing the Vegan cheese bread round in an individual soup bowl and then pouring the hot soup over it.
14. Indulge!

Health: Onions lower cholesterol, maintain healthy blood pressure and are good for your heart
Beauty: Onions are great for your hair especially if you have thinning hair

Did you know that Miso should <u>never</u> be boiled, or it loses its health benefits?

Irish Potato Leek Soup

A creamy coconut cream-based soup with bite size chunks of tender potatoes simmered in caramelized leeks in a rich broth of aromatic herbs garnished with a tinge of roasted garlic

Serves 6

What You Will Need:

1 Large Organic Leek (leaves and bulb) – finely sliced
4 Cups Organic Potatoes – washed and cubed
  (Or you can adjust the amount of potatoes to your
    taste since I like a nibble of potatoes in every bite)
4 TB Organic Vegan Buttery Spread
1 TSP Organic Garlic – Minced
2 TSP Dried Dill
1 TSP Dried Marjoram
3 Sprigs Organic Fresh Curly Parsley
  – thick stems removed & chopped fine
1 Vegetable Bouillon Cube
2 Cups Filtered Water
1 of 13.5 fl Oz Can Organic Coconut milk
2 TSP Himalayan Pink Salt
1 TSP Raw Sugar
2 Cups Organic Dried Potato Flakes

> **Suggested Shopping List:**
> - Earth Balance® Natural Buttery Spread (non-Soy version)
> - Edward & Sons® Not Chick'n Natural Bouillon Cubes
> - Native Forest® Organic Coconut Milk
> - Edward & Sons® Organic Mashed Potatoes

To Make The Soup:

1. In a pressure cooker with lid removed, melt the vegan buttery spread.
2. Add the garlic and leeks and sauté for 3 minutes until leeks become limp. Lower the burner.
3. Mix in the dill, marjoram and parsley and stir well.
4. Increase your burner to high, and add 2 cups of water and the vegetable bouillon cube allowing the bouillon cube to dissolve completely.
5. Add the can of coconut milk. Use the empty can and fill it with water twice, thus adding 2 cans of water.
6. Season with salt and sugar and mix thoroughly.
7. Add the potatoes.
8. Pay attention to your pressure cooker. When you start to hear the pressure cooker begin to whistle, turn your timer on to 5 minutes. (Or check your own pressure cooker for "potato cooking" times).

> Did you know that cooking with a pressure cooker results in healthier and better tasting food prepared in less time and with less energy?

9. After 5 minutes, turn the burner off.
10. Carefully release the steam from the pressure cooker. Then open the lid.
11. Turn the burner back on. Add the dried potato flakes. Mix thoroughly into the soup. When the soup starts to thicken, turn off the burner.
12. Pour soup into bowls and enjoy with homemade bread (see page 155 for recipe)

> **Health:** Potatoes have lots of vitamins and minerals. Vitamins C & B-complex in the potatoes aid in digestion
> **Beauty:** Potatoes contain an abundance of minerals like potassium, magnesium and phosphorus which help give you younger looking skin

Minestrone Soup

A medley of mixed vegetables, kidney beans and macaroni in a hearty herbed tomato broth

Serves 4

What You Will Need:

3 TB Organic Vegan Buttery Spread
1 Large Organic Onion – diced
2 TSP Organic Garlic – minced
2 Cups Organic Carrots – diced
2 Stalks Organic Celery- finely chopped
1 of 15 Oz Can Organic Kidney Beans – drained and rinsed
1 TSP Dried Oregano
1 TSP Dried Basil
1 TSP Dried Marjoram
1 TSP Himalayan Pink Salt
Freshly Ground Pepper to taste
2 TSP Raw Sugar
4 Fresh Organic Tomatoes, puréed
Or 1 of 14 Oz Can Organic Crushed Tomatoes
2 TB Organic Ketchup
2 Vegetable Bouillon Cubes
4 Cups Filtered Water
1 Cup Brown Rice Elbow Pasta
1 Cup Organic Cashew Nuts – soaked in filtered water for at least 30 minutes
2 TB Organic Fresh Basil – chopped (Optional – for garnish)

Suggested Shopping List:
- Earth Balance® Natural Buttery Spread (non-Soy version)
- Edward & Sons® Not Chick'n Natural Bouillon Cubes
- Tree of Life® Organic Ketchup
- Tinkyada® Brown Rice Pasta

 Health: Tomatoes are high in antioxidants (lycopene) and prevent colon, prostate and pancreatic cancer. Tomatoes are "happy food" and help with migraines and depression – so if you're PMS'ing go ahead have a tomato!
Beauty: Tomatoes give you a rosy complexion

To Make The Soup:

1. Once the cashew nuts are soaked, drain water, and process the soaked cashew nuts in a food processor or blender to form a puréed cashew paste. Set aside.
2. Heat the vegan buttery spread in a large pot. On medium heat, sauté garlic and onions for 4-5 minutes until the onions are limp and translucent.

 Did you know that a tomato is a fruit and not a vegetable?

3. Add the carrots and celery. Cover pot, and cook on a low burner for about 10 minutes until the vegetables are softened.
4. Season with oregano, basil, salt, sugar and freshly ground pepper to taste. Stir for another 2-3 minutes for the seasonings and flavors to blend.
5. Add the tomatoes and 4 cups water.
6. Toss in the vegetable bouillon cubes and increase burner to high, bringing the mixture to a boil allowing the bouillon cubes to dissolve.
7. Add the drained kidney beans and elbow pasta and cook for 15-20 minutes based on the pasta cooking times on your pasta package.
8. Whisk in the puréed cashew nut paste mixing it thoroughly into soup.
9. Now lower heat and let the soup simmer for 10 minutes.
10. Add ketchup and mix well.
11. Serve hot in soup bowls.

 Top this soup with freshly chopped basil and vegan rice parmesan and serve with hot garlic bread (or hot gluten-free garlic bread)

Persian Red Lentil Soup

Turkish split red lentils simmered in a tomato and cilantro vegan broth with aromatic spices, garnished with roasted garlic

Serves 4

What You Will Need:
3 Cups Organic Split Red Lentils
4 Organic Large Tomatoes – diced
3 TSP Organic Garlic – minced
2 TSP Turmeric Powder
Dash of Cayenne Pepper or 1 fresh cayenne pepper
- chopped (optional)
1 Cup Organic Cilantro – stems and leaves chopped up
with thick stems removed
3 TSP Himalayan Pink Salt
10 Cups Filtered Water
Grapeseed Oil for cooking

To Make The Soup:
1. Wash the lentils in filtered water.
2. Soak the lentils in filtered water for about 20 minutes before cooking.
3. In a pressure cooker with the lid off, add the 10 cups of water.
4. Add the turmeric and the cayenne pepper (optional – if you like spice) to the water. Bring the water to a boil.
5. Drain the soaked lentils as much as you can (it is okay if you still have a little water at the bottom).
6. Add the soaked lentils to the boiling water.
7. Stir in the tomatoes, cilantro and salt.
8. Secure the lid of the pressure cooker. Leave the burner on high. Set your pressure cooker to start pressurizing.
9. Pay attention to your pressure cooker. When you start to hear the pressure cooker begin to whistle, turn your timer on to 5 minutes.
10. After 5 minutes, turn the pressure cooker off.
11. Carefully release the steam from the pressure cooker. Then open the lid.
12. Using a wooden tamp (available at Indian stores) or a wire whisk, break up the lentils stirring vigorously.
13. In a separate pan, roast minced garlic in a 1-2 TB of oil.
14. Pour the roasted garlic over the top of the cooked lentils and stir into the cooked lentils.
15. Serve lentil soup warm.

An alternative way to enjoy this soup is to serve it over steamed white rice with French fries or potato chips on the side.

Health: Turmeric reduces inflammation and prevents arthritis
It also prevents dementia and diseases like Alzheimer's because of the curcumin present
Turmeric is a natural antibiotic so take it when you get sick
Beauty: Turmeric also gives radiance to your skin

Raw Vegetable Energy Soup

This soup is for those days when you don't feel like cooking but want something delicious and healthy to boost your energy

Serves 4

What You Will Need:

3 Medium Organic Tomatoes – quartered
2 Stalks Organic Celery
1 Large Organic Red or Orange Bell Pepper (or a combination of two Medium sized ones) – cored, deseeded and roughly chopped
1/2 Cup Organic Onions – peeled and roughly
1 TB Nutritional Yeast
1 heaped TSP Himalayan Pink Salt
1 TSP Organic Garlic – minced
<u>Or</u> 1 Organic Garlic clove
Handful of Organic Fresh Basil Leaves
1½ TSP Organic Lemon Juice (juice of 1/2 lemon)
1 Cup Organic Coconut Milk – unsweetened

> **Suggested Shopping List:**
> – Bragg® Nutritional Yeast Seasoning
> – So Delicious® Organic Coconut Milk (unsweetened)

Did you know that these soups are so fast that you can make them in 5-7 minutes flat? That would be the quickest dinner ever! However, take your time to enjoy your soup-sip it slowly, since consuming blended foods too fast doesn't give your body the time to digest and assimilate them properly

To Make Soup:

1. Place all the ingredients in a high powered blender like a Vitamix.
2. Blend everything until you get a smooth texture.
3. Pour into bowls or small glasses and energize!

This soup makes for a delectable dip too – you can use organic tortilla chips or raw veggies to dip into it.

Raw Tomato Soup

Another raw soup to make you feel vitality and vibrance

Serves 4

What You Will Need:

1 Cup Filtered Water or Coconut Water
10 Medium Organic Raw Tomatoes – quartered
1 Cup Organic Cabbage – cut into large chunks
1/2 TB Organic Red Onion
1/2 Cup Organic Red Bell Pepper
  – cored, deseeded and roughly chopped
1/4 Cup Organic Sweet Basil leaves
1 TB Fresh Organic Lime Juice
1 Clove Organic Garlic <u>Or</u> 1 TSP Organic Garlic – minced
1 TSP Himalayan Sea Salt
Dash of Cayenne Pepper (Optional)

 Health & Beauty: Raw Soups – Here are the benefits:

Convenient – you can make them quick and even carry them with you to work or anywhere in a take away cup

Easy to Digest – Blending raw vegetables breaks them down into particles that are easy to assimilate by our bodies. This is especially true for those of us who do not chew our food well enough

Delicious – You'll have no trouble convincing your family and friends especially children to consume these beauties even if they don't like veggies in general

Beautifying – Eating raw soups on a regular basis will give you translucent skin and a beautiful glow. You will feel and look vibrant!

To Make Soup:

1. Place all the ingredients in a high powered blender like a Vitamix.
2. Blend everything until you get a smooth texture.
3. Pour into bowls or small glasses and vitalize!

Russian Beet Borscht (Soup)

A hearty tomato and beet stew made with caramelized onions, cabbage, potatoes and carrots and seasoned with the bold flavors of dill & parsley topped with a dollop of vegan sour cream

Serves 6

What You Will Need:

4 Cups Filtered Water
1 Large Organic Beet- peeled and diced
1/2 Cup Organic Carrots – shredded
1 Cup Organic Onions– diced
1 Cup Organic Potatoes – diced
2 Cups Organic Cabbage – shredded
1 TSP Dried Dill
2-3 Sprigs Fresh Organic Parsley
 Or 1 TB Dried Parsley
1/4 Cup Organic Red Wine Vinegar
2 Vegetable Bouillon Cubes
2 TB Organic Vegan Buttery Spread
1 TSP Organic Garlic – minced
1 of 14 Oz Can Organic Diced Tomatoes
4 TSP Raw Sugar
1 TSP Himalayan Pink Salt
1 Container (340g) Organic Vegan Sour Cream
(Optional)

Suggested Shopping List:
- Spectrum® Organic Red Wine Vinegar
- Earth Balance® Natural Buttery Spread (non-Soy version)
- Edward & Sons® Not Chick'n Natural Bouillon Cubes
- Follow Your Heart® Organic Vegan Sour Cream (Optional)

To Make The Soup:

1. In a pressure cooker with the lid removed, sauté the garlic and onions in the vegan buttery spread until the onions are softened.
2. Add the red wine vinegar and sugar, and let the onions and garlic cook in this mixture on medium heat for about 5 minutes.
3. Season with dill, parsley and Himalayan Pink Salt.
4. Pour in the water and then toss in the bouillon cubes.
5. Increase the burner to high and keep stirring so the bouillon cubes can completely dissolve.
6. Add the can of organic tomatoes, carrots, beets, potatoes and cabbage. Stir the vegetables in.
7. Secure the lid of the pressure cooker. Leave the burner on high. Set your pressure cooker to start pressurizing.
8. Pay attention to your pressure cooker. When you start to hear the pressure cooker begin to whistle, turn your timer on to 5 minutes. (You may want to check your own pressure cooker for cooking times of potatoes– since they take the longest to cook).
9. After the timer goes off after 5 minutes, turn the pressure cooker off.
10. Carefully release the steam from the pressure cooker. Then open the lid.
11. Stir the soup and serve.
    Serve soup in individual bowls by topping with a dollop of vegan sour cream.

Health: Beets benefit healthy circulation, blood pressure, give you energy, improve brain function, and alleviate sexual dysfunctions
Beauty: Red Wine Vinegar helps to keep your weight down because of the presence of resveratrol a powerful antioxidant. Plus it keeps blood sugar levels down. Next time you want to slim your waistline while adding flavor to your food, add a splash of red wine vinegar!

Tom Yum Miso Noodle Soup

This aromatic noodle soup is a fusion of Japanese and Thai bursting with the flavors of miso, spinach, and tom yum with floating chunks of tofu simmered in a sumptuous scallion, ginger and garlic broth

Serves 4-6

What You Will Need:

12 Cups Filtered Water
3 Stalks Organic Scallions – sliced into thin pieces
1TSP Organic Ginger – minced
1 TSP Organic Garlic – minced
Organic Cilantro – 2 to 3 Sprigs – leaves and stems chopped fine
1 TB Tom Yum Paste
1 TB Organic Miso Paste

 Use Chickpea Miso

2 Vegetable Bouillon Cubes
1 of 14 Oz Block Organic Extra Firm Tofu – cut into cubes
1½ Cups Organic Spinach (frozen or fresh)
2 TB Organic Shoyu Sauce

 Use Organic Tamari Sauce

3 TB Bragg® Liquid Amino Acids
6 TSP Raw Sugar
2 Dried Cakes of Chinese Rice Noodles

Suggested Shopping List:
- Bright Star® Tom Yum Paste – sold in Oriental markets
- Miso Master® Barley-Miso or Chickpea Miso (gluten-free)
- Edward & Sons® Not Chick'n Natural Bouillon Cubes
- Wildwood® Organic Sprouted Tofu
- San-J® Organic Shoyu Sauce or Organic Tamari (gluten-free)
- Bragg® Liquid Amino Acids
- Wei-Chuan® Rice Stick (Pasta) – found in Oriental markets

 If you ever crave instant noodles e.g. Ramen®, make this soup instead – it's healthier and just as quick to prepare!

To Make The Soup:

1. Fill a large pot with 12 cups of water, and place over high heat. Add the scallions, ginger, garlic and cilantro to the water.
2. Add the vegetable bouillon cubes, raw sugar, Shoyu sauce, Bragg and Tom Yum paste, stirring consistently to make sure the bouillon cubes have dissolved
3. Stir in the spinach and tofu.
4. When the mixture comes to a rolling boil, add the noodles.
5. Cook for another 1-2 minutes, until noodles get limp. Turn off burner.
6. Place miso in a small separate bowl. Take a few tablespoons of broth from the pot, and mix in with the miso to make a thick paste. Once miso is well whisked, add to the soup.
7. Serve soup with noodles in individual bowls and enjoy!

  Add more health benefits to this soup by adding kelp to it. See a variation recipe on the next page.

Health: Miso is an excellent source of B12, which is necessary to keep the body's nerve and blood cells healthy. B12 is generally difficult for vegans to obtain from plant based foods so eat more miso!
High in protein – 1 tablespoon of miso contains 2 grams of protein
Beauty: Miso contains linoleic acid, which keeps skin supple, and prevents wrinkles and age spots

Tom Yum Kelp Miso Noodle Soup

Same aromatic noodle soup with a variation of kelp salad added to it to give that boost of iodine we all need!

Serves 4-6

What You Will Need:
12 cups Filtered Water
3 stalks Organic Scallions – thinly sliced
1 TSP Organic Ginger – minced
1 TSP Organic Garlic – minced
2-3 Sprigs Organic Cilantro – leaves and stems chopped fine
1 TB Tom Yum Paste
1 TB Organic Miso Paste

 Use Chickpea Miso

2 Vegetable Bouillon Cubes
1 of 14 Oz Block Organic Extra Firm Tofu – cut into cubes
1½ Cups Organic Spinach (frozen or fresh)
2 sheets Organic Kelp – cut into short strips which yields about 1½ cups
2 TB Organic Shoyu Sauce

 Use Organic Tamari Sauce

3 TB Bragg® Liquid Amino Acids
6 TSP Raw Sugar
2 Dried Cakes of Chinese Rice noodles

What You Will Need For The Kelp Salad:
1 TB Mirin (or rice vinegar)
1/2 TB Chinese Sesame Oil
1 TB Bragg Liquid Amino Acids
2 TSP Raw Sugar

Suggested Shopping List:
- Bright Star® Tom Yum Paste – sold in Oriental markets
- Miso Master® Barley-Miso or Chickpea Miso
- Edward & Sons® Not Chick'n Natural Bouillon Cubes
- Wildwood® Organic Sprouted Tofu
- Maine Coast Sea Vegetable® Kelp – Wild Atlantic Kombu
- San-J® Organic Shoyu Sauce or Organic Tamari (gluten-free)
- Bragg® Liquid Amino Acids
- Wei-Chuan® Rice Stick (Pasta) found in Oriental markets
- Eden® Mirin
- Wei-Chuan® 100% Pure Black Sesame Oil

 Health: Kelp has large amounts of iodine which helps with thyroid regulation, and prevention of cancers especially estrogen related cancers, e.g. ovarian, breast, cervix etc. because the fucoidan contained in kelp induces "cell death" in cancer cells
Beauty: Kelp gives you radiant skin and shiny hair!

To Make Kelp Salad:
1. Using a pair of sharp scissors or a knife, cut the kelp sheets into short strips.
2. Mix all ingredients for kelp salad into a bowl. Toss the strips of kelp in the marinade so that they are well coated.
3. Let the strips marinate in this mixture for 2-3 hours or longer. Set aside.

To Make Tom Yum-Miso Kelp Soup:
1. Fill a large pot with 12 cups of water, and place over high heat. Add the scallions, ginger, garlic, cilantro and prepared kelp salad to the water.
2. Add the vegetable bouillon cubes, raw sugar, Shoyu (Tamari) sauce, Bragg and Tom Yum paste, stirring consistently to make sure the bouillon cubes have dissolved
3. Stir in the spinach and tofu.
4. When the mixture comes to a rolling boil, add the noodles.
5. Cook for another 1-2 minutes, until noodles get limp. Turn off burner.
6. Place miso in a small separate bowl. Take a few tablespoons of broth from the pot, and mix in with the miso to make a thick paste. Once miso is well whisked, add to the soup.
7. Serve soup with noodles in individual bowls and enjoy!

 You can enjoy kelp salad by itself – it makes a delicious healthy raw salad

Hummus p. 40 & Baba Ganoush p. 32

Appetizers

Kati Rolls p. 43

Barbecued Tofu p.35

Baba Ganoush

A fire-roasted eggplant dip blended with creamy tahini, garlic, and aromatic herbs and spices. Who can resist this delectable dip?

Serves 4

Suggested Shopping List:
- Tree of Life® Organic Tahini or Organic Peanut Butter

What You Will Need:

9 Organic Thai Eggplants or 9 Small Indian Eggplants – with stems removed
1/8 Cup Organic Lemon juice
1/4 Cup Organic Tahini
Or Organic Creamy Peanut Butter (if you like a sweeter flavor)
1 TB Sesame Seeds (optional)
2 Cloves Organic Garlic
2 Sprigs of Fresh Organic Parsley
1 TSP Ground Cumin
1 TSP Himalayan Pink Salt
Pepper to taste
1½ TB Extra Virgin Olive Oil

To Make The Dip:

1. Lightly grease a baking sheet.
2. Place whole eggplants with stems removed on baking sheet, making holes in the skins with a skewer or a fork.
3. Broil the eggplants for 8 minutes or until they are soft to the touch.
4. Carefully remove the broiled eggplants from the oven.
5. Place eggplants in a bowl of cold water.
6. Remove skins from the broiled eggplants, and discard skins.
7. Place eggplant pulp, lemon juice, tahini (or peanut butter), sesame seeds, garlic, fresh parsley, cumin, salt and pepper and olive oil in a food processor and process until you get a thick pasty-like consistency with all ingredients puréed.
8. Serve the Baba Ganoush dip with pita chips or warmed pita bread triangles or with fresh cut up veggies..

 Have Baba Ganoush with Hummus (see page 40 for recipe) and Greek Millet Salad (see page 59 for recipe) for a delish Mediterranean meal

 Did you know if you don't remove the skins of the eggplant, your dip will be bitter?

 Health: Eggplants are good for your brain and shield the brain cell membranes from any kind of damage and injury.
Beauty: Eggplants prevent water retention and weight gain due to their potassium content so they keep the bloating down hence giving you a slimmer appearance

Basil Rolls

Delicate fresh rice spring roll skins filled with chunks of spicy seitan, fresh basil, and a sautéed tangy mixture of cabbage, carrots, and rice noodles

Makes 20 rolls

What You Will Need for The Filling:

2½ Cups Organic Cabbage
  – shredded (1/2 head – purple or green your choice)
2 Cups Organic Carrots – shredded
2 TSP Chili Garlic Sauce (see page 154 for recipe or store-bought)
2 TB Organic Shoyu Sauce

 Use Organic Tamari Sauce

1 TB Bragg® Liquid Amino Acids
2 TSP Raw Sugar
1 Packet Seasoned Organic Seitan – sliced thin

 Omit Seitan

2 Cups Rice Noodles
4 Cups Filtered Water (for boiling noodles)
1 TSP Himalayan Pink Salt
40 Fresh Organic Basil Leaves
Grapeseed Oil for cooking

What You Will Need for Outer Shell:

1 of 12 Oz Package Circular Spring Roll Wrappers
Filtered Water in large bowl for dipping spring roll wrappers

What You Will Need for The Dipping Sauce:

1 TB Chili Garlic Sauce (see page 154 for recipe or store-bought)
1 TB Organic Ketchup
1 TB Organic Shoyu Sauce

 Use Organic Tamari Sauce

2 TSP Raw Sugar
2 TB Filtered Water

Suggested Shopping List:
- Lee Kum Kee® Chili Garlic Sauce or Sriracha® Chili Garlic Sauce
- San-J® Organic Shoyu Sauce or Organic Tamari (Gluten-Free)
- Bragg® Liquid Amino Acids
- Eco Vegan® "Spicy Bits" for Seitan
- Wei-Chuan® Rice Stick (Pasta) – found in Oriental markets
- BanH Trang® Spring Roll Wrappers found in Oriental markets
- Tree of Life® Organic Ketchup

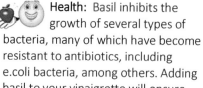 **Health:** Basil inhibits the growth of several types of bacteria, many of which have become resistant to antibiotics, including e.coli bacteria, among others. Adding basil to your vinaigrette will ensure that the fresh salad greens are safe to eat

Beauty: Basil is a pimple eraser. The herb's oil helps combat the bacteria that causes pimples

To Make The Noodles:
1. In a large pot, bring 4 cups of water to boil. Add salt and a tablespoon of oil to the water.
2. Once the water starts to boil, add the dry cake of noodles.
3. Cook noodles for about 1-2 minutes or as soon as they start to break up.
   Note: Do not overcook the noodles or you will have a mushy mess!
4. Drain the noodles in a colander.
5. Cut them up with a pair of kitchen scissors.
6. Set the cooked noodles aside.

Continued…

Basil Rolls (Cont'd)

To Make The Rest of the Filling:

1. In a large skillet, in 3 tablespoons of oil, sauté the chili garlic sauce.
2. Add the cabbage and carrots and stir fry on high heat for 5 minutes.
3. Add the Shoyu sauce (Tamari Sauce), Bragg, and raw sugar. Mix well.
4. Lower heat, and cover the skillet for about 10 minutes to allow the cabbage and carrots to become tender and for the flavors to blend.
5. Turn off heat.
6. Toss the cooked noodles into the cabbage and carrot mixture mixing in thoroughly.

To Make The Basil Rolls:

1. In a large bowl filled with water, submerge 1 spring roll wrapper for 1 minute and 15 seconds; it will become pliable.
2. Carefully remove the wrapper from the water.
3. Place on a smooth working surface.
4. Place 2 tablespoons of carrot and cabbage noodle mixture in wrapper.
5. Place four pieces of sliced seitan on top of the filling.
6. Top with 2 basil leaves.
7. Wrap your spring rolls. (See the six-step diagram below)
8. Mix all the ingredients for the dipping sauce in a small bowl. (See recipe on previous page)
9. Serve your spring rolls with dipping sauce.

Six-Steps To Follow to Wrap The Basil Rolls:

Step 1: Place filling in the middle of the wrapper as shown in Step 1 in the diagram below.
Step 2: Roll the wrapper twice up in the direction of the arrow as shown in Step 2.
Step 3: Fold one flap over as shown in Step 3.
Step 4: Fold the other flap over, overlapping the first flap as shown in Step 4.
Step 5: Keep rolling the wrapper (in the direction of the arrow) until you reach the end and stick in place.
Step 6: Admire your finished masterpiece!

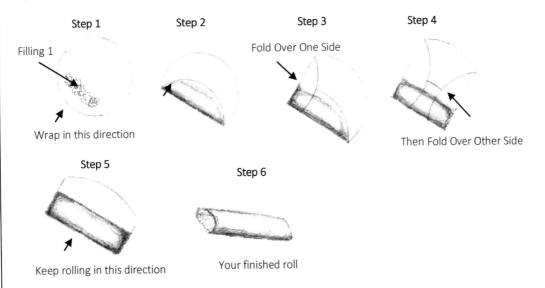

Step 1
Filling 1
Wrap in this direction

Step 2

Step 3
Fold Over One Side

Step 4
Then Fold Over Other Side

Step 5
Keep rolling in this direction

Step 6
Your finished roll

Barbecued Tofu Steaks

Grilled succulent slabs of marinated tofu bursting with flavor – perfect for a Vegan Backyard Barbecue (for best results, marinate tofu for 3 days prior to cooking)

Makes about 24 Tofu Steaks

What You Will Need:

2 Pounds <u>Super Firm</u> or Extra-Firm Organic Tofu – drained – (see freezing preparation process below)

What You Will Need for the Marinade:

1/4 Cup Organic Peanut Butter
1/4 Cup Organic Sunflower Oil
<u>or</u> Organic Canola Oil
1½ TSP Dried Paprika
1½ TSP Himalayan Pink Salt
1/2 TSP Garlic Powder
1 of 15 Oz Can Organic Crushed Tomatoes
1/4 Cup Raw Sugar
4 Sprigs Fresh Organic Parsley (about 2 TB)
 – Chopped fine
1½ TSP Organic Raw Coconut Nectar
<u>or</u> Organic Brown Rice Syrup/Organic Maple Syrup
1/4 TSP Ground Allspice
1/4 TSP Cayenne Pepper (optional – if you like spice)
2 TB Fresh Organic Lime Juice (juice of 1 lime)
1 TB Organic Shoyu Sauce
1 TB Barbecue Vegenaise® or Organic Barbecue Sauce
 (Optional – just to give it that smoked flavor)

Suggested Shopping List:
- Wildwood® Super Firm Organic Sprouted Tofu
- San-J® Organic Shoyu Sauce or Organic Tamari (Gluten-Free)
- Coconut Secret® Organic Raw Coconut Nectar <u>or</u> Lundberg® Sweet Dreams Organic Brown Rice Syrup
- Follow Your Heart® Barbecue Vegenaise

 Did you know that freezing the tofu creates little cracks in the tofu which allows it to take on the flavor of the marinade? Otherwise you'll have bland tofu no matter how long you marinate it

 Health: Tofu is high in calcium (1 serving gives you 10% of daily requirement) protecting against bone weakness & loss, osteoporosis and rheumatoid arthritis.
Beauty: Tofu helps with weight loss because of its lower calorie content, saturated fat and sodium. Having a tofu steak is less fattening than having a meat steak and still gives you lots of protein!

To Prepare the Tofu Steaks:

1. Make sure you use super firm or extra firm tofu – the firmer the tofu the better the results.
2. Slice the tofu into 1/2 inch slabs.
3. Place the tofu slabs in a freezer-proof container and freeze overnight.
4. Remove the container from the freezer and allow the tofu slabs to completely thaw at room temperature. Do not try to separate the tofu slabs until completely thawed or they will break.
5. Mix the marinade ingredients in a bowl. Use a wire whisk to blend well.
6. Arrange tofu slabs in a deep glass dish.
7. Spoon the marinade sauce over tofu slabs completely covering all the tofu slabs. *Note: the slabs can be stacked.*

To Cook the Tofu Steaks:

1. Spray a large ceramic skillet with oil.
2. Place the marinated tofu slabs on the skillet, making sure to brush the marinade well onto the tofu. Fry on one side and then turn over to the other side making sure both sides are nicely browned, pressing gently.
3. Or cook on an outdoor grill.

 To make it a meal, serve with vegan potato salad (see page 61 for recipe).

Variation: For a low fat version you could bake the tofu in a preheated oven at 350° F. Grease a flat baking sheet with oil, then place tofu slabs on the sheet brushing the slabs well with marinade. Bake tofu slabs for 15-20 minutes on one side or until browned. Then turn the slabs over, brush with more marinade sauce, and bake for another 10-15 minutes or until nicely browned and the sauce has soaked in. *Note: Tofu slabs don't come out as crisp when baked as when you cook them on a stove or grill*

Bean Dip

A quick, easy and tasty snack to make when you are feeling hungry but lazy

Serves 6

What You Will Need:

2 of 15 Oz Cans Organic Refried Beans
4 TB of Organic Salsa (see page 48 for recipe or store-bought)
1 Organic Onion – diced
1 TSP Organic Garlic – minced
2 TSP Organic Taco Seasoning
1 TB Organic Barbecue Sauce
3 Sprigs Fresh Organic Cilantro – finely chopped
1/4 TSP Ground Cumin
1/4 Cup Vegan Cheese Shreds (Optional)
Grapeseed Oil for cooking

see page 48 for recipe

Suggested Shopping List:
- Bearitos® Organic Refried Beans (Traditional)
- Pace® Salsa
- Bearitos® or Simply Organic® Southwest Taco Seasoning
- Annie's® Organic BBQ Sauce
- Daiya® Vegan Cheese Shreds – Cheddar

To Make The Bean Dip:

1. In a large skillet, in two to three tablespoons of oil, sauté the garlic and onions until the onions are translucent and you can smell the aroma of the garlic.
2. Add the salsa, taco seasoning, cilantro, cumin powder and mix thoroughly. Reduce the heat to low.
3. Add the cans of beans and mix well into the salsa mixture coating the beans completely. Make sure to keep stirring on very low heat.
4. Mix in the barbecue sauce. Let the mixture cook on a very low burner for 5 to 7 minutes. Don't forget to keep stirring every so often so the bean mixture doesn't stick to the bottom of the skillet.
5. Sprinkle in the vegan cheese and stir it in until it melts. You can omit the cheese, if you like, since this dip even tastes great without cheese.
6. Serve warm with organic corn chips or crackers.

 If you want a low-fat version of this dish, just eliminate the vegan cheese and instead of eating the dip with corn chips enjoy it with low-fat crackers or gluten-free crackers.

 Health: Refried Beans can help promote digestion and regular, easy-to-pass bowel movements. So if you're constipated eat more beans!
Beauty: Refried Beans can contribute to weight loss provided you're not eating them with cheese and chips. They contain fiber and their nutrients stay in the body longer, so they make you stay fuller longer

According to a Harvard School of Public Health Study a 6-ounce broiled porterhouse steak has 40g worth of protein but 38g of fat – 14g of that saturated fat! Compare that to 2 cups of cooked pinto beans which have 32g of protein, but less than 1 gram of fat – Now aren't you happy eating your beans?

Falafels

Fried golden lentil balls of scrumptiousness – a Mediterranean fast food that you can make very simply at home

Makes 20-30 balls

What You Will Need:

1/2 Cup Skinned and Split Organic Green Gram Lentils (Moong Dal)
1/2 Cup Organic Bengal Gram Lentils (Chana Dal)
1 TSP Organic Ginger-minced
1 TSP Organic Garlic-minced
1 TSP Himalayan Pink Salt
1/2 TSP Coriander Powder
1/2 TSP Aluminum-free Baking Soda
Grapeseed Oil for frying

Suggested Shopping List:
- Split Green Gram Lentils and Bengal Gram Lentils can be found in Indian grocery stores under the names Moong dal and Chana dal)
- Coriander Powder – can be found in Indian grocery stores.
- Bob's Red Mill® Aluminum-Free Baking Soda
- So Delicious® Cultured Coconut Milk (plain)
- Follow Your Heart® Soy-Free Vegenaise

To Make Falafels:

1. Wash and soak the lentils in filtered water for several hours, preferably overnight.
2. The next day, drain all the water out of the soaked lentils.
3. Place soaked lentils, ginger, garlic, salt, coriander powder and baking soda into a food processor or high powered blender.
4. Process all the ingredients until a semi-smooth paste is formed. Don't over process since you want the falafel mix to be slightly chunky.
5. Put enough oil in a small deep frying pan so that the balls can be completely submerged.
6. Turn the heat on high, and wait until the oil is very hot.
7. Carefully drop spoonfuls of falafel mixture forming balls into hot oil and deep fry the falafel balls, making sure to turn them over gently every so often.
8. Keep frying the falafels until they are golden brown in color.
9. Carefully remove the hot falafels – making sure to drain the excess oil off. Cover a flat plate or tray with a paper towel. Place fried falafels on the paper towel allowing it to absorb the excess oil.

 Serve in pita pockets (or gluten-free pita pockets) with shredded lettuce, diced tomatoes and Tzatziki sauce (see recipe below)

What You Will Need for Tzatziki Sauce:

2 TB Cultured Organic Coconut Milk (Vegan Yogurt)
1/2 TSP Organic Garlic – minced
2 TB Vegan Mayonnaise (see page 162 for recipe or store-bought)
1/2 TSP Dried Dill
1/4 Cup Cucumber – finely diced (optional)

To Make Tzatziki Sauce:

Mix all the above sauce ingredients in a bowl and spoon over falafels.

 Health: Lentils are filled with B Vitamins – esp. folate and niacin – these help with depression and other neurological disorders. Forget Prozac®, eat more lentils instead, to stay happy! Lentils are protein packed – 26% of the lentil is protein and the rest is fiber. Vegans must incorporate more lentils into their diet!

Beauty: Lentils prevent constipation, and they increase stool size, which speeds the journey of waste products through the gut leading to better complexion and weight loss

Fried "Mock" Chik'N

This is my compassionate version of southern fried chicken. Chunks of crispy seitan strips that pack a big crunch in every bite. Step aside Colonel Sanders® – I think our Vegan version is better!

Serves 4

What You Will Need:

1 Package Seasoned Seitan Strips

 Use Organic Super-Firm Tofu or Tempeh

1 Cup Unbleached Organic Flour

 Use Gluten-free Flour

1 Cup Chickpea Flour
2 TB Aluminum-Free Baking Powder
1/4 Cup Nutritional Yeast
1/2 TSP Thyme
1/2 TSP Mild Madras Curry Powder
1/2 TSP Ground Black Pepper
1/2 TSP Ground White Pepper
1 TSP Onion Powder
1 TSP Dried Parsley
1 TSP Dried Basil
1 TSP Garlic Powder
1 TSP Himalayan Pink Salt
3 TB Organic Yellow Mustard
1/2 Cup Filtered Water
4 Cups Grapeseed Oil for frying

Suggested Shopping List:
- Trader Joe's® Chicken-Less Strips
For Gluten-free use - Wildwood® Organic Sprouted Tofu
Or Lightlife® Organic Tempeh Garden Veggie flavor.
- Bob's Red Mill® Unbleached Unbromated Organic Flour
- Chickpea Flour found in Indian grocery stores
- Bob's Red Mill® Aluminum-Free Baking Soda
- Bragg® Nutritional Yeast
- Kim Thu Thap® Mild Madras Curry Powder
- Eden® Organic Yellow Mustard

 Gluten-free Meal: If you are using tofu, then make sure you use the super firm kind and press out any excess water, pat dry between paper towels, and then cut into strips. If you are using tempeh, then see page 80 for how to prepare tempeh before using in recipe.

To Make Fried Mock Chik'N:

1. In a mixing bowl, mix together flour, chickpea flour, nutritional yeast, thyme, curry powder, black pepper, white pepper, onion powder, parsley, basil, garlic powder and salt.
2. In another bowl whisk together 1/2 cup of filtered water and mustard.
3. Add 1/3 Cup of the flour mixture created in step 1 to the mustard mixture, stirring vigorously to well-combine the flour mixture into the mustard mixture.
4. Add the baking powder to the flour mixture created in step 1.
5. Dredge the seitan(tofu or tempeh) strips first in the mustard batter (made in step 2), then coat the strips with the flour mixture created in step 1 – this forms the crust.
6. Heat 4 cups of oil in a small deep frying pan.
7. Turn the heat on high, and wait until the oil is very hot. (You'll know it's ready when you place a strip and It floats instead of sinking down to the bottom)
8. Carefully place coated strips (a few at a time) into hot oil and deep fry the strips, making sure to turn them over gently every so often. *Note: Don't add too many pieces to the frying pan at once or you will cool the oil down and make the strips greasy.*
9. Keep frying the mock chik'n strips until they are golden brown in color.
10. Carefully remove the fried strips – making sure to drain the excess oil off. Place on a paper towel covering a plate so that the excess oil can be absorbed by the paper towel.

 Make it a Southern meal, and serve with mashed potatoes, vegan gravy (see page 94 for recipe) or with potato salad (see page 61 for recipe), and steamed collard greens or kale.

Guacamole-Oh-So-Easy

Creamy, chunky, irresistible, easy-to-make, ripe avocado dip that you can whip up in 5 minutes for those sudden hungry guests that arrive at your doorstep!

Serves 4

What You Will Need:

2 Ripe Avocados
2 TB Fresh Organic Lime Juice (juice of 1 lime)
2-3 Sprigs Fresh Organic Cilantro – with stems and leaves finely chopped
1/2 Cup of Organic Grape Tomatoes – quartered
1 TSP Fresh Organic Garlic – minced or 1/4 TSP garlic powder
1/2 TSP Ground Cumin
1/2 TSP Himalayan Pink Salt
Minced Organic hot chili peppers (jalapeño, serrano, habanero, etc) – Optional – only if you like it spicy

Suggested Shopping List:
- Ground Cumin – can be found in Indian grocery stores

To Make Guacamole:

1. Cut avocados in half, remove pits and scoop out pulp with a spoon.
2. In a mixing bowl, mash pulp coarsely with a fork.
3. Season with lime juice, cilantro, garlic, cumin and salt.
4. Mix well.
5. Gently stir in the tomatoes and minced peppers (if you are using them).

 You can enjoy this dip with chips or make it a healthy snack by dipping with cut up veggies like broccoli florets, bell pepper strips, baby carrots, celery sticks, zucchini or yellow squash rounds

Guacamole also makes an excellent salad dressing. Next time you make a raw salad, omit the store-bought salad dressing, and use guacamole instead!

 Health: Avocados give you a healthy brain due to the presence of folate which prevents and reverses Alzheimer's disease and dementia.
Also good for your eyes – contains the carotenoid lutein, an antioxidant that specializes with protecting the eyes from oxidative stress damage which leads to poor vision, cataracts, and macular degeneration
Beauty: Eat an Avocado everyday to reverse the aging process. Great for skin disorders too – rub a raw avocado all over face to remove blemishes and pimples

Did you know that contrary to popular belief Avocados are not fattening and actually help in weight loss?

Hummus

A perfect hearty dip made with a blend of garbanzo beans (chick peas), sesame seeds, lemon juice, garlic, and aromatic spices with a hint of olive oil — A Mediterranean staple

Serves 4

What You Will Need:

2 of 15 Oz Cans Organic Garbanzo Beans or Chick Peas
 — with one can drained and the other undrained
4 TB Raw Sesame seeds
1 TB Organic Extra Virgin Olive Oil
1/4 Cup Organic Lemon Juice
1 Clove Organic Garlic
1 TSP Ground Cumin
1 TSP Himalayan Pink Salt
Paprika for garnish

Suggested Shopping List:
– Eden® Organic Garbanzo Cans
– Ground Cumin – can be found in Indian grocery stores.
– Mediterranean Organic® Sun-dried Tomatoes
– Follow Your Heart® Soy-Free Vegenaise

Use Hummus as a delicious dressing in a wrap with sautéed veggies or with falafels (see page 37 for recipe).

To Make Hummus:

1. Put all the ingredients in a food processor or high-powered blender.
2. Process all the ingredients until they reach a smooth paste-like consistency.
3. Sprinkle with paprika over the top.

 Serve hummus with pita chips or warmed cut up triangles of pita bread or sliced veggies like broccoli, bell pepper strips, baby carrots, celery, zucchini or yellow squash rounds.

Sun-Dried Tomato Basil Hummus

A variation to the traditional Mediterranean classic — with a delectable addition of sun-dried tomatoes and basil

Serves 4

What You Will Need:

2 of 15 Oz Cans Organic Garbanzo Beans or Chick Peas
 — with one can drained and the other undrained
1 of 8.5 Oz Jar Organic Sun-Dried Tomatoes
 Or 1 Cup Dried Organic Sun-Dried Tomatoes
 soaked in warm filtered water for 10 minutes and then drained
1/8 Cup Organic Extra Virgin Olive Oil (**only** if you are **not** using the sun-dried tomatoes in a jar)
1/2 TSP Dried Basil or 10 Fresh Organic Basil Leaves
1 TSP Organic Garlic
2 TB Vegan Mayonnaise — (see page 162 for recipe or store-bought)

To Make Sun-Dried Tomato Hummus:

Process all the above ingredients in a food processor or high powered blender until they reach a smooth paste-like consistency.

Kale Chips – Curry Flavor

Take these raw crispy curry snacks with you to the movies or to the ball game – or wherever you would like to munch on some healthy crunch!

What You Will Need:
1-2 bunches of Organic kale – de-stemmed and torn into medium sized pieces (see directions below) (see picture below – actual size)
A Dehydrator

Suggested Shopping List:
- Tree of Life® Organic Tahini
- Bragg® Organic Raw Apple Cider Vinegar
- Bragg® Nutritional Yeast Seasoning
- Coombs® Organic Maple Syrup (Grade B)

What You Will Need for the Seasoning:

1 TSP Organic Tahini
1 TSP Organic Raw Apple Cider Vinegar
4 TB Organic Extra Virgin Olive Oil
1 TB Nutritional Yeast
1 TSP Organic Maple Syrup (Grade B)
1/2 TSP Ground Cumin
1/4 TSP Ground Turmeric
1/2 TSP Himalayan Pink Salt
1½ TSP Garlic Powder
Dash of Cayenne Powder to taste
  (Optional – omit if you don't like spice)

To Make the Kale Chips:
1. Tear the leafy part of the kale away from the stem into large pieces (size to scale – see picture above). Leaves shrink a lot when dehydrated and thus if your leaves are too small – you end up with tiny crumbs and not bite size chips. Discard stems.
2. Wash the torn leaves in a large bowl of water discarding and refilling water in the bowl until all the dirt on leaves has been washed away. Kale can be quite dirty with dirt hiding in the curly edges of its leaves. Set aside.
3. In another bowl, mix all the ingredients for the seasoning, making sure to whisk well until all the tahini has blended in with the other ingredients since tahini can get lumpy if not mixed in well.
4. Pour the seasoning mixture over the torn kale leaves.
5. Now with clean hands, massage the mixture into the kale making sure to coat the mixture well into every piece of kale. Squeezing, kneading and pressing the kale between your fingers. It's messy but it's fun!
6. Pick up handfuls of coated kale pieces and scatter them carefully on your dehydrator trays on top of the plastic sheets with the holes. Do make sure to spread them out evenly over several trays. *Note: you don't have to lay every piece of kale individually.*
7. Dehydrate at 115°F for 10-14 hours. Check at 10 hours – if your chips are crisp, you can remove them from the dehydrator, but if they are still not that crisp, then dehydrate for another 4 hours.
8. When you are finished dehydrating the chips will be crunchy.
9. You can store them in an airtight container for up to a month!

Variation: For another tasty flavor of Kale Chips see the recipe on the next page – Soy Sesame Kale Chips

Health: Kale is high in calcium. Per calorie, kale has more calcium than milk. Kale aids in preventing bone loss, preventing osteoporosis and maintaining healthy metabolism. Kale is also a great detox food, filled with fiber and sulfur keeping your liver healthy
Beauty: Kale is filled with antioxidants, and Vitamins A & C which gives you younger looking skin

Kale Chips – Soy-Sesame Flavor

Same crunchy raw goodness except this time with an Oriental flair to them

What You Will Need:
1-2 bunches of Organic kale – de-stemmed
and torn into medium sized pieces (see directions below)
(see picture below – actual size)
A Dehydrator

What You Will Need for the Seasoning:

1 TB Bragg® Liquid Amino Acids
1 TB Organic Shoyu Sauce

 Use Organic Tamari Sauce

2 TB Chinese Sesame Oil
2 TB Organic Extra Virgin Olive Oil
2 TSP Organic Maple Syrup (Grade B)
1 TSP Organic Tahini
Dash of Garlic Powder
1½ TB Raw Sesame Seeds

To Make the Kale Chips:
1. Tear the leafy part of the kale away from the stem into large pieces (size to scale – see picture above). Leaves shrink a lot when dehydrated and thus if your leaves are too small – you end up with tiny crumbs and not bite size chips. Discard stems.
2. Wash the torn leaves in a large bowl of water discarding and refilling water in the bowl until all the dirt on leaves has been washed away. Kale can be quite dirty with dirt hiding in the curly edges of its leaves. Set aside.
3. In another bowl, mix all the ingredients for the seasoning, making sure to whisk well until all the tahini has blended in with the other ingredients since tahini can get lumpy if not mixed in well.
4. Pour the seasoning mixture over the torn kale leaves.
5. Now with clean hands, massage the mixture into the kale making sure to coat the mixture well into every piece of kale. Squeezing, kneading and pressing the kale between your fingers. It's messy but it's fun!
6. Pick up handfuls of coated kale pieces and scatter them carefully on your dehydrator trays on top of the plastic sheets with the holes. Do make sure to spread them out evenly over several trays. *Note: you don't have to lay every piece of kale individually.*
7. Dehydrate at 115°F for 10-14 hours. Check at 10 hours – if your chips are crisp, you can remove them from the dehydrator, but if they are still not that crisp, then dehydrate for another 4 hours.
8. When you are finished dehydrating the chips will be crunchy.
9. You can store them in an airtight container for up to a month!

 Health: Raw Food⇨Enzymes⇨More Energy⇨Less Needed Sleep⇨More Productivity
Raw Food gives us natural enzymes that we require to digest food. This leaves us with so much more energy since a lot of our energy is spent in digestion. This leads to better sleep and even less required sleep, which in turn brings in more productivity.
Beauty: Raw Food gives us more regularity hence clearing up toxin build-up in our bodies – which brings about brighter looking hair and skin

Kati Rolls A.K.A Frankies

Here you get to try popular Indian style burritos sold daily on the busy streets of India! Intoxicatingly flavorful soy protein granules seasoned with Indian spices and stuffed into a roti paratha (puffed bread)

Makes 10-15 Rolls

What You Will Need:

1½ Cups Vegan Ground Beef – (see page 161 for recipe)
1½ Cups Organic Onions – diced
3 Sprigs Fresh Organic Cilantro – chopped fine
1 TSP Himalayan Pink Salt
1 TSP Cumin Seeds ("Jeera" in Indian)
1 TSP Garam Masala (see 156 for recipe or store-bought)
10-15 Roti Parathas also called Roti Canai
2 TB Grapeseed Oil

Suggested Shopping List:
- Cumin Seeds (called "Jeera" and available in Indian grocery stores)
- Garam Masala – available in Indian grocery stores
- Kawan® brand Roti Parathas/Roti Kanai – available in the freezers in Indian stores or online.

To Make the Kati Rolls:

1. In a large skillet, in 2 tablespoons of oil, sauté onions until they are translucent and limp. Lower heat.
2. Season with cumin seeds, garam masala, cilantro, and salt. Stir consistently until you can smell the aroma of the spices – about 2-3 minutes.
3. Add the vegan ground beef. Mix well until the TVP granules are well coated with the onion mixture. Cover skillet, and let the mixture cook on low heat for about 5 minutes to blend flavors.
4. Turn off burner. Set TVP mixture aside.
5. On a flat skillet, place 1 frozen roti paratha and cook on both sides until both sides are slightly browned and start to fluff up.
6. Place the TVP mixture in the center of each roti paratha, roll up like a burrito (see page 34 for instructions on how to wrap a basil roll) and enjoy!
7. Repeat steps 5-6 until all the TVP mixture is used up.

 Unfortunately I have not listed this dish as gluten-free as it would take hours of your time in the kitchen making your own roti parathas

 Did you know that Kati roll is a street-food originating from Kolkata, India? It is known by various names in different parts of India, e.g. In Western India it is called Kati Kebab roll, In Southern and Eastern India it is called Frankie and in Northern India it is known as Unda roll or Roti roll. So many names for the same yummy rolls!

Meatless Meatballs

Succulent, spicy, sweet and sour meat-less balls of absolute delight which can be eaten as they are, in a submarine sandwich on hoagie bread or with a bed of spaghetti – very versatile

Makes 20 Balls

What You Will Need:

1½ Cups Vegan Ground Beef (see page 161)
1½ Cups Organic Onions – finely diced
1 Cup Organic Green Bell Peppers – finely diced
3 Sprigs Fresh Organic Cilantro – stems and leaves chopped fine
1 TSP Organic Garlic – minced
1 TSP Organic Ginger – minced
1 TSP Himalayan Pink Salt
Freshly Ground Pepper to Taste
1 TSP Ground Cumin
1 TSP Garam Masala (see page 156 for recipe
  or store-bought)
2 Slices of Organic White Bread – crumbled

 Use Gluten-free Bread

3 TSP Egg Replacer mixed with
  4 TB warm filtered water
Grapeseed Oil for frying
6 Oz Chili Garlic Sauce (see page 154 for recipe
  or store-bought)
5 Oz Organic Red Currant Jelly or Concord
  Grape Jelly

Suggested Shopping List:
- Ground Cumin and Garam Masala –
available in Indian grocery stores
- Ener-G® Egg Replacer
Optional – Tinkyada® Spaghetti Style
Brown Rice Pasta
<u>Or</u> Hoagie rolls for sub sandwich

To Make Meatless Meatballs:

1. In a large skillet, on medium heat, in 2 tablespoons of oil, sauté garlic, ginger, cilantro, onions and peppers until the onions are translucent and limp. (about 5 minutes). Lower heat.
2. Season with cumin, garam masala, salt and pepper. Stir consistently until you can smell the aroma of the spices – about 2-3 minutes.
3. Add the vegan ground beef. Mix well until the TVP granules are well coated with the vegetable mixture. Cover skillet, and let the mixture cook on low heat for about 5 minutes to blend flavors.
4. Turn off burner. Set this mixture aside.
5. In a large bowl, combine the cooked mixture, crumbled white bread, and egg replacer. Mix thoroughly until a dough forms.
6. Using your hands, form the dough into 1-inch balls.
7. Heat 4 cups of oil in a small deep frying pan.
8. Turn the heat on high, and wait until the oil is very hot. (You'll know it's ready when you place a ball in and It will float instead of sinking down to the bottom)
9. Carefully place meatless meatballs (a few at a time) into hot oil and deep fry the balls, making sure to turn them over gently every so often. *Note: Don't add too many balls into the frying pan at once or you will cool the oil down and make the balls greasy.*
10. Keep frying the meatless meatballs until they are golden brown in color.
11. Carefully remove the fried balls– making sure to drain the excess oil off. Place on a plate covered with a paper towel to absorb excess oil.
12. In a small saucepan, heat the chili garlic sauce and jelly together, mixing well to combine the two.

Spoon the sauce over the meatballs and serve as is, or enjoy meatless meatballs with your favorite cooked spaghetti or place in hoagie rolls to enjoy a meatless meatball sub

Millet Burgers

Once you discover these tasty, healthy veggie burger alternatives, you may not go back to the processed store-bought veggie burgers – plus with the benefits of millet these are so good for you too!

Makes 8 Burger Patties

What You Will Need:

1/2 Cup Dry Organic Millet
  – soaked overnight in 1½ cups filtered water
1½ Cups Filtered Water for cooking millet
1 TSP Organic Garlic – minced
1 TSP Organic Ginger – minced
1 TSP Garam Masala (see page 156 for recipe or store-bought)
1 TSP Coriander Powder
2 TSP Himalayan Pink Salt
1 TSP Raw Sugar
3 TB Organic Coconut Oil
Dash of Cayenne pepper (optional)
1/4 Cup Chopped Almonds (or buy blanched almonds)
(soak almonds & remove skins before using)
1 Cup Organic Onions – finely diced
2 Cups Organic Spinach or Kale leaves – finely chopped
2 Stalks Organic Celery – finely diced
1 Cup Organic Carrots – shredded
1 Cup Chickpea Flour – sifted
2 TB Grapeseed Oil for cooking burgers

To Make Burgers:

1. Soak millet in a small bowl overnight.
2. Soak almonds in another small bowl overnight.
3. Next day remove skins from almonds. Chop up almonds and set aside. (Eliminate steps 2 and 3 if using blanched almonds)
4. Drain millet.
5. Pour 1½ cups filtered water in a small saucepan. Bring water to a rolling boil.
6. Then add soaked millet to boiling water and cook on high heat for about 5 minutes.
7. Reduce heat to low, and let millet simmer for about 10-15 minutes or until all the water has evaporated. Set aside.
8. In a large skillet, in 3 TB of coconut oil, sauté the garlic, ginger and onions on medium heat, until the onions are translucent and limp (about 5 minutes).
9. Add the celery, carrots and spinach (or kale) leaves, and stir well. Cover your skillet and let the vegetables steam for 10 minutes on low heat.
10. Once vegetables are cooked, uncover skillet, and season the vegetables with salt, sugar, coriander powder, garam masala and cayenne pepper.
11. Stir in the cooked millet grains and mix well into vegetable mixture.

Suggested Shopping List:
– Chickpea Flour (called "Besan" is available in Indian grocery stores)
– Coriander Powder and Garam Masala – available in Indian grocery Stores
– Dr. Bronner's® Fresh Pressed Virgin Organic Coconut Oil

 Did you know eating almonds with the skins limits the nutrients your body can absorb from the almonds, also making them difficult to digest?

Serve hot with organic ketchup, vegan mayonnaise, or mustard and enjoy as a salad on romaine leaves or as a burger between two buns dressed with lettuce and tomatoes.

12. Turn off heat. Add the chickpea flour to the millet mixture. Stir thoroughly making sure to coat the entire mixture with chickpea flour. The mixture will start to bind together into a dough-like formation.
13. Allow the mixture to cool.
14. Rolling in between the palms of your hands, form the dough into large balls (about 1/2 cup each) and then flatten each ball into a flat burger patty.
15. Continue to make burger patties out of the entire dough mixture.
16. Lay out the millet burgers on a tray or a flat plate.
17. Grease a flat ceramic skillet with oil. Carefully place 4 to 5 burgers at a time on greased skillet. Be careful not to overcrowd the burger patties on the skillet, as it will be harder to flip them over.
18. On medium heat, cook the burgers on the first side about 3-5 minutes, allowing them to become golden brown. Once they move easily and are no longer sticking to the pan, they are ready to be flipped. *(Note: You may need to turn the heat down as the pan heats up).*
19. Cook on the other side for the same amount of time.
20. Transfer the cooked burgers on a plate lined with a paper towel to absorb any excess oil.

Onion Pakodas

Crunchy, crispy golden brown onion fritters – a tasty Indian appetizer that will wow your palette

Makes about 12 fritters

What You Will Need:
1½ Cups Chickpea Flour – sifted
1/2 Cup Filtered Water
1 TSP Himalayan Pink Salt
1 TSP Coriander Powder
1 TSP Aluminum-free Baking Soda
1/2 Cup Organic Onions – finely diced
2 Sprigs Organic Cilantro – stems and leaves finely chopped
Grapeseed oil for frying

Suggested Shopping List:
- Chickpea Flour (called "Besan" is available in Indian grocery stores)
- Coriander Powder – available in Indian grocery stores
- Bob's Red Mill® Aluminum-Free Baking Soda

To Make the Pakodas:
1. In a large bowl, whisk chickpea flour, water, baking soda and mix into a thick cake-like batter.
2. Add salt, coriander powder, onions and cilantro and stir well into the pakoda batter.
3. Put enough oil in a small deep frying pan so that the fritters can be completely submerged.
4. Turn the heat on high, and wait until the oil is very hot.
5. Carefully drop spoonfuls of the pakoda batter into hot oil, forming balls, and deep fry the pakoda balls (fritters), making sure to turn them over gently every so often.
6. You will see the fritters swell up and float to the top and they will be dark yellow in color.
7. Carefully remove the hot pakodas – making sure to drain the excess oil off. Place on a plate covered with a paper towel to absorb excess oil.
8. Let the fritters cool. Using your fingers tear apart each fritter into two pieces.
9. Then fry the broken pieces again in hot oil until they are golden brown and crisp.
10. Serve hot with any of the chutneys on pages 154, 156 or 159.

Variation: You can add other vegetables to the batter instead of just onions e.g. potatoes (sliced in circles), whole green chilies, jalapeno peppers, pumpkin pieces, and even slices of bread cut into squares. Follow steps 1 and 2 and then, dip vegetables into the batter until sufficiently coated. Then deep fry the vegetables covered in batter only once until they are golden brown (eliminating steps 8 and 9).

Health: Chickpea Flour – prevents digestive disorders, constipation and increases stool bulk. Great for detoxifying your body due to the presence of molybdenum
Beauty: Give your face instant radiance with a mixture of chickpea flour (which absorbs oil), turmeric (which is anti-inflammatory and antiseptic), and almond oil. Your skin will be instantly exfoliated, softened and brightened

Potato Burger Patties

A great alternative to soy burgers – try these hearty mashed potato patties delicately flavored with fragrant herbs and spices

Makes about 17-18 small burger patties

What You Will Need:

3 Large Organic Potatoes – any kind (about 4 Cups)
1 TSP Cumin Seeds
1 TSP Turmeric Powder
1 Organic Onion – finely diced
1 TSP Organic Ginger – Minced
1 TSP Organic Garlic – Minced
1 TSP Coriander Powder
1 TSP Garam Masala (see page 156 for recipe or store-bought)
1 Heaping TSP – Himalayan Pink Salt
Dash of Cayenne Pepper
1 TB Chickpea Flour – sifted
1 TB Organic Lemon Juice
3 Sprigs – Fresh Organic Cilantro – finely chopped
Grapeseed Oil

Suggested Shopping List:
- Cumin Seeds, Turmeric Powder, Coriander Powder, Garam Masala – available in Indian grocery stores
- Chickpea Flour (called "Besan" is available in Indian grocery stores)

 Did you know that when you remove the peel from potatoes they become acidic otherwise they are an alkaline forming food?

To Make the Potato Burger Patties:

1. In a pot, boil your potatoes with the skins for about 20-25 minutes (depending on what kind of potatoes you use – Yukons boil faster and Russets take longer). You will know they are done when you poke them with a fork and they are soft.
2. Once boiled, immediately remove potatoes from the water with tongs and place them in a colander. If you leave them in the water too long, they get water logged – this ruins your dish.
3. In a large mixing bowl, mash the boiled potatoes with a fork or potato masher until the mixture is no longer lumpy.
4. In a skillet, in 2 tablespoons of oil, on high heat, sauté the cumin seeds and turmeric powder until the seeds start to sizzle, about 30-40 seconds, then lower heat.
5. Add the onions, ginger, and garlic and mix well with the cumin and turmeric, and cook for another 5 minutes to blend flavors.
6. Turn off burner, and transfer this mixture to the bowl with the mashed potatoes, pouring the mixture gently over the potatoes.
7. Season with coriander powder, garam masala, cayenne pepper, and salt.
8. Add the fresh cilantro, chickpea flour and lemon juice.
9. Mix everything well into the mashed potatoes with a wooden spoon.
10. To evenly blend all ingredients into the potatoes, knead the potato mixture like cookie dough with your hands.
11. Rolling in between the palms of your hands, form the dough into small balls (about 1/4 Cup each) and then flatten each ball into a flat burger patty.
12. Continue to make burger patties out of the entire potato dough.
13. Lay out the potato patties on a tray.
14. Grease a flat skillet with oil. Carefully place 4 to 5 patties at a time on greased skillet. Be careful not to overcrowd the patties on the skillet, as it will be harder to flip them over.
15. On medium heat, cook the patties on the first side about 3-5 minutes, allowing them to become golden brown. Once they move easily and are no longer sticking to the pan, they are ready to be flipped. (Note: You may need to turn the heat down as the pan heats up).
16. Cook on the other side for the same amount of time.
17. Transfer the cooked patties on a plate lined with a paper towel to absorb any excess oil.
18. Serve hot with organic ketchup or chutney (see page 156 for recipe).

 These patties are a great alternative to burger patties and can be placed in between burger buns dressed with ketchup, mustard, lettuce, tomatoes, and pickles

Salsa – Fresh

Making your own Salsa is not only more nutritious but also very cost effective – This version is mostly raw too made with delicious red ripe tomatoes, peppers and fresh cilantro

Makes 1 half gallon sized jar

What You Will Need:

6 Organic Ripe Roma Tomatoes – quartered
6-7 Sprigs Organic Fresh Cilantro (about 1/2 cup)
1/2 Medium Organic Onion (1 Cup) – roughly chopped
1 Large Organic Jalapeno Pepper – with stem removed
 (optional: you can omit this if you don't like spice)
1/2 Organic Green Bell Pepper (with stem and seeds removed) (about 1 Cup)
1 TSP Organic Fresh Lime or Lemon Juice
1 TSP Himalayan Pink Salt
1 Organic Garlic Clove
2 TB Organic Tomato Paste
1/2 TSP Raw Sugar

To Make Salsa:

Blend or process all ingredients in a food processor or powerful blender and process until you get a thick chunky consistency. Enjoy with Organic Corn chips or use in recipes in this book that call for "Salsa".

To make different flavorful salsas:
Variation 1: Add 1/2 cup of organic pineapple chunks to the above recipe
Variation 2: Add 1/2 cup of organic peaches to the above recipe

Health: Salsa contains lots of Vitamin C which protects the cells from damage, plus with added cilantro it neutralizes toxins. It also contains loads of Vitamin A which helps keep your vision in tip top shape. Additionally Vitamin A contributes to healthy functioning of the thyroid thus helping you to maintain a strong immune system
The peppers in Salsa contain capsaicin which helps relieve indigestion and prevents stomach ulcers
Beauty: Salsa is very low in fat, thus you can replace your fattening sauces and dressings with salsa, and contribute to quick weight loss. Peppers are known to promote weight loss.
Who knew Salsa could be so good for you? Go ahead, eat your salsa today – but instead of chips, use gluten-free crackers or cut up veggies and you can snack away!

Samosas

Flaky puff pastry stuffed with savory potatoes and green peas seasoned with fragrant Indian herbs and spices

Makes 18 large triangles and 36 small triangles

What You Will Need:

2 Puff Pastry sheets
3 Cups of Organic Potatoes (any kind)
1½ Cup Organic Onions – diced
1 of 15 Oz Can Organic Sweet Peas – drained
1 TSP Coriander Powder
1 TSP Garam Masala (see page 156 for recipe or store-bought)
1 TSP Madras Curry Powder
1 TSP Organic Garlic – minced
1 TSP Organic Ginger – minced
1 TSP Himalayan Pink Salt
1 TSP Organic Lemon Juice
3 TB Grapeseed oil

Suggested Shopping List:
- Pepperidge Farms® Puff Pastry Sheets
- Westbrae® or Field Day® Organic Sweet Peas
- Coriander Powder and Garam Masala can be found in Indian grocery stores
- Kim Thu Thap® Mild Madras Curry Powder

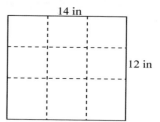

To Make Samosas:

Unfortunately I have not listed this dish as gluten-free as it would take hours of your time in the kitchen making your own puff pastry

1. Thaw puff pastry at room temperature for a couple of hours.
2. In a pot, boil your potatoes with the skins for about 20-25 minutes (depending on what kind of potatoes you use – Yukons boil faster and Russets take longer). You will know they are done when you poke them with a fork and they are soft. Once boiled, immediately remove potatoes from the water with tongs and place them in a colander. If you leave them in the water too long, they get water logged – this ruins your dish.
3. When cooled, slice the potatoes into small cubes and set aside.
4. Preheat oven to 350°F.
5. In a large skillet, in 3 tablespoons of oil, sauté the ginger, garlic, and onions until onions are limp and translucent. Turn the burner to low.
6. Add the coriander powder, garam masala, curry powder, salt, and lemon juice. Stir well into the onions.
7. Add the boiled cubed potatoes and peas and stir well so that the potatoes and peas are well coated with the spice mixture.
8. Cover the skillet, allowing the flavors to blend. Make sure your burner is set to very low. After 5 minutes turn off stove. Set aside allowing the potato mixture to cool.

 Serve with green chutney (see page 156156), organic ketchup, or vegan gravy (see page 94).

9. Roll out the puff pastry sheets on a lightly floured board until each sheet is about 14 inches x 12 inches.
10. Cut the rolled out pastry into 9 squares. (See diagram below).

```
          14 in
 ┌─────┬─────┬─────┐
 │     ┆     ┆     │
 ├ ─ ─ ┼ ─ ─ ┼ ─ ─┤  12 in
 │     ┆     ┆     │
 ├ ─ ─ ┼ ─ ─ ┼ ─ ─┤
 │     ┆     ┆     │
 └─────┴─────┴─────┘
```

11. Place 1 tablespoon of potato mixture in the middle of each square, and fold pastry over diagonally forming a triangle. Secure the edges by pressing firmly together to seal each samosa pastry. Use a fork to crimp and

seal the edges.

12. Repeat step 11 until all the potato mixture and pastry squares are used up.
13. Place filled triangles on a lightly greased baking tray.
14. Bake in a preheated oven at 375°F for 20-25 minutes or until the samosa pastries are golden brown. (Note: cooking times may vary for different ovens)

Spanakopita

Mediterranean version of yummy spinach pies – Flaky Pastry Triangles stuffed with a savory spinach mixture baked to perfection

Makes 18 large triangles and 36 small triangles

What You Will Need:

1 of 10 Oz Package Organic Frozen Chopped Spinach
  (thawed and drained)

<u>Or</u> 1 Pound Fresh Organic Spinach – chopped (6 cups)
1 TSP Organic Garlic – minced
1 TSP Dried Dill
2 Organic Tomatoes – finely diced
1 Cup Organic Onions – finely diced
2 Organic Green Cayenne Peppers – finely sliced
(use gloves when slicing peppers)
3 TSP Cultured Coconut Milk (Vegan Yogurt)
3 TB Organic Lemon Juice
Himalayan Pink Salt and Pepper to taste
2 Puff Pastry Sheets
3 TB Grapeseed oil

Suggested Shopping List:
- So Delicious® Cultured Coconut Milk (plain)
- Pepperidge Farms® Puff Pastry Sheets

 Health: Spinach nourishes the eyes since it is loaded with lutein and carotenoids.
Plus it strengthens bones because of Vitamin K, calcium and magnesium
Beauty: Spinach gives quick relief from dry, itchy skin and lavishes you with a radiant complexion.

 Unfortunately I have not listed this dish as gluten-free as it would take hours of your time in the kitchen making your own puff pastry

To Make Spinach Filling:

1. In a large skillet, in 3 tablespoons of oil, on medium heat, sauté garlic and onions for 4-5 minutes until the onions are limp and translucent.
2. Add the tomatoes, spinach, cayenne peppers, cultured coconut milk, lemon juice, dill, salt and pepper.
3. Cook for about 5 minutes on low heat.
4. Set spinach filling aside allowing it to cool.

To Make Spanakopita:

1. Thaw puff pastry at room temperature for a couple of hours.
2. Preheat oven to 350°F.
3. Roll out the puff pastry sheets on a lightly floured board until each sheet is about 14 inches x 12 inches.
4. Cut the rolled out pastry into 9 squares. (See Figure 1)

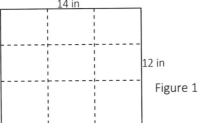
Figure 1

Figure 2

5. Place 1 tablespoon of the spinach mixture in the middle of each square, and fold pastry over diagonally forming a triangle. Secure the edges by pressing firmly together to seal each spinach triangle. Use a fork to crimp the edges (see Figure 2)
6. Repeat step 5 until all the spinach mixture and pastry squares are used up.
7. Place filled triangles on a lightly greased baking tray. .
8. Bake in a preheated oven at 375°F for 20-25 minutes or until the Spanakopitas are golden brown. *(Note: cooking times may vary for different ovens).*

 Serve with Tzatziki sauce (see recipe on page 75)
Variation: Try my other version of Spanakopita using Phyllo pastry and tofu – see following page)

Spanakopita with Vegan Feta

My other Mediterranean version of Spanakopita – whole wheat flaky phyllo pastry stuffed with savory spinach, tomatoes, pine nuts, tofu, and fragrant herbs

What You Will Need:

1 Package Whole Wheat Organic Phyllo Dough
2 of 10 Oz Packages Organic Frozen spinach
<u>Or</u> 2 pounds Fresh Organic Spinach (12 cups)
1 Small Organic Onion – diced
1 TSP Organic Garlic – minced
Grapeseed Oil for cooking
1/2 TSP Dried Dill
1/2 TSP Dried Parsley
1/2 Cup of Pine Nuts
1 Cup Vegan Cheese Shreds

Suggested Shopping List:
– Fillo Factory® Organic Phyllo Dough
– Daiya® Vegan Cheese Shreds – Mozzarella
– Bragg® Organic Raw Apple Cider Vinegar
– Wildwood® Organic Sprouted Tofu

 Instead of using Pam® spray, fill your own oil sprayer bottle with a higher grade of oil – it's cheaper and healthier. I use a Misto® stainless steel oil sprayer and fill it with grapeseed oil

What You Will Need for Vegan Feta:

1/4 Cup Organic Extra Virgin Olive Oil
1/4 Cup Sun-Dried Tomatoes
 – soaked in warm filtered water
   for 10 minutes and then drained
1/4 Cup Filtered Water
1/4 Cup Organic Raw Apple Cider Vinegar
1/2 TSP Himalayan Pink Salt
1 TB Dried Basil
1/2 TSP Dried Oregano
1/2 TSP Pepper
1 of 14 Oz Package Organic Extra Firm Tofu

To Make Vegan Feta:

1. Place olive oil, drained sun-dried tomatoes, filtered water, apple cider vinegar, salt, basil, oregano, pepper in a food processor and process until all the ingredients are puréed.
2. Drain the tofu and dry thoroughly with paper towels to remove all moisture. Chop up the tofu until it is crumbly.
3. Add tofu to blended ingredients, stir, and let it sit covered in the refrigerator for at least an hour to blend flavors and harden.

To Make Spanakopita:

1. Steam the spinach, drain, and squeeze dry between two paper towels. Then set aside.
2. In a large skillet, in 3 tablespoons of oil, on medium heat, sauté garlic and onions for 4-5 minutes until the onions are limp and translucent.
3. Season with dill, parsley and salt, and mix well.
4. Add the steamed spinach and vegan feta and toss well.
5. Cook on low heat for about 3 minutes to combine flavors. Turn off stove.
6. Grease a baking tray.
7. Place one sheet of phyllo dough on the tray. Fold sheet into thirds (like folding a letter) in the wide direction producing a strip that is about 5.5"wide x 12.5" long. (see diagram) Spray the surface with oil.

Fold down	5.5 in
Phyllo Pastry	5.5 in
Fold up	5.5 in

12.5 in

8. Carefully spoon the cooked mixture onto the folded phyllo sheet. Sprinkle the top of mixture with vegan cheese shreds.
9. Top with another folded phyllo sheet. Repeat steps 7 and 8 until you have used up all the cooked mixture and vegan cheese.

10. End the last layer with another folded phyllo sheet which acts like a cover. (I use about 8 phyllo sheets all total. You can use more or less.)
11. Bake in an oven at 350°F for 20 minutes until the sheets look slightly brown and are crisp.
12. Slice the cooked pastry and serve immediately.

Spring Rolls

Spicy savory cabbage and carrot mix wrapped in a thin crackly crisp shell

Makes about 25 Spring Rolls

What You Will Need:

1/2 Head Organic Cabbage (about 2 Cups) – shredded
4 to 5 Medium Organic Carrots – shredded
1/2 TSP Organic Ginger – minced
1/2 TSP Organic Garlic – minced
1/2 TSP Chili Garlic Sauce (see page 154 for recipe or store-bought)
1 TSP Raw Sugar
1/2 Cup Organic Shoyu Sauce
1 Packet of Spring Roll Wrappers
Grapeseed Oil for cooking

To Make Spring Rolls:

1. In a large skillet, sauté the ginger, garlic and chili garlic sauce in 3 tablespoons of oil,
2. Add the shredded carrots and cabbage. Stir-fry on high heat.
3. Season with sugar and shoyu sauce.
4. Mix well and continue cooking on high heat, consistently tossing the mixture until the moisture from the cabbage has evaporated, and the mixture is relatively dry.
5. Wrap the vegetable mixture in spring roll wrappers (see instructions on next page).
6. Put enough oil in a small deep frying pan so that the spring rolls can be completely submerged.
7. Turn the heat on high, and wait until the oil is very hot.
8. Carefully drop a few spring rolls at a time into the hot oil and fry them, making sure to turn them over gently every so often.
9. You will see the spring rolls float to the top and they will be golden brown in color when they are ready.
10. Carefully remove the hot spring rolls – making sure to drain the excess oil off. Place on a plate or tray covered with a paper towel so that the excess oil can be absorbed by the paper towel.
11. Serve spring rolls with Special Chinese Sauce (see recipe below).

What You Will Need for the Special Chinese Sauce:

1 TB Chili Garlic Sauce (see page 154 for recipe or store-bought)
2 TB Organic Shoyu Sauce
1 TSP Raw Sugar
1 TB Organic Ketchup

To Make Sauce:

Whisk all the ingredients in a small bowl until thoroughly mixed in.

 Unfortunately I have not listed this dish as gluten-free as it would take hours of your time in the kitchen making your own spring roll wrappers

Continued…

Spring Rolls (Cont'd)

How to wrap a spring roll:

1. Place a teaspoon of mixture in the corner of the spring roll wrapper as shown in Step 1 in the diagram below.
2. Roll the wrapper twice up in the direction of the arrow as shown in Step 2.
3. Fold one flap over as shown in Step 3.
4. Fold the other flap over, overlapping the first flap as shown in Step 4.
5. Keep rolling the wrapper (in the direction of the arrow) until you reach the end and *stick in place.

*Place 1 TB flour and 2 TB water in a bowl and mix well to make a thick paste. Use this paste to seal the end of the spring roll wrapper in place.

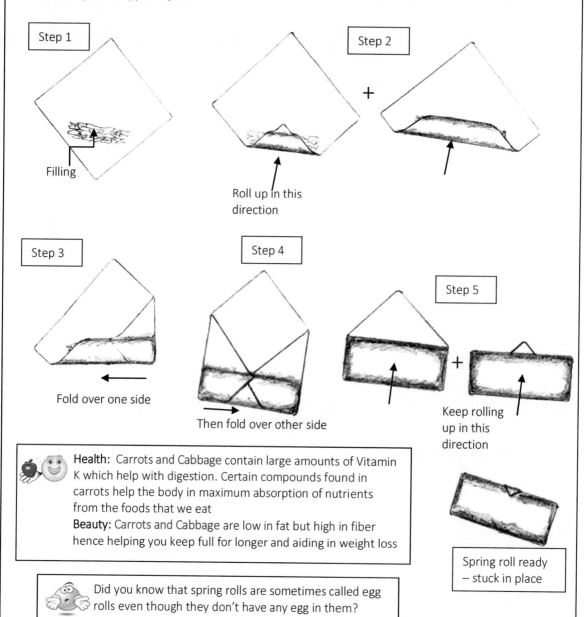

Step 1
Filling

Step 2
Roll up in this direction

Step 3
Fold over one side

Step 4
Then fold over other side

Step 5
Keep rolling up in this direction

Spring roll ready – stuck in place

Health: Carrots and Cabbage contain large amounts of Vitamin K which help with digestion. Certain compounds found in carrots help the body in maximum absorption of nutrients from the foods that we eat

Beauty: Carrots and Cabbage are low in fat but high in fiber hence helping you keep full for longer and aiding in weight loss

Did you know that spring rolls are sometimes called egg rolls even though they don't have any egg in them?

Sushi

Bite-sized morsels of Japanese Bundles of Joy – Become a Sushi Chef today!

Makes 40-50 Sushi Pieces

What You Will Need:
2 Cups Organic Sushi Rice
3 Cups Filtered Water
2 TB Rice Vinegar
2 TB Brown Rice Syrup
Or 4 TSP Raw Sugar
1 TSP Himalayan Pink Salt

To Make Sushi Rice:
1. Cook rice using 2 cups rice to 3 cups water ratio.
2. Once cooked, place hot sushi rice in a wide shallow glass bowl (not metal).
3. In a small saucepan, heat vinegar, brown rice syrup (or Raw Sugar) and salt on low heat, stirring consistently until the salt dissolves.
4. Pour the vinegar mixture over the cooked sushi rice, and toss the mixture into the rice gently using a wooden spoon.
5. The sushi rice is now ready for use in your favorite sushi rolls. Use rice as soon as it is cool enough that you can comfortably handle it. *Note: Do not refrigerate rice, since it will harden.*

What You Will Need for Sushi fillings:
1 Cup Roasted Peanuts
1 Avocado
1 of 8 Oz Container Vegan Cream Cheese
1/2 Cup Organic Spinach – steamed
1/2 Cup Organic Carrots – sliced like thin matchsticks
1/2 Cup Diced Vegan Fish
 Avoid this for Gluten-Free

1 Organic Cucumber – sliced like thin matchsticks
1/2 Cup Vegan Ham – diced
 Avoid this for Gluten-Free

1/2 Cup Vegan Mayonnaise (see page 162 for recipe or store-bought)
Wasabi Powder

To Make Wasabi:
Mix 1 tablespoon wasabi powder with a teaspoon of hot water to make a paste. Cover and let it sit for 5 minutes to release its flavor. Make it 5 minutes before you are ready to eat sushi.

Continued...

Sushi (Cont'd)

Makes 1/2 a quart jar

8 ounces (4 small pieces) Galangal Root (or if you can find it: Fresh Young Ginger – Shin Shoga – not easily available – but can be found in some Asian markets)
1/4 Cup Rice Vinegar
2 TB Mirin
7 TSP Raw Sugar (if you use Raw Sugar your ginger will be brownish in color but if you use organic cane sugar then your ginger will be more like the store-bought one – white to pink in color)

To Make Pickled Ginger:

1. Scrub the young ginger or galangal root under running water as you would a potato for baking.
2. Blanch in boiling water for one minute and drain.
3. Use a potato or carrot peeler to make very thin slices.
4. Combine rice vinegar, Mirin & sugar in small pan.
5. Bring to a boil, stirring until the sugar has dissolved.
6. Remove from heat and let cool.
7. Place the ginger into a sterilized jar and pour the cooled vinegar mixture over the ginger.
8. Cover and put in the refrigerator. Keep for 3-4 days before using. This ginger will keep well if refrigerated for up to 1 month.
9. The pale pink color will develop only if you use the fresh young ginger. Otherwise, it will remain white.

What You Will Need for Rolling Sushi:

Sushi Nori – seaweed sheets
Sushi filling ingredients (as listed on previous page)
1 Bamboo Sushi Mat
1 Bowl of cold water with 1 TSP of Himalayan Pink Salt dissolved in it
Sesame Seeds

To Roll Sushi:

1. Place nori or seaweed sheet on a bamboo mat.
2. Dip your fingers in the cold salt water to prevent the rice from sticking to your fingers.
3. Spread the rice with your fingers evenly over the nori about 3/8 inch thick, covering all but a 2 inch strip along the edge farthest from you. (figure 1)

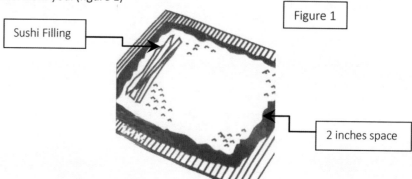

Sushi Filling

Figure 1

2 inches space

4. Lay first choice of fillings (see step 5 a through e for list of fillings) in a row at the near edge (see figure 1 above).

Continued…

Sushi (Cont'd)

5. Here are all the combinations of ingredients of the 5 different Sushi rolls that you can make with this recipe:
    a. "Piinatsu Maki" – Peanut Roll – Roasted peanuts
    b. "Abokado Cream Chīzu Maki – Avocado and Soy Cream Cheese Roll
    c. "Kariforunia maki" – Vegan California roll – Vegan California Roll (with steamed spinach, carrots, seaweed seitan)
    d. "Kappa maki" – Cucumber Roll
    e. "Vegan Hamu maki" – Vegan Ham and Dollops of Vegan Mayonnaise

Place each set of sushi fillings in each roll

6. Garnish your toppings with wasabi and sesame seeds if you like.
7. Moisten the far edge of the nori with fingers dipped in water, and roll the mat firmly. Remove the mat as you go (see figure 2).

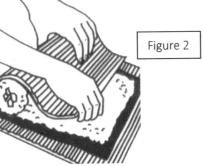

Figure 2

8. Press the moistened edge against the roll to seal.
9. Place the roll seam side down, moisten knife in salt water to prevent sticking, and carefully slice roll into 6 to 8 pieces (see figure 3).

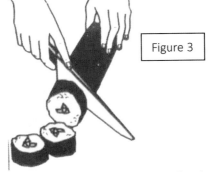

Figure 3

 To serve, pour shoyu sauce or tamari sauce (for gluten-free) in a shallow bowl, mix in some wasabi paste, dip Sushi slices in it, and enjoy!

 Health: The Nori used to wrap sushi rolls is a seaweed that is rich in magnesium, calcium, folic acid, iron, iodine and various antioxidant compounds
Beauty: Sushi is low in fat and good for your complexion

 Did you know that the original type of sushi, known today as nare-zushi was first made in Southeast Asia, possibly along what is now known as the Mekong River? The sushi cuisine then spread to Southern China before it was introduced in Japan. That would make Sushi Chinese food wouldn't it?

Salads

Beet and Carrot Salad

A "pretty in pink" raw medley of two roots – a combination of sweet, sour and salty. Raw never tasted this good!

Serves 4 to 6

What You Will Need:

2 Cups (1 pound) Organic Carrots – shredded
2 Cups (1 pound) Organic Beets (Beetroots) – shredded
2 TSP Organic Garlic – minced
1 TB Extra Virgin Organic Olive Oil
1 TB Balsamic Vinegar
1 TB Vegan Mayonnaise (see page 162 for recipe or store-bought)
1 TSP Dried Dill
1 TSP Himalayan Pink Salt
1 TSP Raw Sugar
1 Cup Organic Raisins or Organic Dried Cranberries
1/2 Cup Organic Raw Slivered Blanched Almonds (optional)

Suggested Shopping List:
– Vegenaise® – Vegan Mayonnaise
– Spectrum® Organic Balsamic Vinegar

To Make The Salad:

1. Peel and grate the carrots and beets. This is where a food processor comes in handy. If you have food processor with a grater attachment, this job will take you 5 minutes. It is a worthwhile investment just to do jobs like these.
2. Place shredded carrots and beets in a large mixing bowl.
3. Add the garlic, olive oil, balsamic vinegar, vegan mayonnaise, dill, salt, sugar, raisins, and almonds, and mix in well making sure to the toss all the ingredients sufficiently to coat the shredded veggies until everything is well combined.
4. Taste your salad, if you require more salt or sugar, go ahead add it now, and toss again.
5. Refrigerate the salad for at least 30 minutes before serving. Serve chilled.

 Health: Beets are good for your liver: The presence of betaines in the beet juice stimulates the functions of the liver
Beauty: Beets give you a rosy complexion. Who needs blush when you have beets!

 Bring this salad instead of traditional coleslaw to your next picnic

Greek Millet Salad

A spicy and tangy Mediterranean salad made with healthy millet
Serves 4

What You Will Need to Cook the Millet:
1 Cup Organic Millet
2 Vegetarian Bouillon Cubes
3 Cups Filtered Water
Grapeseed Oil for cooking

What You Will Need for the Salad:
1 Organic Yellow Bell Pepper – diced
1 Organic Green Bell Pepper – diced
1 Organic Medium Onion – diced
3 Organic Tomatoes – diced
1 Cup Organic Black Olives – sliced
Vegan Cheese (block) – cut into small cubes

What You Will Need for the Dressing:
1/4 Cup Organic Salsa (see page 48 for recipe
  or store-bought)
2 TSP Organic Maple Syrup (Grade B)
1 TB Organic Mustard
1 Cup Organic Cranberries or Organic Raisins
1 TSP Garlic – Minced

Suggested Shopping List:
- Edward & Sons® Not Chick'n Natural Bouillon Cubes
- Daiya® Jack Style Wedge
- Pace® Salsa

 Did you know that a lot of vegans are deficient in protein and zinc? Incorporating millet into a Vegan diet would definitely eliminate that problem!

To Make Salad:
1. In a pot place 3 cups of water and 2 bouillon cubes. Bring to a boil and stir to dissolve the cubes. Set vegetarian broth aside.
2. Lightly grease a large ceramic skillet with some oil.
3. Toast the millet in the ceramic skillet over medium heat until slightly golden brown about 5-7 minutes.
4. Transfer the toasted millet into the pot with the vegetarian broth. Turn the heat onto high.
5. Once the broth comes to a boil. Reduce the heat to low and let simmer for about 35 minutes until the broth is absorbed by the millet.
6. Turn off stove. Remove the millet from the heat, and fluff with a fork.
7. While the millet is cooking, make the dressing by mixing salsa, maple syrup, mustard, cranberries (or raisins), and garlic into a small bowl and whisking until well blended.
8. In another larger bowl, toss together all the diced raw vegetables, olives, and vegan cheese cubes.
9. Add the cooked millet, pour in the dressing, and gently stir until well combined.

 You can serve this salad warm, at room temperature or chilled in the fridge for a few hours – It tastes just as good either way!

 Health: Millet is high in protein – A one cup serving of cooked millet contains 6 g of protein, meeting 12 percent of your daily value
Beauty: Millet contains high levels of Zinc a mineral required for a number of biochemical reactions in our body including beautiful hair and nails

Pineapple Chik Salad

This salad celebrates the best of summer! Taste the fresh and light flavors as you dream of the waves rolling on the ocean shore in Hawaii

Serves 4

What You Will Need:

1 Cup Seasoned Seitan Strips – cut into cubes
1 of 14 Oz Can Organic Crushed Pineapple
 – with all the juice drained and the pineapple squeezed dry
2 Stalks Organic Celery – cut into small pieces
1/2 Cup Slivered Blanched Almonds
1/4 Cup Organic Raisins (optional)
1 Cup Brown-Rice Pasta Spirals – boiled (optional)
3 TB Vegan Mayonnaise (see page 162 for recipe
 or store-bought)
1 TSP Organic Mustard
1 TSP Raw Sugar
1 TSP Himalayan Pink Salt
Freshly Ground Pepper to taste

Suggested Shopping List:
- Trader Joe's® Chicken-Less Strips (for seasoned seitan)
- Native Forest® Organic Crushed Pineapple
- Tinkyada ® Brown Rice Pasta Vegetable Spirals
- Follow Your Heart® Soy-Free Vegenaise

To Make Salad:

1. If you are planning to add pasta to your salad, then boil the pasta according to instructions on package, and set aside to cool.
2. In a large mixing bowl, combine seitan strips, pineapple, celery, almonds, raisins (optional), and boiled cooled pasta (optional).
3. Season with vegan mayonnaise, mustard, sugar, salt, and pepper. Mix well to combine all seasonings.
4. Store in refrigerator covered for at least 1 hour before serving.
5. Serve chilled.

 Health: Pineapples are rich in Vitamin C which can fight off viruses that cause coughs and colds. They also contain bromelain, which is effective in suppressing coughs and loosening mucus and boosting the immune system
Beauty: Pineapples give you a pretty smile by making your gums and teeth healthy and strong

 Did you know that American colonists regarded pineapples as a luxurious treat because of their rarity and cost? Who would have thought the pineapple was food for royalty?

 Unfortunately this dish cannot be made gluten-free – there is no gluten-free substitute for seasoned seitan

Potato Salad

No picnic or barbecue is complete without potato salad – Make this vegan creamy version and get everyone's attention, even the carnivores!

Serves 4-6

What You Will Need:

8 Medium Organic Potatoes (about 6 Cups)
I used Purple and Yukon Gold potatoes (see picture below)
2 Stalks Organic Scallions – finely chopped
1 Organic Bell Pepper (your choice – green, yellow, or red)
   (about 1/2 Cup) – finely chopped
I used half of a red bell and half of an orange bell (see picture below)
1 Stalk Organic Celery (about 1/2 Cup) – finely diced
1 TB Organic Mustard
1 TB Organic Sweet Relish
1/2 Cup Vegan Mayonnaise (see page 162 for recipe or store-bought)
1 TSP Dried Dill
Dash of Cayenne Pepper or Hot Sauce e.g. Tabasco® (optional)
1 TSP Himalayan Pink Salt
1 TSP Raw Sugar
1/4 Cup Filtered Water

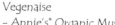

Suggested Shopping List:
– Follow Your Heart® Soy-Free Vegenaise
– Annie's® Organic Mustard
– Woodstock Farms® Organic Sweet Relish
– Tabasco® Hot sauce

To Make Potato Salad:

1. Cover potatoes with skins intact completely with filtered water in a large pot.
2. Boil for 25-30 minutes or until the potatoes are tender in the middle. Different potatoes cook at different times e.g. Yukon Golds cook faster whereas Russets take longer.
3. Finely chop the scallions, bell peppers, and celery and place in a large mixing bowl.
4. Let potatoes cool to room temperature and cut into cubes. Toss these in with other vegetables into the mixing bowl.
5. Add all the remaining ingredients: the vegan mayonnaise, mustard, sweet relish, salt, sugar, dried dill and filtered water and combine with potatoes and vegetables. Toss well and stir thoroughly to combine flavors.
6. Drizzle with hot sauce or cayenne pepper. Then mix again. (Optional step – only if you like that extra spicy kick)
7. Refrigerate until ready to serve.

Did you know that potatoes are in no way related to sweet potatoes? Potatoes belong to the nightshade family whereas sweet potatoes belong to convolvulaceae, commonly known as the morning glory family

Probiotic Couscous/Quinoa Salad

An array of flavors that will tickle your taste buds – plus you'll be pumped with probiotic goodness!

Serves 6

What You Will Need for Cooking the Grains:

2 Cups Organic Couscous

 Use 2 Cups Organic Quinoa

2½ Cups Filtered Water (if cooking couscous)
  Or 4 Cups Filtered Water (if cooking quinoa)
1/2 TSP Himalayan Pink Salt
1 TB Grapeseed Oil

What You Will Need for the Salad:

Juice of 1 Fresh Organic Lime (about 1 TB)
1 TSP Organic Garlic – minced
2 TSP Madras Curry Powder
2 TSP Raw Sugar
1 TSP Himalayan Pink Salt
1 Cup Organic Carrots – shredded
1 Cup Organic Grape Tomatoes – quartered
1/2 Cup Fresh Organic Parsley – finely chopped
Vegan Cheese – cut into small cubes
1/2 Cup Raw Sauerkraut (see page 157 for recipe)
1 Cup Organic Raisins
1/2 Cup Walnuts – roughly chopped
1/2 Cup Pecans – roughly chopped
1 TB Extra Virgin Olive Oil

Suggested Shopping List:
- Fantastic® Organic Couscous
- For Gluten-free meal – Earthly Delight® or Ancient Harvest® for Organic Quinoa
(Make sure that whatever brand you buy, the quinoa is pre-washed)
- Kim Thu Thap® Mild Madras Curry Powder
- Daiya® Jack Style Wedge

 Health: Probiotics can improve intestinal function and preserve the integrity of the intestinal lining
Some digestive disorders happen when the balance of friendly bacteria in the intestines becomes disturbed. This can happen after an infection or after taking antibiotics. Intestinal problems can also arise when the lining of the intestines is damaged
Beauty: If your gut flora is healthy, then this will reflect on your skin and hair, giving you an overall healthy look

To Make Salad:

1. If you are using a rice cooker, place the couscous (or quinoa) with 2½ cups water (if cooking couscous) or 4 cups water (if cooking quinoa) with 1/2 teaspoon of salt and a tablespoon of oil into the rice cooker. Stir the couscous (or quinoa) well before pressing the "cook" button on your cooker.
2. If you choose to use a regular pot, mix the quinoa (or couscous), water, oil and salt together in a saucepan; bring to a boil. Cover, reduce heat, and simmer until quinoa (couscous) is tender and water is absorbed, about 15 minutes. Once it is cooked, set aside.
3. Juice 1 fresh lime, and set the juice aside.
4. In a large mixing bowl toss the carrots, tomatoes, parsley, and sauerkraut.
5. Mix in the raisins, walnuts and pecans.
6. Add the cooked couscous (or quinoa) and toss well with the vegetables and nuts.
7. Add the lime juice and olive oil.
8. Season with minced garlic, raw sugar, salt, and curry powder.
9. Mix the salad thoroughly until all the seasonings are well mixed in. Serve immediately.

 You can add raw sauerkraut (page 157 for recipe) to many dishes to give yourself an extra probiotic boost!

Seaweed Salad

A gift from the ocean turned into an appetizing aquatic adventure for your palette – Take a healthy dip in this salad and "sea" for yourself!

Serves 4

What You Will Need:

2 Oz Packet of Wakame Seaweed
1 TSP Organic Garlic – minced
1 TB Sesame Oil
1 Stalk Organic Scallion – finely chopped up
4 TB Organic Shoyu Sauce

 Use Organic Tamari Sauce

1 TB Mirin or Rice Vinegar
2 TSP Raw Sugar
1 TSP Sesame Seeds
1/2 Cup Raw Cashews
1/2 Cup Cranberries

Suggested Shopping List:
– Eden® Wakame
– Wei-Chuan® 100% pure black sesame oil
– San-J® Organic Shoyu Sauce or Organic Tamari Sauce (for gluten-free)
– Eden® Mirin

To Make Salad:

1. Soak the wakame seaweed in 10 cups hot water for 20-30 minutes.
2. Drain the water.
3. Cut the wakame seaweed with kitchen scissors into short strips.
4. In a large bowl, mix garlic, scallions, sesame oil, shoyu (or tamari), mirin, and sugar. Whisk well until the sugar is well dissolved.
5. Pour the sauce over the wakame strips and toss well to combine ingredients.
6. Sprinkle in the sesame seeds, cashews and cranberries, and again toss well into the seaweed.
7. Refrigerate for at least 1 hour and then serve.

 Health: Vegans often complain that they don't get enough Omega-3s that often come from fish and other seafood
Wakame is a rich source of eicosapentaenoic acid, an omega-3 fatty acid. A typical 1-2 tablespoon serving of wakame contains roughly 3.75-7.5 kcal and provides 15-30 mg of omega-3 fatty acids; the highest omega-3 fatty acids from a vegetarian source.
Iodine deficiency is also common amongst vegans. Iodized salt just doesn't give you enough iodine. Wakame provides a natural source of iodine which is important for the immune system, and female hormone regulation, especially thyroid hormones
Beauty: Wakame contains a compound fucoxanthin which can help burn fatty tissue. So if you want to lose weight fast, eat more seaweed! Looking at all those slim Japanese and Korean girls is proof enough!

 Do you know the difference between Mirin (rice wine) and rice vinegar? "Rice wine" is made by a fermentation process involving yeast that transforms the sugars from glutinous rice into alcohol. "Rice vinegar", also called "Rice Wine Vinegar", takes the fermentation process one step further, adding bacteria to turn the alcohol into an acid

Burritos p. 66

Sandwiches

Fish-Less Spicy Soft Tacos p. 72

Beef-Less Soft Tacos

Make it a Mexican night with marinated "TVP" – textured vegetable protein sautéed with onions and bell peppers simmered in a zesty sauce infused with tomatoes, cilantro, cumin, and melted vegan cheese served on flour tortillas. Olé!

Serves 6

What You Will Need:

1½ Cups Vegan Ground Beef
 (see page 161 for recipe or store-bought)
1½ Cups Organic Onions – diced
2 Cups Organic Green Bell Peppers – diced
1 Cup Organic Tomatoes – diced
1 Cup Organic Fresh Cilantro – stems and leaves chopped fine
2 TB Salsa (see page 48 for recipe or store-bought)
1 TSP Ground Cumin
2 TSP Organic Taco Seasoning
Grapeseed Oil for cooking
12 Organic 6 inch Flour Tortillas

GF Use Organic Gluten-Free Flour Tortillas

2 Cups Vegan Cheese Shreds

Suggested Shopping List:
–Trader Joe's® Beef-Less Ground Beef
– Pace® Organic Salsa
– Ground cumin can be bought in Indian grocery stores
– Bearitos® or Simply Organic® Southwest Taco Seasoning
– La Tortilla Factory® Sonoma "Traditional" **or** "Ivory Teff" (for gluten-free) Tortillas 6 pack
– Daiya® Vegan Cheese Shreds – Pepper Jack

 You can dress up your tacos with shredded fresh romaine lettuce, sliced jalapenos, diced black olives, salsa (see page 48), and guacamole (see page 39)

To Make Tacos:

1. If making your own Vegan Ground Beef – follow recipe on page 161. Set aside.
2. In a large skillet, in 3 tablespoons of oil, sauté onions and bell peppers until they are limp (about 5 minutes). Then lower heat.
3. Add the tomatoes, cilantro, and salsa.
4. Sprinkle in the ground cumin and taco seasoning. Stir thoroughly and let the mixture cook until the tomatoes are softened (about 2-3 minutes).
5. Add the prepared Vegan Ground Beef (TVP granules) or store-bought vegan ground beef. Toss well until the TVP granules are well mixed into the vegetable mixture. Cover skillet, and let the mixture cook on low heat for about 5 minutes to blend flavors.
6. Raise the heat slightly, and add the vegan cheese, allowing it to melt into the vegan ground beef mixture.
7. Once the cheese has melted, turn off burner.
8. Warm tortillas on a lightly greased skillet.
9. To make the tacos, fill tortillas with the vegan beef mixture, fold tortillas in half and enjoy!

I did this quick comparison on the CalorieKing™ website to see how 1/4 Cup serving of TVP compares nutritionally to 1/4 Cup serving of Ground Beef. Boy was a pleased with the results – see for yourself! Look at the numbers on Calories, Fat, and Cholesterol

Reproduced from CalorieKing ™

TVP dry – 1/4 Cup serving

Calories 80		(334 kJ)
		% Daily Value 1
Total Fat	0g	0%
Sat. Fat	0g	0%
Trans Fat	0g	
Cholesterol	0mg	0%
Sodium	2mg	< 1%
Total Carbs.	7g	2%
Dietary Fiber	4g	16%
Sugars	3g	
Protein	12g	
Calcium		
Potassium		

Beef: Ground, 85% lean 15% fat, raw – 1/4 Cup serving

Calories 243		(1016 kJ)
		% Daily Value 1
Total Fat	17g	26%
Sat. Fat	6.6g	33%
Trans Fat	1.1g	
Cholesterol	77mg	26%
Sodium	75mg	3%
Total Carbs.	0g	0%
Dietary Fiber	0g	0%
Sugars	0g	
Protein	21g	
Calcium	17mg	
Potassium	333.4mg	

Breakfast Burritos

Zesty southwest tofu scramble sautéed with peppers and onions, hash brown potatoes, a touch of salsa and dollops of vegan sour cream wrapped in flour tortillas

Makes 6 Burritos

What You Will Need:

1 of 14 Oz package Organic Extra Firm Tofu
1 of 16 Oz package Organic Hash Browns
1/4 TSP Himalayan Pink Salt to season potatoes
1 Cup Organic Onions – finely diced
1 Cup Organic Green Bell Peppers – finely diced
1 Cup Salsa or Picante Sauce
 (For Salsa – see page 48 for recipe or store-bought)
4-5 Sprigs Organic Cilantro – stems and leaves chopped fine
2 TSP Organic Taco Seasoning
1 TSP Ground Turmeric
1 TSP Organic Garlic – minced
1 TSP Himalayan Pink Salt
1 Cup Vegan Cheese Shreds
6 Organic 8 inch Flour Tortillas

 Use Organic Gluten-Free Flour Tortillas

1 Container (340g) Organic Vegan Sour Cream
Grapeseed Oil for cooking

Suggested Shopping List:
- Wildwood® Organic Sprouted Tofu – Extra Firm
- Cascadian Farms® Organic Hash Browns
- Pace® Salsa or Picante Sauce
- Bearitos® or Simply Organic® Taco Seasoning
- Ground turmeric can be bought in Indian grocery stores
- Daiya® Vegan Cheese shreds – any flavor Cheddar, Mozzarella or Pepper Jack
- La Tortilla Factory® Sonoma "Traditional" **or** "Ivory Teff" (for gluten-free) Tortillas 6 pack
- Follow Your Heart® Vegan Sour Cream

To Make Breakfast Burritos:

1. Drain the water from the tofu, and pat dry with paper towels. On a chopping board, mince the tofu really well with a large knife. Set aside.
2. Place frozen potatoes in a bowl and toss with 1/4 TSP salt.
3. In a large ceramic skillet, heat three tablespoons of oil, and then carefully place the frozen hash brown potatoes in a single layer.
4. Cover the skillet for 12 minutes, allowing potatoes to cook on medium heat. They will turn crispy and golden brown.
5. After 12 minutes, sprinkle some oil on the surface of the potatoes, and then flip the layer of potatoes. Cover the skillet again, and fry the other side for another 12 minutes, until crispy and golden brown. Once done, turn off burner, and set aside.
6. In another large skillet, in three tablespoons of oil, sauté the garlic, onions, cilantro, and peppers until the onions are limp and translucent (about 5 minutes).
7. Mix in the salsa.
8. Season with taco seasoning, turmeric, and salt.
9. Add the minced tofu and mix well to completely coat the tofu with the seasoned mixture.
10. Sprinkle in the vegan cheese, and keep stirring until the cheese is all melted into the tofu mixture.
11. Once the cheese melts, turn off burner.
12. Warm tortillas on a flat skillet.
13. To make the burritos, fill tortillas with the tofu mixture, and line with a few broken pieces of fried hash brown potatoes.
14. Top with dollops of vegan sour cream. Wrap tortillas up like a burrito and enjoy! (To wrap like a burrito – See page 34 on instructions on how to wrap a basil roll)

Chik'N Salad Sandwich

 Ireland

A mixture of celery and onions sautéed in vegan butter tossed with faux chik'n (made of seitan) topped with granny smith apples and raisins and a touch of vegan mayonnaise seasoned with exotic spices like caraway, cumin, and anise on Irish soda bread or sourdough bread

Serves 6

What You Will Need:

1 of 21.2 Oz package of Vegan Ham Paste
 Or 1 Package Seasoned Seitan Strips
1/4 TSP Ground Cumin
1/4 TSP Caraway Seeds
1/4 TSP Anise Seeds
1/2 Organic Yellow Onion (1 cup) – diced
Grapeseed Oil for cooking
1 Organic Granny Smith Apple – finely diced
2 Stalks Organic Celery – finely chopped
7 TB Vegan Mayonnaise (see page 162 for recipe
 or store-bought)
1 TSP Himalayan Pink Salt
1 Loaf Irish Soda Bread or Sourdough bread
Lettuce and Tomatoes for garnish

Suggested Shopping List:
–All Vegetarian Inc° Vegan Ham Paste (Thit Chay Nhao) – buy online
 Or Trader Joe's° Chicken-Less Strips
– Ground cumin, Caraway Seeds and Anise Seeds can be bought in Indian grocery stores
– Follow Your Heart° Soy-Free Vegenaise

 Did you know that cumin, caraway and anise seeds all come from the same family of plants, i.e. the Apiaceae or Umbelliferae commonly known as the carrot or parsley family?

To Make Sandwich:

1. Defrost the package of Vegan Ham paste. Once it is defrosted, tear up the block into finer shreds. Set aside.
2. If you are using Trader Joe's® Chicken-Less Strips, then run them through a food processor to finely shred them. Set aside.
3. In a large skillet, add three tablespoons of grapeseed oil, and sauté the onion and celery for 2 minutes.
4. Lower heat. Stir in the cumin, caraway and anise seeds. Sauté for another 3-4 minutes until onions are softened.
5. In a large mixing bowl. Add the vegan ham shreds (or shredded Chicken-Less Strips) and add the cooked onions and celery and mix thoroughly so the vegan ham (or shredded chicken-less strips) is well blended with the onions and celery mixture.
6. Season with vegan mayonnaise, raisins and diced apple.
7. Sprinkle in the salt and mix well to combine all the ingredients. Now your vegan chik'n salad is ready.
8. Place the vegan chik'n salad on one slice of bread. Layer with tomatoes and lettuce. Spread another slice of bread with additional vegan mayonnaise. Place this slice on top of the vegan chik'n salad side and Voila! Your Vegan Chik'N Salad Sandwich is ready to be devoured!

 Unfortunately this dish cannot be made gluten-free – there is no gluten-free substitute for seasoned seitan

 Health: Cumin, Caraway & Anise Seeds all improve digestion and relieve many common digestive ailments by stimulating the production of pancreatic enzymes. Eating them on a regular basis can give relief from constipation, flatulence, bloating, diarrhea, nausea and indigestion
Beauty: Cumin, Caraway & Anise are also effective treatments for insomnia. We all know that if we get our beauty sleep we will remain beautiful!

Chik'N Tandoori Wraps

If you're looking for a quick, zesty, healthy sandwich, then try making one of these beauties. A wholesome wrap filled with seitan, veggies, fruit, nuts seasoned with Tandoori and Tulsi (Holy Basi). Makes a terrific lunchbox filler. Tantalize your taste buds today!

Makes 4-5 Wraps

What You Will Need:

1/2 Cup Organic Onions – julienned
1/2 Cup Organic Bell Peppers (any color) – julienned
1 TSP Organic Garlic – minced
1/2 TSP Organic Ginger – minced
3 Sprigs Fresh Organic Cilantro – finely chopped
1/2 Cup Organic Carrots – shredded
1/2 Cup Organic Broccoli – separated into smaller florets
1 Small Organic Apple (any kind) – finely diced
4-5 Tulsi Leaves (Holy Basil leaves) – finely chopped
1/4 Cup Walnuts – chopped up
1 Package Seasoned Seitan Strips
1 TB Organic Lemon Juice
1 TB Organic Raw Apple Cider Vinegar
1 of 8oz Container Vegan Cream cheese
1 TB Tandoori powder
1 TSP Himalayan Pink Salt
2 TSP Raw Sugar
6 Organic 8 inch Flour Tortillas
2 Leaves Organic Romaine Lettuce – shredded
1/4 Cup Organic tomatoes – diced
Grapeseed Oil for cooking

Unfortunately this dish cannot be made gluten-free – there is no gluten-free substitute for seasoned seitan

To Make The Wrap:

1. In a large skillet, in three tablespoons of grapeseed oil, on medium heat, sauté the garlic, ginger, and onions until onions are translucent and you can smell the aroma of the roasted garlic.
2. Raise heat. Add the bell peppers and cilantro and sauté for another 3-4 minutes until bell peppers are tender.
3. Add the carrots and broccoli, lower heat, and cover skillet to allow the vegetables to steam for about 10-15 minutes.
4. Toss in the seasoned seitan strips, apple pieces, tulsi leaves (holy basil), and walnuts.
5. Add the lemon juice and apple cider vinegar.
6. Season with tandoori powder, salt, and sugar, making sure to mix thoroughly.
7. Whisk in the vegan cream cheese until the mixture is of a thick creamy consistency. Turn off heat.
8. Put 1 TB of filling in a flour tortilla, top with shredded lettuce and diced tomatoes, and wrap like a soft taco or a burrito (see page 34 for instructions on how to wrap a basil roll) or wrap it any way you like and enjoy!

Health: Tulsi (Holy Basil) helps in immune support. If ever a pandemic breaks out, make sure to have tulsi on hand – it can save your life. It protects against all kinds of flu and even radiation. In 2011 a study in the "Journal of Ethnopharmacology," 24 volunteers were given tulsi on an empty stomach. After 4 weeks, scientists concluded that there were increases in interferon and T-helper cells in these individuals confirming the immune modulation benefits of tulsi leaves
Beauty: Tulsi contains Ursolic acid which diminishes wrinkles and age spots by strengthening your skin's collagen. Make a tea from tulsi leaves and apply it to your face

Collard Green Wraps with Lemon Nut Pâté

Fresh collard green leaves smeared with a tangy lemon nut pâté wrapped around the goodness of avocados, tomatoes, carrots and other nuggets of raw happiness

Makes 8 Big Wraps or 16 Small Wraps

What You Will Need:

8 Organic Collard Green Leaves – with stems removed

What You Will Need For the Filling:

3 Ripe Avocados – sliced thin
2 Fresh Organic Tomatoes – diced
2 Cups Organic Carrots – shredded
4-5 Sprigs (about 1 Cup) Fresh Organic Cilantro – leaves and stems chopped fine
Black Sesame Seeds (optional)

 Did you know that when you incorporate more raw food into your diet, there is less cleanup, i.e. there aren't any pots and pans to wash? Maybe that can be reason alone to eat more raw food?

What You Will Need For the Lemon Nut Pâté:

2/3 Cup Almonds
2/3 Cup Walnuts
2/3 Cup Pecans
2 TB Liquid Amino Acids
10 Leaves Fresh Organic Basil or 2 TSP Dried Basil
1 TSP Organic Garlic – minced
2 TB Organic Lemon Juice
1/2 Cup Organic Green Bell Peppers
1 Stalk Organic Scallion

Picture 1   Picture 2

To Make Collard Green Wraps:

1. Chop and prepare all the ingredients for the filling and set aside.
2. Put all the ingredients for the nut pâté in a food processor and process until you get a paste-like consistency.
3. If you're using a whole collard green leaf, spread a layer of pâté on the leaf. Then place the filling in the middle. Tuck In the sides of the leaf to secure the filling, and then roll up the leaf (see picture 1). You can also use a toothpick to hold the leaf closed.
4. If you're using a half a leaf (see picture 2) – cut the collard green along the middle and follow step 3 for the rest of the procedure.

Collard Green Wraps with Sun-Dried Tomato & Macadamia Nut Pâté

Same healthy wraps as above but with a zesty sun-dried tomato and macadamia nut pâté

What You Will Need For the Sun-Dried Tomato & Macadamia Nut Pâté:

1/2 Cup Sun-Dried Tomatoes – soaked in warm distilled water for 10 minutes and then drained
1 Cup Raw Macadamia Nuts – soaked for 1/2 to 1 hour in filtered water
1 TSP Organic Garlic – minced
1 TB Organic Lemon Juice
1 TB Organic Maple Syrup (Grade B)
2 TB Organic Parsley – finely chopped

Health: Collard Greens contain tons of Phytonutrients which help the body with the process of detoxification
Beauty: When your body detoxes, it automatically gives you brighter eyes and a glow to your complexion

To Make Collard Green Wraps:

1. Soak your nuts and sun-dried tomatoes in separate bowls.
2. Process soaked nuts, sun-dried tomatoes, garlic, lemon juice and maple syrup in a food processor until you get a thick paste-like consistency.
3. Top pâté with chopped parsley and wrap in collard green leaves (as per instructions given in step 3 above.

Dulse Potato Rolls

Fluffy flour tortillas rolled and filled with a palatable potato, cilantro and dulse mixture simmered in fragrant Indian spices topped with vegan cheese

Makes 24 Rolls

What You Will Need:

12 Organic 6 inch Flour Tortillas

 Use Organic Gluten-Free Flour Tortillas

1 TSP Organic Garlic – minced
1 TSP Organic Ginger – minced
2 Cups Fresh Organic Tomatoes – diced
1 Cup Fresh Organic Cilantro
  – leaves and stems chopped fine
6 Cups Organic Potatoes – washed, scraped, and cubed
2 TB Dulse Flakes
1½ Cups Filtered Water
1 TSP Himalayan Pink Salt
1 TSP Coriander powder
1 TSP Turmeric
2 Cups Vegan Cheese Shreds
Grapeseed Oil for cooking

Suggested Shopping List:
- La Tortilla Factory® Sonoma "Traditional" **or** "Ivory Teff" (for gluten-free) Tortillas 6 pack
- Maine Coast Sea Vegetable® Dulse Flakes
- Coriander Powder and Turmeric can be found in Indian grocery stores
- Daiya® Vegan Cheese Shreds – Cheddar or Mozzarella – your choice
- Follow Your Heart® Soy-Free Vegenaise
- Tree of Life® Organic Ketchup

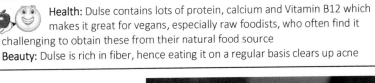

Health: Dulse contains lots of protein, calcium and Vitamin B12 which makes it great for vegans, especially raw foodists, who often find it challenging to obtain these from their natural food source
Beauty: Dulse is rich in fiber, hence eating it on a regular basis clears up acne

To Make Rolls:

1. In a pressure cooker, in three tablespoons of oil sauté the garlic and ginger for a minute.
2. Add the tomatoes and cilantro and mix thoroughly.
3. Sprinkle in the coriander powder, turmeric, and salt.
4. Now add the cubed potatoes and mix thoroughly.
5. Pour in the filtered water and give it a good stir.
6. Close the pressure cooker with its lid.
7. Once the pressure starts, time your cooker for 5 minutes. Then turn off pressure cooker (check your pressure cooker on timings for cooking potatoes).
8. Once all the steam is released, carefully open the pressure cooker.
9. If the potato mixture is too runny, drain the water, and set this liquid aside to use as a savory broth for use in another dish (you can store in the refrigerator for 3 days).
10. Turn the burner back on to low, and stir in the vegan cheese until it is completed melted into the potato mixture. Then turn off stove.
11. Mix the dulse flakes into the potato and cheese mixture.
12. Place two tablespoons of potato mixture in the center of each tortilla wrapper.
13. Roll up the filled tortilla like a burrito (see page 34 for instructions on how to wrap a basil roll)
14. Repeat steps 12 and 13 using up the remaining tortillas.
15. Cut each potato burrito in half and serve.

*Dulse Rolls Special Sauce:

1 TB Vegan Mayonnaise
  (see page 162 for recipe or store-bought)
3 TB Organic Ketchup
2 TB Filtered Water
1/2 TSP Ground Cayenne pepper
1/2 TSP Ground Cumin
1/2 TSP Taco Seasoning

 Did you know Dulse can be used as a substitute for table salt? Next time you want to salt your dish just sprinkle in some dulse flakes. Plus you'll be adding nutritional benefits

You can enjoy the potato rolls by themselves or to make them even tastier by dipping them in the Dulse Rolls Special Sauce* (see recipe on this page)
To Make Sauce: Whisk all the ingredients for Dulse special sauce in a mixing bowl.

Eggless Egg Salad Sandwiches

A creamy delectable faux egg preparation made with tofu and aromatic herbs and spices, topped with chunks of avocado, tomatoes, lettuce, and sprouts on a crispy baguette

Makes 8 Large Sandwiches

What You Will Need for the Eggless Egg Salad:
1 of 14 Oz Package Organic Extra Firm Tofu
1 TSP Organic Lemon Juice
1 TB Extra Virgin Olive Oil
1 TSP Organic Garlic – minced
1/2 TSP Himalayan Pink Salt
1/4 TSP Dried Basil
1/4 TSP Dried Dill
Dash of Freshly Ground Black Pepper
2 TB Vegan Mayonnaise
  (see page 162 for recipe or store-bought)
1/4 TSP Ground Turmeric
1 TSP Organic Yellow Mustard
1/4 TSP Celery Seed
1 TSP Nutritional Yeast
1 TSP Organic Sweet Relish
1/2 TSP Raw Sugar

Suggested Shopping List:
- Wildwood® Organic Sprouted Tofu – Extra Firm
- Follow Your Heart® Soy-Free Vegenaise
- Turmeric can be found in Indian grocery stores
- Eden® Organic Yellow Mustard
- Bragg® Nutritional Yeast Seasoning
- Woodstock Farms® Organic Sweet Relish

 Health: When it sprouts, a seed converts some of its sugar content into Vitamin C. It also begins to produce new enzymes and other stored nutrition which multiplies. Sprouts are thus richer in protein, Vitamin C, enzymes, and fiber than when they become more mature plants. When we eat them we get high doses of nutrition from a tiny amount. They also help us better digest the food we eat. Better digestion leads to better health!
Beauty: Sprouts with their abundant antioxidants, prevent aging

What You Will Need for the Bread:
Bread: 1 big loaf Italian bread or French baguette or make your own (see page 155 for recipe)

What You Will Need for the Garnish:
1 ripe Avocado – sliced
1 Organic Tomato – sliced into circles
1-2 Organic Romaine Lettuce Leaves
Organic Clover, Sunflower or Alfalfa Sprouts

To Make Sandwiches:
1. Place all the ingredients listed above for the eggless egg salad into a food processor and process until you get a creamy smooth texture.
2. Slice the bread into two halves (see picture).

 Leftover eggless egg salad can be refrigerated for up to 3 days and can be enjoyed by itself minus the bread

3. Spread eggless egg salad mixture onto one half of the bread.
4. Top eggless egg salad with avocados, tomatoes, lettuce and sprouts.
5. Spread some Vegan Mayonnaise or vegan butter (your choice) on the other half.
6. Place this half on top of the other half that contains the eggless egg salad.
7. Then slice the bread across the top to make sandwiches. (see picture on the right)

Fish-Less Spicy Soft Tacos

Pan fried vegan fish strips topped with a mildly spicy cabbage and scallions relish infused with a chili garlic sauce and topped with creamy avocados and fragrant cilantro on flour tortillas

Serves 6

What You Will Need:

1 Cup Vegan Sour Cream
1 Fresh Organic Lime juice (about 2 TB)
1/4 TSP Himalayan Pink Salt
1/4 TSP Freshly Ground Black Pepper
1 TSP Raw Sugar
1/2 Head Organic Purple Cabbage (about 5 cups)
  – finely shredded
5 Organic Scallions – thinly sliced
1 TSP Chili Garlic Sauce (see page 154 for recipe or store-bought)
3 TB Grapeseed oil for frying the Vegan Fish fillets
15 slices of Vegan Fish Fillets
12 Organic 6 inch Flour Tortillas
1 Cup Fresh Organic Cilantro – leaves and stems chopped fine
3 Avocados – sliced

What You Will Need for the Tartar Sauce:

2 TSP Organic Sweet Relish
4 TB Vegan Mayonnaise (see page 162 for recipe
 or store-bought)
1 TB Filtered Water

Suggested Shopping List:
- Follow Your Heart® Vegan Sour Cream
- Sriracha® **or** Lee Kum Kee® Chili Garlic Sauce
- All Vegetarian Inc® Vegan Fish Ham **or** EcoVegan® Ocean's Delight for vegan fish fillets
- La Tortilla Factory® Sonoma "Traditional" Flour Tortillas
- Woodstock Farms® Organic Sweet Relish
- Follow Your Heart® Soy-Free Vegenaise

 Unfortunately this dish cannot be made gluten-free – there is no gluten-free substitute for vegan fish fillets

To Make Fish-Less Tacos:

1. Make the tartar sauce by combining all the ingredients for "Tartar Sauce" above in a small bowl and set aside.
2. In a large bowl, combine vegan sour cream, lime juice, salt, black pepper, raw sugar and chili garlic sauce.
3. Toss in cabbage and scallions. Mix well.
4. Add 3 tablespoons of oil to a large skillet, swirl to coat the bottom of the skillet with oil.
5. Pan-fry the vegan fish fillets until they are golden brown on both sides. About 5-6 minutes.
6. Remove the vegan fish fillets from the skillet, and transfer to your chopping board. When cooled, cut the vegan fish into short strips using kitchen scissors.
7. Warm tortillas on a flat skillet.
8. To make the tacos, fill tortillas with the cabbage slaw, and line with a few strips of vegan fish
9. Top with cilantro leaves and a few pieces of sliced avocado.
10. Drizzle with tartar sauce.
11. Fold your tortillas in half and enjoy!

 Did you know that the way they get vegan fish fillets to taste like fish is because they put seaweed in them? The ingredients in the fish filets are soy protein, black soy bean sauce, sunflower oil, potato, laver, wheat flour, white sesame, unbleached sugar (non-bone char), glutinous rice, trehalose (from seaweed), licorice, and seaweed – so by eating these fish-less tacos you get all the health and beauty benefits of seaweed too!

Quick Quesadillas

If you're ever hankering for a quick snack, make yourself a batch of these quick quesadillas – they literally can be made in 5-10 minutes flat!

Serves 4-6

What You Will Need:

6 Organic 8-10 inch Flour Tortillas

 Use Organic Gluten-Free Flour Tortillas

1 of 10 Oz Package Organic Frozen Chopped Spinach (thawed and drained)

Or 1 Pound Fresh Organic Spinach-chopped (6 cups)

1 Small Organic Onion (1 Cup) – julienned

1 Medium Organic Green Bell Pepper (1 Cup) – julienned

1 TSP Organic Garlic – minced

1 TSP Organic Taco Seasoning

1 TSP Himalayan Pink Salt

1/4 TSP Freshly Ground Black Pepper

1 Cup Organic Salsa (see page 48 for recipe or store-bought) – you may omit this if you don't want it spicy

1 Cup Vegan Cheese Shreds

Grapeseed Oil for cooking

Suggested Shopping List:
- La Tortilla Factory® Sonoma "Traditional" **or** "Ivory Teff" (for gluten-free) Tortillas 6 pack
- Bearitos® or Simply Organic® Southwest Taco Seasoning
- Pace® Salsa
- Daiya® Vegan Cheese Shreds – Mozzarella or Cheddar
- Follow Your Heart® Vegan Sour Cream

To Make Quesadillas:

1. In a large skillet, in three tablespoons of oil, on medium heat sauté garlic, onions and bell peppers until onions and bell peppers are cooked. About 5-7 minutes.
2. Add spinach and continue to stir-fry on medium heat.
3. Season with taco seasoning, salt and pepper. Turn off burner.
4. Lay 1 flour tortilla out on a flat plate or tray.
5. Sprinkle the vegetable mixture all over the tortilla.
6. Dot with spoonfuls of salsa (optional: only if you like spice).
7. Sprinkle vegan cheese shreds all over vegetable mixture.
8. Place another tortilla on top covering the first tortilla. Set quesadilla aside.
9. Repeat steps 4-8 until all tortillas are used up.
10. Lightly grease a flat ceramic pan and gently place the quesadilla on the pan.
11. Pan-fry the filled quesadilla on high heat and pat gently with flat spatula until slightly browned and crisp on one side (about 2-3 minutes).
12. Carefully turn over the quesadilla to brown the other side (another 2-3 minutes).
13. Cut into quarters and serve with guacamole (see page 39 for recipe) and vegan sour cream.

For a quick variation for an even faster and easier version, see directions below. I usually make this for picnics and everyone always wants a piece!

1. On a flat plate or tray, place one tortilla.
2. Spread salsa all over the tortilla using a spoon or a butter knife.
3. Place pieces of frozen spinach all over the salsa.
4. Add dashes of Italian seasoning or garlic powder.
5. Sprinkle vegan cheese shreds all over the frozen spinach.
6. Top with another flour tortilla
7. Cook your quesadillas as explained in steps 10-12 above. Or just microwave for 1 minute (not a healthy option but if you are in a real hurry you can opt to do this).
8. Cut into quarters, place in to-go containers, and take on your picnic!

Roasted Eggplant & Tofu Pita-Wich

A truly delicious way to enjoy eggplants! Roasted eggplant seasoned with zesty sauces topped with pan-fried tofu and melted vegan cheese stuffed into pita pockets. No deli could ever make a sandwich this good!

Makes 4-5 Pita-Wiches

What You Will Need:

1 of 14 Oz Package Organic Extra Firm Tofu
4-5 Chinese Eggplants – sliced lengthwise into 1/2-inch-thick rectangles
1 Cup Organic Onions – diced
1 Cup Organic Bell Peppers (any color your choice)- diced
1 TSP Organic Garlic – minced
1 TSP Organic Ginger – minced
1 Cup Organic Tomatoes – diced
1 TB Liquid Amino Acids
1/2 Cup Enchilada Sauce
2 TB Organic Ketchup
10 Fresh Organic Basil Leaves
1/4 Cup Organic Sliced Jalapenos (optional)
1 Cup Vegan Cheese Shreds
Grapeseed Oil for cooking
8 Inch Pita Bread Rounds

 Use Gluten-Free Pita Bread

Suggested Shopping List:
– Wildwood® Organic Sprouted Tofu "Extra Firm"
– Bragg® Liquid Amino Acids
– Frontera® Red Chile Enchilada Sauce
– Tree of Life® Organic Ketchup
– Daiya® Vegan Cheese Shreds – Mozzarella

 Did you know that there are more than 60 types of flat bread made worldwide and that Pita bread is one of the oldest recipes known to mankind?

1. Slice tofu into 1/2 inch slabs.
2. Grease a flat non-stick skillet by swirling the bottom with grapeseed oil.
3. Place tofu slabs onto skillet spreading them out so that they aren't touching.
4. Pan-fry the tofu slabs on one side until crisp and browned, then turn over and pan-fry the other side until golden brown. Set aside.
5. Lightly grease a baking sheet with oil, and place sliced eggplant on the tray carefully spreading them out so that they aren't overlapping.
6. Broil eggplant for 5 minutes or until eggplant is softened.
7. In a large skillet, in 3 tablespoons of oil, on medium heat, sauté ginger, garlic, onions, green peppers, and tomatoes, stirring well. Cook for about 5-7 minutes or until vegetables are tender.
8. Season the vegetables with liquid amino acids, enchilada sauce, ketchup, fresh basil, and sliced jalapenos (you can omit these if you don't want it spicy).
9. Add pan-fried tofu and broiled eggplant pieces.
10. Stir in vegan cheese to melt.
11. Warm the pita breads on a flat skillet.
12. Cut the pita breads in half and fill with prepared vegetable mixture. Enjoy!

 Health: Pita Bread, provided it is made with whole grains, contains a wide array of vitamins and minerals – especially B vitamins. It also contains lots of fiber which aids in digestion and prevents constipation
Beauty: Pita Bread helps you lose weight. Because of its high fiber it helps you to become fuller faster; hence you tend to consume less of it compared to loaf bread

Tandoori Faux Chicken Pita Pockets

Faux chicken (seitan) marinated in a mouth-watering cultured coconut mixture blended with tandoori spices, then sautéed with peppers and onions served in pita pockets and topped with a Vegan Tzatziki dressing. Everyone loves the taste of tandoori – now make it in your own kitchen!

Makes 48 Mini Pita Pockets

What You Will Need:

2 Packets 8 Oz Seitan Strips

 Use Organic Tempeh

1 Cup Organic Onions – julienned
1 Cup Organic Green Bell Peppers – julienned
24 Mini Pita Breads

 Use Gluten-Free Pita Bread

Grapeseed Oil for cooking

What You Will Need for Marinade:

3 TB Tandoori Powder
3 TB Organic Lemon juice
3 TB Organic Raw Apple Cider Vinegar
3 TB Cultured Coconut Milk (Vegan Yogurt)
1 TSP Raw Sugar

What You Will Need for Tzatziki Sauce:

2 TB Cultured Coconut Milk (Vegan Yogurt)
1/2 TSP Organic Garlic – minced
2 TB Vegan Mayonnaise (see page 162 for recipe or store-bought)
1/4 Cup Organic Fresh Cucumber or Organic Zucchini – finely diced

Suggested Shopping List:
- WestSoy® Seitan Strips "Wheat Protein"
  or Lightlife® Organic Tempeh
- Tandoori Powder – you can buy this at Indian grocery stores
- Bragg® Organic Raw Apple Cider Vinegar
- So Delicious® Cultured Coconut Milk
- Follow Your Heart® Soy-Free Vegenaise

To Make Sauce: Mix all ingredients in a bowl, and set aside.

To Make Tandoori Faux-Chicken Pita Pockets:

1. In a large bowl, mix all the ingredients for the marinade and then toss seitan strips in this mixture until completely coated.
2. Place marinated seitan, covered in the refrigerator, for at least 5 hours (or preferably overnight) so that the seitan can fully absorb the marinade. The longer you marinate the seitan, the tastier it will be.

Health: Seitan is high in protein, it's also known as "Wheat Protein" and essential amino acids, A four ounce serving of seitan supplies between 6 and 10 percent of the U.S daily requirement of Vitamin C, thiamin, riboflavin, niacin, and iron
Beauty: Seitan is great for dieters; there are only 130 calories in a three ounce serving. It is low in fat, less than two grams per serving. Plus it has very few saturated fats and carbs

3. When you are ready to serve your pita pockets and seitan is fully marinated, you can start the process of garnishing your seitan with sautéed onions and peppers.
4. In a large skillet, in three tablespoons of oil on high heat, sauté the onions and green peppers until they are well cooked, if they are slightly charred, even better, since this adds to the flavor (about 5-7 minutes).
5. Add the marinated seitan to the skillet and stir-fry on high heat until the juice of the marinade evaporates and the mixture is pretty dry. Turn off burner. Your tandoori faux chicken is ready. Set aside.
6. Cut the pita breads in half. Make sure to open them up a little so they are fill-able after heating.
7. Lightly grease a flat ceramic pan, and place the cut pita pockets on the surface. Heat the pita halves until they are slightly brown on each side. Alternatively you can place the pita bread halves on a baking tray, and spray the surfaces with a little oil, and bake in an oven at 350°F for 10 minutes.
8. Once the pita halves are warmed up, stuff them with the tandoori faux chicken. Top with Tzatziki sauce and indulge!

Tempeh Reuben

Slabs of marinated tempeh on a bed of raw sauerkraut slathered with Russian dressing grilled to perfection on foccacia bread with melted vegan cheese. Can you taste gourmet?

Makes 12 Bite-Size Sandwiches

What You Will Need:

1 large Organic Focaccia Bread
(**Or** you can use any other hearty bread like Sourdough or Rye)

 Use Any Gluten-Free Bread

2 Slabs of 8 Oz Organic Tempeh
1 Cup Organic Raw Sauerkraut (see page 157 for recipe or store-bought)
4 Cups Filtered Water
1 TB Organic Vegan Buttery Spread
1 Cup Vegan Cheese Shreds
Grapeseed Oil for cooking

What You Will Need For The Marinade:

2/3 Cup Organic Raw Apple Cider Vinegar
2/3 Cup Liquid Amino Acids
1 Cup Filtered Water
2 TSP Organic Garlic – minced
1½ TSP Ground Cumin
1 TSP Dried Dill
1 TSP Caraway Seeds
1/2 TSP Dried Paprika
1½ TSP Raw Sugar

What You Will Need For the Russian Dressing:

3 TB Vegan Mayonnaise (see page 162 for recipe or store-bought)
3 TB Organic Ketchup
3 TB Organic Sweet Relish

To Make the Tempeh Reuben:

Slice the Tempeh:

1. Slice each tempeh slab through the middle splitting it into two thinner pieces.
2. Then cut each split half into 2 equal pieces.
3. You will end up with 8 pieces for 2 slabs of Tempeh.

Poach the Tempeh:

4. Bring 4 cups of water to boil in a pot. When the water starts to boil, place the tempeh slices in and boil for 10 minutes.
5. Remove tempeh with a slotted spoon and set aside. This step of poaching the tempeh is very important – the secret to yummy tempeh!

Marinate the Tempeh:

6. Mix the ingredients of the marinade in a glass container big enough to submerge all the tempeh slabs.
7. Place poached tempeh slices in marinade making sure that they are completely immersed in it.
8. Let the tempeh marinate in this mixture for at least 2-3 hours or preferably overnight.

Continued...

> **Suggested Shopping List:**
> - Organic hearty bread or gluten-free bread
> - Lightlife® Organic Tempeh – flavor of your choice (For Gluten-free only use Soy, Wild Rice or Garden Veggie Tempeh flavor)
> - Farmhouse Culture® Raw Sauerkraut
> - Earth Balance® Organic Vegan Buttery Spread (non-Soy version)
> - Daiya® Vegan Cheese Shreds – Mozzarella
> - Bragg® Organic Raw Apple Cider Vinegar
> - Bragg® Liquid Amino Acids
> - Follow Your Heart® Soy-Free Vegenaise
> - Tree of Life® Organic Ketchup
> - Woodstock Farms® Organic Sweet Relish

> Did you know that eating too much soy can be harmful to our bodies since it contains phytic acid? This binds with certain nutrients, including iron, to inhibit their absorption. Plus it increases estrogen in the body. Fermented soy, on the other hand (e.g. tempeh, miso, soy sauce, and natto) doesn't have the same effect

Tempeh Reuben (Cont'd)

Fry the Tempeh:

9. Grease a flat skillet with a few tablespoons of oil, making sure to swirl the oil to coat the bottom of the pan.
10. Carefully remove the tempeh slices from the marinade with a slotted spoon, and fry only the tempeh slices in the skillet on medium heat. You can save the marinade in the fridge for about a week and use it as a salad dressing or pasta sauce.
11. Make sure you flip the tempeh slices from time to time to keep them from burning.
12. Fry the tempeh slices on both sides until they look golden brown (about 5 minutes). Set aside.

Make the Dressing:

13. Mix the vegan mayonnaise, ketchup, and sweet relish in a bowl to make your very own Russian dressing. Set aside.

 You can substitute tempeh for tofu in certain dishes to get the benefits of fermented soy. Just "Prepare Tempeh" before using in recipes (see page 80) since tempeh straight out of the package is not very appetizing

Prep the Sandwiches:

14. If you are using a large piece of foccacia bread, cut the bread in half to create two rectangular pieces. (you skip these steps if you are using regular loaf bread and go straight to step 16)

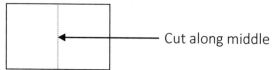

Cut along middle

15. Create a top and bottom by slicing horizontally with a long serrated knife through the middle of each half.

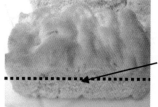

Slice through the middle with a long serrated knife.

Health: Tempeh is high in protein – Just 4 Oz of tempeh provides 41.3% of the Daily Value of protein. It also contains necessary enzymes to help with many bodily functions especially with the brain. It aids the body in making melatonin (a hormone that regulates sleep patterns), serotonin, and norepinephrine (mood influencers)

Beauty: Tempeh can help keep your skin firm and strong since it is a fermented soy product. It has been proven to increase the hyaluronic acid (HA) in your skin. HA keeps skin tight and moisturized. Plus it helps keep hair from turning gray prematurely

16. Spread vegan butter on the inside of each part of the bread.
17. Heat <u>two</u> of the buttered pieces of bread on a skillet, buttered face down on high heat or on an electric griddle, until slightly browned. Set aside.
18. Sprinkle the vegan cheese shreds on the other two buttered pieces of bread.
19. Place the cheese-covered bread in an oven or toaster oven for 3-5 minutes or until the cheese melts.
20. Remove from oven. Set aside.

Warm the sauerkraut:

21. In a small pot, heat the sauerkraut on very low heat, until it is fairly dry, taking care not to overheat (i.e. don't let the temperature get to 115°F – since it is raw and you don't want to lose the benefits by killing the healthy bacteria and overheating it). Heat for less than a minute or so.

Putting the Masterpiece Together!

22. Spread the Russian dressing on the non-cheesy side of the bread.
23. Place 3 fried Tempeh slabs on top of each of the melted cheese sides of the bread.
24. Place the warmed sauerkraut on top of the Tempeh.
25. Cover with the bread pieces that have the dressing on them.
26. Slice the sandwiches and enjoy!

Un-Tuna Sandwich

A mixture of celery and onions sautéed in vegan butter tossed with faux tuna (made of seaweed flavored gluten) and a touch of vegan mayonnaise topped with fresh sweet basil leaves on crispy Italian bread

Makes 8 Large Sandwiches

What You Will Need:
2 TB Organic Vegan Buttery Spread
1 Cup Organic Onions (1 small onion) – diced
1 Cup Organic Celery (1 stalk) – finely chopped
2½ Cups Vegan Tuna (about 21 Oz)
  GF – For gluten-free version see recipe below
3 TB Vegan Mayonnaise (see page 162 for recipe or store-bought)
6-7 Fresh Organic Sweet Basil Leaves

Bread: 1 big loaf Organic Italian bread or French Baguette

Suggested Shopping List:
- Earth Balance® Organic Vegan Buttery Spread (non-Soy version)
- Vegetarian Plus® Vegan Tuna Rolls (2 packages for this recipe) or All Vegetarian Inc ® 21 Oz package Vegan Ocean Paste "Thit Chay Nhao"
Or Eden® Organic Garbanzo can (Gluten-free)
- Follow Your Heart® Soy-Free Vegenaise
- Organic Italian or French bread (or gluten-free bread)
- Miso Master® Chickpea Miso

To Make Sandwiches:
1. In a large skillet, melt the vegan buttery spread.
2. Sauté the onions and celery in the vegan butter until they are softened.
3. Stir in the vegan tuna and toss well. Turn off heat.
4. Add the vegan mayonnaise and mix thoroughly.
5. Refrigerate the vegan tuna mixture for about 1 hour.
6. Slice the bread into two halves (see picture).

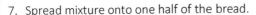

 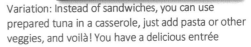
Variation: Instead of sandwiches, you can use prepared tuna in a casserole, just add pasta or other veggies, and voilà! You have a delicious entrée

7. Spread mixture onto one half of the bread.
8. Add the basil leaves on top of the mixture.
9. Spread some vegan mayonnaise or vegan butter (your choice) on the other half.
10. Place this half on top of the other half.
11. Then slice the bread across the top to make sandwiches. (see picture)

12. Leftover vegan tuna can be refrigerated for up to 1 week or frozen for up to 1 month.

For Gluten-free Version:
What You Will Need:
1 of 15 Oz Can Organic Garbanzo Beans
  (also called chickpeas)
  – drained
1 TB Organic Mustard
2 TB Chickpea Miso
1/2 Cup Vegan Mayonnaise
1 TSP Organic Garlic – minced
1/4 Cup Organic Sweet Relish
1 TSP Celery Seeds
2 TB Dulse Flakes
1 Cup Organic Onions (1 small onion) – diced
1 Cup Organic Celery (1 stalk) – finely chopped

To Make Gluten-free Vegan Tuna:
1. In a food processor or blender roughly mash the garbanzo beans making sure not to over process since you want them to be of chunky consistency or mash by hand with a fork.
2. In another smaller mixing bowl, combine the mustard, miso paste. vegan mayonnaise, garlic, sweet relish, celery seeds, and dulse flakes and stir together until well mixed.
3. Transfer saucy mix to the mashed garbanzo beans and toss them well into the saucy mix to combine well. Refrigerate your vegan tuna for about 1 hour.
4. Now follow directions 1-12 as shown above "To Make Sandwiches".

Entrees

Baked Bean Burritos p.82

Pineapple Fried Rice p.111

Biryani p.125

Ma Po Tofu p.102

Palak Tofu Paneer p.108

Spaghetti Bolognese p.118

Raw Pesto Pasta p.110

Quiche p.128

Eggplant Vegasan p. 91

Adzuki Beans and Kale Medley

This dish takes macrobiotic cooking to the next level creating an eastern/western medley of adorable adzuki beans, curly kale leaves, and tempting tempeh all blended with savory spices and herbs

Serves 4

What You Will Need:
1 Cup Uncooked Organic Adzuki beans
 Or canned Aduki beans – drained
1 TB Grapeseed Oil
1 TSP Organic Garlic – minced
1 Cup Organic Onions – diced
6 Cups Kale leaves – roughly chopped with stems removed
1 Packet Organic Tempeh – sliced into thin strips
1/4 Cup Organic Shoyu Sauce

 Use Organic Tamari Sauce

1 TSP Ground Cumin
1 TSP Curry Powder
1 TSP Coriander Powder
1/2 TSP Himalayan Pink Salt
2 TSP Raw Sugar
Dash of Cayenne Pepper

What You Will Need For Seasoning the Tempeh
2-3 Springs Organic Cilantro
  – leaves and stems chopped up fine
1 TSP Organic Garlic – minced
1 TSP Organic Ginger – minced
2 TB Organic Shoyu

 Use Organic Tamari Sauce

2 TSP Raw Sugar

 Did you know that the Adzuki bean is also called Azuki, Aduki, Red Chori, Red Cow Pea, and Red Bean? So many names for the same bean!

 Health: Adzuki Beans are considered in Macrobiotics to be the most "Yang" or warming, of all beans, and thus are known to give strength to our bodies. In Traditional Chinese Medicine, Adzukis are known for their healing properties, and help support kidney, bladder and reproductive functions. Plus they are easy to digest so they usually do not give you gas as other beans do

Beauty: Adzukis are called "the weight loss bean" since they are low in calories and fat, but high in nutrition

To Cook Adzuki Beans:
1. Put Adzuki beans in a pressure cooker with lid removed, adding enough water to cover the beans.
2. Close the pressure cooker. Once it starts to whistle, start your timer for 15 minutes. Turn off the pressure cooker after 15 minutes. (Or check your own pressure cooker for "bean cooking" times). Once the pressure has all been released. Open the pressure cooker. Set aside.

Note: You can eliminate steps 1 & 2 if using canned Adzuki.

To Prepare Tempeh:
3. Bring 3 cups of water to boil in a pot. When the water starts to boil, place the tempeh block in and boil for 10 minutes.
4. Remove Tempeh with a slotted spoon, pat dry with paper towels, slice into strips and set aside

5. Lightly grease a flat ceramic skillet and shallow fry tempeh strips until browned on both sides. Set aside.
6. In a small saucepan, in 1 tablespoon of oil, sauté garlic, ginger and cilantro for 1 minute on low heat.
7. Add the Shoyu sauce (or Tamari) and sugar and mix well.
8. Add the fried tempeh strips and toss them in the sauce mixture until tempeh strips are well coated. Set seasoned tempeh aside.

To Put it all Together:
9. In a medium skillet, heat 3 tablespoons oil over medium heat and sauté garlic and onions for about 5 minutes until the onions are limp and translucent.
10. Season with Shoyu (or Tamari) sauce, cumin, coriander and curry powder.
11. Add kale and cook for 15 minutes until kale is tender.
12. Stir in the cooked adzuki beans or drained canned beans.
13. Reduce heat to low, cover and simmer for 5 minutes to allow flavors to blend.
14. Season with salt, sugar and cayenne.
15. Toss in seasoned tempeh strips.
16. Serve over rice or eat as is.

Asperges À La Béchamel

Tender asparagus spears smothered in a cheesy béchamel sauce infused with aromatic dill and garlic, garnished with capers

Serves 8

What You Will Need:

50 Organic Asparagus spears – with 2 in. from the stem ends cut off
1 TB Organic Vegan Buttery Spread
2 TB Vegan Mayonnaise (see page 162 for recipe or store-bought)
2 TSP Organic Maple Syrup (Grade B)
1 TB Organic Mustard
1 Cup Vegan Sour Cream
2 TSP Organic Garlic – minced
1 TSP Dried Dill
1 Cup Water – reserved from cooked asparagus
1 Cup Vegan Cheese Shreds
1 TSP Raw Sugar
1 TSP Himalayan Pink Salt
1/4 Cup Capers *(optional)*

Suggested Shopping List:
– Earth Balance® Natural Buttery Spread (non-Soy version)
– Follow Your Heart® Soy-Free Vegenaise
– Follow Your Heart® Vegan Sour Cream
– Daiya® Vegan Cheese Shreds – Mozzarella

To Make Asperges À La Béchamel:

1. Cook the asparagus in a pressure cooker. Remove from the water. Set aside. Save the water.
2. In a separate saucepan, on low heat, melt the vegan butter.
3. Sauté the garlic, until you can smell the aroma of the roasted garlic.
4. Lower heat, add the vegan mayonnaise, maple syrup, mustard, raw sugar, salt, and vegan sour cream and mix well.
5. Sprinkle in the dried dill.
6. Stir in the vegan cheese.
7. Add a cup of the reserved water that you saved from the cooked asparagus.
8. Increase the burner to high, and keep stirring until the cheese melts. Your béchamel sauce is ready.
9. Turn off burner. Stir in the capers (optional).
10. Arrange the asparagus in a glass baking dish.
11. Pour the béchamel sauce over the cooked asparagus.

 Variation: If you want to serve this dish truly French style, then place 3-4 asparagus pieces on a plate, drizzle the béchamel sauce over the asparagus spears, and top with garnish to impress!

 Did you know there are many vitamins and minerals lost from cooking the vegetables which end up in the water? This cooking water can be added to homemade soups or sauces with its added nutrition benefits. You should only do this if you are using organic vegetables though, because non-organic vegetables would leach pesticides and herbicides into the cooking water which will do more harm than good!

 Health: Asparagus is good for digestion because it contains Inulin, a carbohydrate that encourages the growth of Bifidobacteria and Lactobacilli, two bacteria that boost nutrient absorption. It also lowers the risk of allergy and colon cancer, and helps prevent unfriendly bacteria from taking hold in our intestinal tract
Beauty: Asparagus is known for reducing belly fat because of its high potassium content (288 milligrams of potassium per cup). Plus it contains a lot of fiber which cleanses the digestive system. Thus Asparagus is a wonderful detox agent

Baked Bean Burritos

Take sautéed onions, tomatoes and the bold flavor of baked beans garnished with my own version of mole sauce, sprinkle with vegan cheese, roll in tortillas and bake until warm and bubbly and you end up with a harmony of sweet & sour Mexican...Yum!

Serves 4

What You Will Need:
6 Organic 8-10 inch Flour Tortillas

 Use Organic Gluten-Free Flour Tortillas

1 of 15 Oz Can Organic Baked Beans
1/2 Cup Organic Onions – diced
1/2 Cup Organic Tomatoes – diced
1 TSP Organic Garlic – minced
1/2 TSP Organic Ginger – minced
2 Cups Vegan Cheese Shreds
1 TB Organic Ketchup
1 TB Organic Barbecue Sauce
1 TSP Organic Taco Seasoning
1 TSP Ground Cumin
1/2 TSP Paprika Powder
1/2 TSP Dried Oregano
1 TSP Himalayan Pink Salt

Suggested Shopping List:
- La Tortilla Factory® Sonoma "Traditional" **or** "Ivory Teff" (for gluten-free) Tortillas 6 pack
- Walnut Acres® Organic Baked Beans
- Daiya® Vegan Cheese Shreds – Cheddar
- Tree of Life® Organic Ketchup
- Follow Your Heart® Barbecue Vegenaise or Annie's® Organic Barbecue Sauce
- Bearitos® or Simply Organic® Southwest Taco Seasoning

To Make Burritos:
1. Pre-heat oven to 350°F.
2. In a large skillet, on medium heat, sauté ginger, garlic, and onions in 3 tablespoons of oil until onions are slightly limp and translucent.
3. Add the tomatoes, lower the heat, and cook for about five minutes.
4. Season with taco seasoning, cumin, paprika, oregano and salt. Mix thoroughly allowing mixture to cook on low heat for about 3 minutes to blend flavors.
5. Add the baked beans, ketchup, and barbecue sauce.
6. Allow the bean mixture to simmer for about 10 minutes on low heat. Turn off stove.
7. Once the bean mixture is cooled, place 1 TB of mixture into a tortilla wrapper, top with vegan cheese shreds (about 1-2 TB – depending on how cheesy you like it), and wrap like a burrito (see page 34 on instructions on how to wrap a basil roll).
8. Repeat step 6 until all the tortillas are used up.
9. Place wrapped burritos in a glass baking dish side by side.
10. Pour left over bean mixture over the top and sprinkle with vegan cheese shreds.
11. Bake in oven at 350°F for 10-15 minutes.

 You can dress up your burritos with, sliced jalapenos, diced black olives, salsa (see page 48), guacamole (see page 39), and vegan sour cream (Follow Your Heart® brand)

Beef-Less Rendang

An Indonesian specialty made vegan – Chunks of vegan beef slices (or tempeh) and broccoli florets simmered in a sumptuous sauce with coconut cream and a rich blend of lemongrass, coriander and ginger

Serves 4

What You Will Need:

1/2 of 8 Oz Package Dried Seitan Slices (about 4 cups)

 Use 1 Packet Organic Tempeh – sliced into thin strips

1 of 1.2 Oz Package of Rendang Paste
4 Cups Organic Broccoli Florets (about 2 big heads of broccoli)
1 of 13.5 fl Oz Can Organic Coconut Milk
1 Cube Vegetable Bouillon
2 Cups Filtered Water
1 Cup Organic Yellow Onions – diced
1 TSP Organic Garlic – minced
1/2 TSP Organic Ginger – minced
1 TSP Himalayan Pink Salt
2 TSP Raw Sugar
3 TB Grapeseed Oil for cooking
Organic Cilantro – 4 to 5 sprigs (about 1/4 Cup)
 – leaves and stems chopped up fine

Suggested Shopping List:
- VegeUSA® Vegan Beef Slices (see picture below)
- Lightlife® Organic Tempeh – Soy, Wild Rice or Garden Veggie Tempeh flavor)
- Bamboe® Rendang Paste – available online
- Native Forest® Organic Coconut Milk can
- Edward & Sons® Not Chick'n Natural Bouillon Cubes

Enlarged to show texture

To Make Rendang:

1. In a large skillet, in 3 tablespoons of grapeseed oil sauté the garlic, ginger, cilantro, and onions on medium heat for about 5 minutes, or until the onions are softened.
2. Add the Rendang paste. Add 1 cup filtered water to dilute paste.
3. Stir in the coconut milk and mix thoroughly.
4. Add 1 more cup of filtered water, and 1 bouillon cube. Keep stirring until the cube is dissolved.
5. Season with salt and sugar. Mix well.
6. Add the broccoli florets and dried soy slices making sure they are well coated with the liquid mixture. (For gluten-free version see suggestion below)
7. Lower heat and cover skillet to let the broccoli steam for about 10-15 minutes. Turn off burner.
8. Serve over steamed brown or white rice.

 Note: If you are making this dish gluten-free then follow the instructions on page 80 for how to season and prepare Tempeh for use in this dish

 Did you know Rendang is traditionally prepared by the Indonesian and Malaysian community during festive occasions such as traditional ceremonies, wedding feasts, and New Year? In an online poll held by CNN International, people chose Rendang as the number one dish for their 'World's 50 Most Delicious Foods"

Beef-Less Stroganoff

From Russia with Love we bring chunks of tender seasoned seitan soy protein and spinach stewed in a creamy vegan sauce served over a bed of fettuccine brown rice noodles

Serves 4

What You Will Need:

1 Cup Seasoned Seitan Soy Protein Chunks – thinly sliced
1 TSP Organic Garlic – minced
1 Small Onion – julienned
2 TB Organic Vegan Buttery Spread
1 of 8 Oz Container Vegan Cream Cheese
1 TSP Himalayan Pink Salt
1 TSP Freshly Ground Pepper
2 TSP Raw Sugar
2 TB Organic Ketchup
1 Cube Vegetable Bouillon
2 Cups Filtered Water
2 Cups Organic Spinach (fresh or frozen)
14 Oz Packet Fettuccine Style Pasta
For boiling pasta: 1½ TSP Himalayan Pink Salt and 1 TB Grapeseed Oil
Drizzle of Olive Oil

Suggested Shopping List:
- EcoVegan® Blissful Bits for seasoned seitan soy protein
- Earth Balance® Vegan Buttery Spread (non-Soy version)
- Follow Your Heart® Vegan Cream Cheese
- Tree of Life® Organic Ketchup
- Edward & Sons® Not Beef Natural Bouillon Cubes
- Tinkyada® Brown Rice Pasta (Fettuccine Style)

To Make Stroganoff:

1. Fill a large pot of filtered water to boil, add salt and oil to the water. Bring the water to a rolling boil.
2. Add the fettuccine style noodles, and cook for the amount of time noted on the pasta package instructions. Make sure to stir the pasta every so often to prevent sticking. Drain the pasta, then drizzle the surface of the cooked pasta with olive oil, and set aside.
3. In a large skillet, on medium heat, melt the vegan buttery spread.
4. Sauté the garlic and onions until the onions are limp and translucent.
5. Add the bouillon cube and 2 cups water. Increase the burner to high, and stir until the bouillon cube is completely dissolved.
6. Season with salt, sugar, pepper, and ketchup.
7. Stir in the spinach.
8. Add the thinly sliced seasoned seitan pieces.
9. Add the tub of vegan cream cheese, thoroughly whisking it in until the cream cheese is well blended into the sauce.
10. Reduce heat, cover the pot and let the sauce simmer on low heat for 5 minutes to allow flavors to blend.
11. Toss the boiled fettuccine noodles into the sauce.
12. Serve hot.

 Unfortunately this dish cannot be made gluten-free – there is no gluten-free substitute for seasoned seitan

 Did you know that Rice Pasta is better than other grain pasta, since it is not mushy and always has a consistent texture? Plus it is lower in cholesterol and easier to digest than regular pasta. You won't get that stuffed feeling that you get when you eat most pasta

Black-Eyed Peas Stew

Who can resist those precious little black-eyed peas when they are simmered in the most fragrant of Indian spices and eaten with Indian Breads?

Serves 2-3

What You Will Need:

2 Medium Organic Tomatoes (about 3 Cups) – halved
1 Large Organic Onion (about 2 Cups) – quartered
1 TSP Organic Garlic – minced
1 TSP Organic Ginger – minced
1 of 15 Oz Can Organic Black-Eyed Peas
  – with half of the liquid drained
1 TSP Himalayan Pink Salt
1 TSP Coriander Powder
1 TSP Garam Masala (see page 156
  for recipe or store-bought)
2 TB Organic Barbecue sauce
Grapeseed Oil for cooking

Suggested Shopping List:
- Eden® Organic Black-Eyed Peas can
- Coriander Powder and Garam Masala can be found in Indian grocery stores
- Annie's® Organic BBQ Sauce

To Make The Stew:

1. Place tomatoes, onions, garlic and ginger in a food processor or blender. Process the ingredients until they are completely pulverized.
2. In a large skillet, in three tablespoons of oil, sauté the processed mixture and cook for ten minutes on low heat with the pot covered.
3. Uncover lid, season with salt, coriander powder, garam masala, and barbecue sauce and mix well, allowing mixture to simmer on low heat for another five minutes to blend flavors.
4. Add the half-drained black-eyed peas can. Stir well.
5. Let the black-eyed peas simmer on low heat for 20 minutes. Turn off stove.

 You can enjoy your stew by itself or you can eat it over toasted slices of bread or with Indian breads like "naan", "paratha" or "roti"

 Did you know Black-Eyed Peas are actually beans and not from the pea family?

 Health: Black-eyed Peas are high in iron – 1/2 cup has 2.2 mg of iron. Iron helps prevent anemia, which causes fatigue and weakness. Iron carries oxygen throughout your body to your organs, cells and muscles, and if the supply is low you experience sluggishness. Plus black-eyed peas are rich in protein and calcium too
Beauty: Black-eyed peas are a low-fat and low-calorie food, making them a healthy addition to a weight-loss meal plan

Chow Faan-Fried Rice

Here's a delectable way to use your left over rice from the previous night... Crank out some Chow Faan (Chinese Fried Rice) – very fast...very easy...and very tasty!

Serves 2-3

What You Will Need:
1 Cup Cooked Left-Over rice (I like Jasmine rice)
 (hot rice doesn't make good chow faan or fried rice
   so if you want to use fresh rice, make sure it is refrigerated
   and cooled before using in this recipe)
1 Cup Organic Frozen Mixed Vegetables
 – beans, peas, carrots, and corn
1 TSP Organic Garlic – minced
1 TSP Organic Ginger – minced
5 Stalks of Organic Scallions – thinly sliced
Grapeseed Oil for cooking
1 TB Organic Shoyu Sauce

 Use Organic Tamari Sauce
1 TB Liquid Amino Acids
1 TB Mirin (or Rice Vinegar)
1 Cup Organic Eggplant – cut into tiny cubes

For Eggplant Cubes Marinade:
1 TB Sesame Oil
1 TB Liquid Amino Acids
1 TB Mirin (or Rice Vinegar)
1 TSP Raw Sugar

Suggested Shopping List:
- Jasmine Rice
- San-J® Organic Shoyu or Tamari Sauce (for gluten-free)
- Bragg® Liquid Amino Acids
- Eden® Mirin
- Wei-Chuan® 100% pure black sesame oil

To Prepare Chow Faan:
1. Mix the marinade ingredients in a large bowl. Toss the eggplant cubes in marinade until they are well coated. Marinate the cubes for about 20 minutes. Set aside.
2. In the meantime, in a large skillet, in about 3 tablespoons of oil, sauté the ginger, garlic and scallions until you can smell the aroma of the garlic and ginger about 3-4 minutes.
3. Add the organic mixed vegetables, lower the heat, cover skillet and let the vegetables steam for 10 minutes.
4. Lay the marinated eggplant cubes on a baking tray and broil for about 5-7 minutes, until the cubes are soft. Or alternatively, in a small frying pan, fry the eggplant cubes until the eggplant cubes are well cooked. Set aside.
5. Your steamed veggies in the other skillet should be done by now. Uncover the skillet. Season with the shoyu sauce or tamari sauce (for gluten-free), liquid amino acids, and Mirin. Mix well making sure to coat all the vegetables with the seasonings.
6. Toss the cooked left-over rice into the seasoned vegetables until all the rice is well mixed in. *Note: If you use freshly cooked rice, make sure rice is cool before you stir it in – otherwise it will turn to mush.*
7. Stir in the cooked eggplant cubes making sure to toss them well into the fried rice.
8. Enjoy!

Creamy Celery Risotto

A savory celery flavored "soy-creamy" rice dish that can accompany any Italian feast

Serves 6

What You Will Need:

3 TB Organic Vegan Buttery Spread
1 Cup Organic Onions – diced
1 TSP Organic Garlic – minced
4 Stalks Organic Celery – finely chopped
2 Organic Tomatoes – diced
1 of 8oz Container Vegan Cream Cheese
1½ Cup Organic Coconut Milk
3 TB Unbleached Organic Flour

 Use Gluten-free Flour or Arrowroot

1 Cube Vegetable Bouillon
1 TSP Himalayan Pink Salt
1/2 TSP Dried Celery Seed
1 TSP Dried Italian Seasoning
1 Cup Vegan Cheese Shreds

For cooking rice you will need:

5 cups White Rice (I like Jasmine Rice)
1½ Heaping TSP Himalayan Pink Salt
1 TB Grapeseed Oil

 Health: Celery prevents cancer, since it contains phthalides and polyacetylenes. These anti cancer components detoxify carcinogens in your body – so if you have cancer cells in your body, celery neutralizes them!
Beauty: If you follow an exercise regime, celery supports your workout by giving you healthy joints. It also prevents rheumatism and arthritis

To Make Risotto:

1. Cook the white rice and set aside. I generally cook mine in a rice cooker, wash and rinse the rice well, then put it in my rice cooker, stir in 1 TB of oil and 1½ heaping TSP of salt, and then press cook. You can cook it on the stove if you like. For white rice, the ratio is 1:1 so 5 cups of white rice to 5 cups of water.
2. In a large skillet, on medium heat, melt 3 tablespoons of vegan buttery spread, and sauté onions and garlic until onions are limp and translucent. Lower heat.
3. Add tomatoes. Cook for a few minutes until tomatoes are softened.
4. Sprinkle 3 tablespoons of flour to the onion and tomato mixture. Mix thoroughly until it forms a lump.
5. Add the coconut milk, increase the heat to high, and keep stirring the mixture until there are no more lumps and the mixture thickens.
6. Season with salt, celery seed, and Italian seasoning and mix well.
7. Toss in the vegetable bouillon cube. Keep stirring until the cube dissolves.
8. Stir in the celery. Lower the heat and cover your pot. Let the mixture simmer on very low heat for about 15 minutes to soften celery and bring out the flavors of the herbs and seasonings.
9. Add the vegan cream cheese. If the sauce is too thick at this point you can add a little water to dilute it. It should resemble a thick creamy consistency. Break up the vegan cream cheese if you need to with a wire whisk.
10. Toss the cooked white rice well until it is completely coated with the sauce mixture.
11. Transfer to a baking dish, and top with vegan cheese shreds. Place dish in oven at 400°F for 5-7 minutes to allow the cheese to melt. Do not leave the dish in the oven for too long because vegan cheese tends to dry out and turn crusty if overcooked.

Crockpot Spinach Lasagna

Want some lasagna quick but don't want to go through the hassle of spending hours in the kitchen? Well use this recipe and make it in a crockpot! It's fast, easy and yummy

Serves 4

What You Will Need:
1 of 10 Oz package Organic Brown Rice Lasagna Noodles
1 of 24 Oz jar of Organic Pasta Sauce-Tomato blend
2 Cups Vegan Cheese Shreds
6 Cups Organic Fresh Spinach (fresh or frozen)
Dried Oregano

Suggested Shopping List:
- Tinkyada® Organic Brown Rice Lasagna
- Bertolli® Organic Pasta Sauce -Tomato & Basil
- Daiya® Vegan Cheese Shreds – Mozzarella
- Wildwood® Organic Sprouted Tofu

What You Will Need for Tofu Ricotta:
1 of 14 Oz Block Organic Firm Tofu
2 TSP Organic Lemon Juice
2 TSP Extra Virgin Olive Oil
1 TSP Garlic – minced
1/4 TSP Himalayan Pink Salt
A Handful Fresh Basil leaves or 1/4 TSP Dried Basil
Dash of Freshly Ground Black Pepper

To Make Tofu Ricotta:
1. Place tofu, lemon juice, olive oil, garlic, salt, basil and black pepper in a food processor or blender. Process all the ingredients until you get a creamy texture. Set aside.
2. Grease your crockpot. Plug it in and set it to low setting.

To Make Lasagna:
1. Using a spoon or butter knife to spread the tofu ricotta over 3 lasagna noodles. (If lasagna noodles are too large for your crockpot, break them in half)
2. Place these in crock pot.
3. Ladle some organic pasta sauce over the tofu ricotta making sure to cover the noodles well.
4. Place a few spinach leaves on top of the sauce.
5. Top generously with vegan cheese shreds.
6. Sprinkle some oregano over the cheese.
7. Repeat procedures 1-6 until all the noodles are used up.
8. End with a layer of vegan cheese shreds.
9. Cook on high in the crock pot for 2 hours. Don't leave cooking for too long, or the lasagna will turn mushy.

 To Make the same Lasagna in the traditional way:
1. Preheat oven to 350°F.
2. Bring a large pot of water to a rolling boil, adding a teaspoon of salt and a tablespoon of oil to the water before boiling.
3. When the water comes to a rolling boil add your lasagna noodles and start your timer for the cooking time as directed on the packaging. When done, drain the noodles. Spray some olive oil over them to prevent them from sticking to one another, and set aside.
4. Spread 1/4 of the pasta sauce on the bottom of a baking dish (about 13 x 9)
5. Lay 4 or 5 boiled noodles over the sauce.

6. Top noodles with tofu ricotta and spinach.
7. Ladle pasta sauce over the tofu ricotta and spinach.
8. Generously top with vegan cheese shreds.
9. Sprinkle with oregano.
10. Repeat steps 5-9 until all the noodles are used up.
11. End with a layer of vegan cheese shreds.
12. Bake in an oven at 375°F for 20 minutes or until the lasagna starts to bubble.

Curried Singapore Noodles

Intoxicatingly flavorful curried rice noodles stir fried with juicy tomatoes and green peppers

Serves 4

What You Will Need:

1 LB Rice Noodles (Mai Fun)
 Or Bean Thread (Sai Fun) or Cellophane Noodles
   (about 6 Cups) – I used 6 dried cakes of noodles
3 Medium Organic Roma Tomatoes – diced
1 Medium Organic Green Bell Pepper – diced
1 TB Madras Curry Powder
2 TB Liquid Amino Acids
1 TSP Himalayan Pink Salt
1 TSP Organic Garlic – minced
1 Stalk Organic Scallion – finely chopped – for garnish
Grapeseed Oil for cooking
4 Cups Filtered Water

Suggested Shopping List:
– Rice Stick (Pasta) Wei-Chuan* – found in Oriental markets – also called "Mai Fun"
Or Orchids* Sai Fun Bean Threads
– Kim Thu Thap* Mild Madras Curry Powder

To Make Noodles:

1. In a large pot, bring water to a boil, adding a teaspoon of salt and a few drops of oil before boiling.
2. When the water comes to a rolling boil, add the rice noodles. Stir the noodles to break them up. Leave the noodles in boiling water for 2 minutes only. (Make sure you don't leave them in the boiling water for any longer since the noodles will turn too limp and become unsuitable for stir-frying.)
3. Drain the noodles in a colander. Cut the noodles in the colander with kitchen scissors to shorten the strands. Set noodles aside.
4. In three tablespoons of oil, sauté garlic, tomatoes and green peppers until they are softened (about 5 minutes), stirring constantly.
5. Season with curry powder and salt and mix well until the tomatoes and green peppers are well coated with the seasonings.
6. Add the boiled noodles to the tomato and bell pepper mixture, making sure to toss the noodles well into mixture.
7. Season with Liquid Amino Acids, and work it thoroughly into the noodles. You may add more liquid amino acids to suit your taste.
8. Garnish with scallions.

> Do you know the difference between Mai Fun and Sai Fun?
> Sai Fun – also known as cellophane noodles, bean threads, bean thread noodles, Chinese vermicelli, crystal noodles, or glass noodles – is a type of transparent noodle made from starch (such as mung bean, yam, potato or cassava starch and water. Mai Fun also known as rice noodles, rice vermicelli or rice sticks are thin noodles made from rice and water. Well now you know!

> **Health:** Curry contains the beneficial curcumin which helps in fighting cancer. In 2008 in an International Medical Journal called "Cancer Letters" it was reported that curcumin interferes with multiple cell signaling pathways that affect the life cycle of cancer cells. This means that it fights off the onset and spread of cancer in the body. The study showed cures for many different types of cancer, such as leukemia, lymphoma, skin cancer, lung cancer and breast cancer
> **Beauty:** Curry gives you healthy shiny hair and strong nails

Curried Vegetable Pot Pie

This dish is great for when the weather gets cooler – its bold flavors warm you all over

Serves 4

What You Will Need:

2 Organic Pie Crusts

 Use gluten-free Pie Crusts

1 Cup Organic Frozen Mixed Vegetables
  (peas, beans, carrots, corn)
1 Cup Organic Potatoes – boiled and cubed
Grapeseed Oil for cooking
1 Organic Onion – finely diced
1 TSP Organic Garlic – minced
2 TSP Madras Curry Powder
1 TSP Himalayan Pink Salt
1 TSP Coriander Powder
1/2 Cup Vegan Cheese Shreds

Suggested Shopping List:
- Wholly Wholesome® Organic Pie Crusts
- Kim Thu Thap® Mild Madras Curry Powder
- Coriander Powder found in Indian grocery stores
- Daiya® Vegan Cheese Shreds – Mozzarella

To Make Pie:

1. In a small saucepan, boil the cubed potatoes in enough filtered water to cover the potatoes for about 20-25 minutes or until they are soft. Set aside.
2. Bake one empty pie crust for 7 minutes at 350°F. Set aside.
3. In a large skillet, in 3 tablespoons of oil, sauté garlic and onions until onions are limp and translucent.
4. Add the organic frozen mixed vegetables and sauté until they are tender.
5. Stir in boiled cubed potatoes and toss well with the vegetables.
6. Season with curry powder, salt and coriander powder, and mix well until all the vegetables are well coated with seasonings.
7. Fill the baked pie crust with the curried vegetable mixture.
8. Top with vegan cheese shreds. Set aside.

> Did you know the pie originated in ancient Egypt around 9500 BC? They were called galettes – these were made with oat, wheat, rye, and barley, then filled with honey and baked over hot coals. Drawings of this can be found etched on the tomb walls of Ramses II.
> Also in the 13th Century live birds were baked into pies as a form of entertainment. When the pies were open the birds were released alive – hence the nursery rhyme "Sing A Song of Sixpence says "When the pie was opened, the birds began to sing wasn't that a dainty dish to set before the king"

9. Bake the other empty pie crust in the oven for 2 minutes at 350°F. Then remove pie crust.
10. Position the empty pie crust over the filled pie crust. The foil pan holding the pie crust should easily lift off – discard it.
11. Using your fingers, fold and press the edges to seal the curried vegetable mixture in.
12. Carefully prick holes in the top shell with a fork.
13. Bake in the oven for 30 minutes at 350°F.
14. Slice into wedges and serve.

Eggplant Vegasan

This is not your typical eggplant parmesan because it's not made with breaded and fried eggplant, plus there's no parmesan cheese – so here's my own version which is low in fat, and tastes great even though it's not authentic. Thin slices of broiled eggplant and tomatoes, fried tofu, fresh basil, sautéed peppers and onions topped with marinara sauce and vegan cheese baked to perfection. Mmm Mmm...

Serves 4

What You Will Need:

12 Japanese or Chinese Organic Eggplants
  – sliced lengthwise into 1/2 inch-thick 1.5 inch long rectangles
4 Organic Tomatoes – thinly sliced
1 Cup Organic Onions – julienned
1 Cup Organic Green Bell Peppers – julienned
1 TSP Organic Garlic – minced
1 of 14 Oz Block Organic Extra Firm Tofu – sliced into 3 x 5 x 1/4 inch rectangles
30 Fresh Organic Basil Leaves
1 of 24 Oz jar of Organic Pasta Sauce – Tomato blend
2 Cups Vegan Cheese Shreds
Organic Breadcrumbs

 Use gluten-free bread crumbs

Grapeseed Oil for cooking

> **Suggested Shopping List:**
> - Wildwood® Organic Sprouted Tofu
> - Bertolli® Organic Pasta Sauce –Tomato & Basil
> - Daiya® Vegan Cheese Shreds – Mozzarella
> - Edward & Sons® Organic Breadcrumbs
> _Or_ Orgran® All Purpose Rice Crumbs (for gluten-free)

To Make Eggplant:

1. Lightly grease a large baking tray.
2. Place sliced eggplants and tomatoes on the tray. Drizzle the surface of the eggplants and tomatoes with oil.
3. Broil the vegetables in an oven for 8 minutes.
4. In a small pan, in three tablespoons of oil on medium heat, sauté the garlic, onions, and green bell peppers until onions and peppers are limp (about 5 minutes). Set aside.
5. Grease a non-stick flat pan with 1 tablespoon of oil. Shallow fry the tofu rectangles on one side until golden brown in color, then turn over the tofu pieces, and fry the other side (about 3 minutes on each side). Set aside.
6. In a glass baking dish, first place a layer of the broiled eggplants and tomatoes.
7. Then place the fried, tofu on top of the layer of eggplants and tomatoes.
8. Top each piece of tofu with a basil leaf.
9. Top with a layer of onions and peppers.
10. Ladle some organic pasta sauce over everything.
11. Sprinkle with vegan cheese and breadcrumbs.
12. Repeat steps 6-11 until all the ingredients are used up, finishing with a layer of vegan cheese and breadcrumbs.
13. Bake in a preheated oven at 375°F for 10 minutes or until the dish starts to bubble.

 Did you know that eggplant is also known as aubergine, brinjal, melongene, garden egg, or guinea squash and that it is related to tomatoes and potatoes and comes from the nightshade family?

Eggplant in Szechuan Sauce

Braised eggplant and zucchini sautéed in a mildly spicy garlic sauce served over a bed of intoxicatingly fragrant jasmine rice. Who needs Chinese takeout when you can have this!

Serves 4

What You Will Need:

3 Chinese Organic Eggplants (about 4 cups)
– sliced lengthwise into 1/2 inch-thick 1.5 inch long rectangles
2 Organic Zucchinis – diced (about 3 cups)
3 Stalks Organic Scallions – finely chopped into pieces
1/2 Cup Organic Cilantro – leaves and stems chopped up fine
1 TSP Organic Ginger – minced
1 TSP Organic Garlic – minced
1 TB Organic Shoyu sauce

 Use Organic Tamari Sauce

4 TSP Raw Sugar
1 TB Organic Raw Apple Cider Vinegar
1 TB Mirin
1 TB Chili Garlic Sauce
  (see page 154 for recipe or store-bought)
1 Cube Vegetable Bouillon
2 Cups Filtered Water
3 TB Organic Cornstarch mixed in 2 TB
  of water to thicken the sauce (optional)
 Or Arrowroot to thicken the sauce (optional)
1 TB Chinese Sesame Oil for garnish
Grapeseed Oil for cooking

Suggested Shopping List:
- San-J* Organic Shoyu Sauce or Organic Tamari (gluten-free)
- Bragg* Organic Raw Apple Cider Vinegar
- Lee Kum Kee* Chili Garlic Sauce
Or Sriracha* Chili Garlic Sauce
- Edward & Sons* Not Chick'n Natural Bouillon Cubes
- Wei-Chuan* 100% pure black sesame oil

Did you know that Szechuan is a style of Chinese cuisine originating from Sichuan province in Southwest China? Szechuan food is composed of 7 basic flavors: sour, pungent, hot, sweet, bitter, aromatic, and salty

To Make Eggplant in Szechuan Sauce:

1. In a large skillet, in 4 tablespoons of oil, braise the eggplant and zucchini for 10-15 minutes or until vegetables are limp to the touch. (Alternative method of cooking: This method is not as authentic tasting, but definitely healthier: you can place vegetables on a baking tray, drizzle them with oil, and then roast them in an oven at 350°F for 20 minutes or until the eggplant is limp to the touch).
2. After braising the vegetables, turn off the heat, and remove cooked vegetables from the skillet and set aside.
3. Add 1 tablespoon of oil to the skillet, and sauté the ginger, garlic, cilantro, and scallions for a few moments until you can smell the aroma of the ginger and garlic (about 2 minutes). Lower heat.
4. Pour in 2 cups of water.
5. Toss in the bouillon cube increasing the heat to high to allow the bouillon cube to dissolve.
6. Season with shoyu sauce (or tamari sauce for gluten-free), apple cider vinegar, mirin, raw sugar, and chili garlic sauce.
7. Toss the braised/roasted eggplant and zucchini into the sauce until the vegetables are well coated with the sauce.
8. Lower the heat, and let the eggplant and zucchini simmer in the sauce for 5-10 minutes to blend flavors.
9. Steps 9-10 are optional; you can thicken the sauce by adding a mixture of cornstarch dissolved in water or a mixture of arrowroot.
10. Increase the heat, and mix in the cornstarch mixture. Keep stirring until you see the sauce thicken.
11. Turn off the burner. Drizzle with sesame oil and enjoy over steamed white/brown jasmine rice.

Faux Chik'N Makhanwala a.k.a. Faux Chik'N Tikka Masala

This is a popular culinary dish served in most Indian restaurants but rarely do you find a vegan version of it...so let's make it with its tasty tandoori, tomato, buttery, and creamy flavors, but yet completely vegan! How is that possible you might ask?

Serves 4

What You Will Need:

2 Cups Seasoned Seitan Strips

 Use 1 Block Organic Super Firm Tofu – sliced into cubes

1 Cup Frozen Organic Mixed Vegetables
  – peas, carrots, corn etc.
3 TB Organic Vegan Buttery Spread
1 Organic Onion (about 1½ Cups) – finely diced
3½ TB Organic Tomato Paste
1 of 13.66 fl Oz Can Organic Coconut Milk Can
1/2 Cup Filtered Water
1 Cup Raw Organic Cashews – soaked in 1/2 Cup Filtered
  Water for at least 1 hour (retain water)
1/4 TSP Garam Masala (see page 156 for recipe or store-bought)
1/2 TSP Cinnamon Powder
1 TSP Dried Fenugreek Leaves (Kasuri Methi)
2 TSP Organic Garlic – minced
1 TSP Organic Ginger – minced
1 TSP Tandoori Powder
1 TSP Himalayan Pink Salt
1/2 TSP Raw Sugar
Cayenne Pepper to taste (if you like it spicy)

Suggested Shopping List:
- Trader Joe's® Chicken-Less Strips or All Vegetarian Inc. Vegan Ham Paste (Thit Chay Nhao) – shredded
<u>Or</u> for Gluten-free use Wildwood® Organic Sprouted Tofu
- Earth Balance® Natural Buttery Spread (non-Soy version)
- Native Forest® Organic Coconut Milk Can
- Garam Masala, Kasuri Methi and Tandoori Powder can be found in Indian grocery stores

To Make Faux Chik'N Makhanwala:

If using Tofu:

1. Drain the tofu, pat dry between paper towels, and cut into cubes. Sprinkle with 1/2 TSP salt and toss well.
2. In a flat non-stick skillet, in 1 tablespoon of oil, pan-fry the salted tofu cubes until they are browned on both sides, making sure to continuously flip them to prevent charring the tofu. Set aside.

 Did you know that the original non-vegan version of this dish "Chicken Makhanwala" is also known as: "Chicken Tikka Masala", "Chicken Makhani", "Butter Chicken", "Murgh Makhani", and "Murgh Makhanwala"?

If using Seitan – Eliminate steps 1 and 2 above:

1. In a food processor, place the soaked cashews with the water, and process until completely puréed. Set aside.
2. In a large skillet, on medium heat, sauté the garlic, ginger, and onions in the butter until the onions are limp and translucent.
3. Add the tomato paste and mix into the onions to form a large lump.
4. Season with garam masala, cinnamon powder, fenugreek leaves, and tandoori powder.
5. Increase the heat to high, stir in the coconut milk, and mix well until the mixture resembles thick gravy.
6. Add the cashew nut paste, salt, and sugar. Stir well. Bring to a boil and then lower heat to low.
7. Add the frozen mixed vegetables and fried tofu <u>or</u> seitan strips and cook on very low heat for 15-20 minutes to blend flavors. Then enjoy!

 You can serve this dish with Indian breads like "naan", "paratha" or "roti" or steamed rice

Faux Turkey & Vegan Stuffing

This dish makes a delightful centerpiece to a Vegan Thanksgiving Meal!

Serves 6

Suggested Shopping List:
- Arrowhead® Organic Cornbread Stuffing
- Pepperidge Farms® Puff Pastry Sheets
- Tofurky® Deli Slices (any flavor)
- Earth Balance® Natural Buttery Spread (non-Soy version)
- Edward & Sons® Not Chick'n Natural Bouillon Cubes
- So Delicious® Coconut Milk (unsweetened)
- Bob's Red Mill® Organically Grown Unbromated Unbleached White Flour
- Simply Organic® Brown Gravy Mix

What You Will Need For The Stuffing:

1 of 10 Oz Package Organic Classic Herb Cornbread Stuffing
4 Stalks Organic Celery (about 1 cup) – diced
1 Medium Organic Onion (about 1 cup) – diced
2 Puff Pastry Sheets (1/3 of 1 sheet cut for faux turkey legs)
7 Vegan Turkey Deli slices
1/3 Cup Organic Vegan Buttery Spread
2 Cups Vegetable Broth made from 1 Vegetable Bouillon Cube

What You Will Need For the Vegan Gravy

2 TB Organic Vegan Buttery Spread
1/4 Cup Organic Onions – diced
1½ Cup Organic Coconut Milk
2 TB Unbleached Organic Flour
1/4 TSP Himalayan Pink Salt
1 Oz Package Vegetarian Brown Gravy Mix

> **GF** Unfortunately I have not listed this dish as gluten-free as it would take hours of your time in the kitchen making your own puff pastry

To Prepare:

Thaw puff pastry at room temperature for a couple of hours.

To make Vegan stuffing:

1. Sauté onions and celery in vegan buttery spread until browned or for about 10 minutes.
2. Mix vegetable bouillon cube in hot water to make vegetable broth, and set aside.
3. Add vegetable broth to celery and onion mixture bringing the mixture to a boil.
4. Turn off heat, and stir in the organic stuffing packet, mixing it in thoroughly.

To make Vegan Gravy:

1. Melt 2 tablespoons of vegan buttery spread in a pot on medium heat.
2. Sauté onions in vegan butter spread until browned (about 5 minutes). Lower heat.
3. Add 2 tablespoons flour to onion mixture. Mix thoroughly.
4. Pour in the coconut milk, and keep stirring the mixture until it is creamy and smooth.
5. Season with salt.
6. Add package of vegetarian brown gravy mix. Stir well. If the gravy is too thick you can add some more coconut milk to dilute.

Continued...

Faux Turkey & Vegan Stuffing (Cont'd)

To Make Faux Turkey   **(See Photos Below)**

1. Preheat oven to 350°F.
2. Cut 1/3 of one of the thawed puff pastry sheets and set it aside.
3. Roll out the sheets of the thawed puff pastry sheets on a lightly floured board until the sheets are about 14 inches x 12 inches.
4. Place one rolled out sheet on a lightly greased baking tray. Attach the other sheet to the edge of it by pressing it firmly in place.
5. Place most of the stuffing in the middle of the puff pastry sheet, setting aside a cup of filling to fill the faux legs.
6. Place vegan turkey deli slices over the stuffing, evenly distributing them all over the stuffing.
7. Cover the stuffing and the vegan turkey deli slices with this other sheet of pastry to seal in mixture.
8. Fold and crimp the edges with a fork to make sure all the edges are sealed tightly.
9. Take the reserved 1/3 of the sheet of dough which we had cut earlier, cut it into two equal pieces.
10. Stuff each piece with the reserved stuffing and 1/2 vegan turkey deli slice.
11. Seal the edges of the faux legs to close in the mixture.
12. Place these faux legs on the side of the faux turkey forming the faux legs.
13. Bake in the oven for 25 minutes or until browned (varying times for different ovens)

Serve faux stuffed turkey with organic cranberry sauce

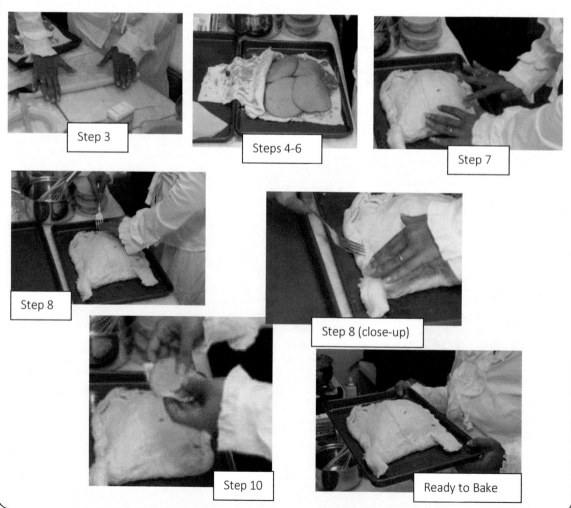

Step 3

Steps 4-6

Step 7

Step 8

Step 8 (close-up)

Step 10

Ready to Bake

Fettuccine Alfredo (Partially Raw Version)

Raw Alfredo sauce made with succulent sun-dried tomatoes and creamy avocado, tofu, and coconut milk on a bed of tender brown rice fettuccine noodles topped with capers and vegan parmesan

Serves 6

What You Will Need:

Pasta
2 of 14 Oz packages of Brown Rice Pasta – fettuccine style (for gluten-free)
Or any other "eggless" fettuccine noodles
1½ TSP Himalayan Pink Salt
3 TB Grapeseed Oil
12 Cups Filtered Water
Olive Oil for keeping the pasta from drying out

Raw Alfredo Sauce
1 Ripe Avocado
1/2 Cup Dried Organic Sun-Dried Tomatoes – soaked and drained (soak in 1 cup warm water for 20 minutes to soften them. Then drain the water and set aside)
Or if you use the sun-dried tomatoes in oil – use 6-7 pieces
2 TSP Organic Garlic – minced
1 of 14 Oz Package Organic Extra-Firm Tofu-drained
1½ Cup Organic Coconut Milk
1/2 Cup Filtered Water
1/2 TSP Himalayan Pink Salt (or adjust as per your taste since sun-dried tomatoes add their own salt)
2 TSP Raw Sugar
1 TSP Dried Basil or 6 Fresh Basil Leaves
2 Heaping TB Organic Vegan Buttery Spread

Garnish
1/2 Cup Capers
1 Cup Vegan Cheese Shreds
Hot sauce (optional)
Vegan Parmesan Cheese

Suggested Shopping List:
- Tinkyada® Brown Rice Fettuccine Style pasta
- Mediterranean Organic® Sun-dried Tomatoes in Oil
- Wildwood® Organic Sprouted Tofu
- So Delicious® Organic Coconut Milk (unsweetened)
- Earth Balance® Natural Buttery Spread (non-Soy version)
- Daiya® Vegan Cheese Shreds – Mozzarella
- Mediterranean Organic® Capers
- Tabasco® for hot sauce
- Galaxy Nutritional Foods® Vegan Grated Topping – Parmesan flavor

To Make Fettuccine Alfredo:

1. Break fettuccine noodles in half. Bring water to boil in a big pot, adding salt and oil to the water before boiling. When the water comes to a rolling boil, add the pasta. Set the timer from this point for the cooking time. See pasta package for cooking time (16-17 minutes for brown rice pasta) Stir often to prevent pasta from sticking. Once pasta is done, drain the pasta and transfer back to the big pot. Toss with olive oil. Set aside.
2. Place all the ingredients listed above under the heading "Raw Alfredo Sauce" in a food processor or blender and process until the consistency is smooth and creamy.
3. Toss the sauce in with the pasta in the pot. If you find the sauce too thick, you can add 1/4 cup of filtered water to dilute it. (To enjoy the pasta with a raw sauce, skip Steps 4-5).
4. Turn on the burner. Add the vegan mozzarella cheese shreds. Keep stirring until the cheese melts.
5. Turn off burner. Garnish with capers.
6. Sprinkle with vegan parmesan.
7. Optional: Add a few drops of hot sauce and enjoy!

Raw Fettuccine Alfredo

Raw Alfredo sauce made with succulent sun-dried tomatoes and creamy avocado, tofu, and coconut milk on a bed of crisp raw zucchini noodles topped with capers

Serves 6

What You Will Need:

Raw Zucchini Pasta
2 Organic Zucchinis (makes about 2 Cups)
1 TSP Himalayan Pink Salt
1-2 TB Extra Virgin Olive Oil

Raw Alfredo Sauce
1 Ripe Avocado
1/2 Cup Organic Sun-Dried tomatoes – soaked and drained
 (soak in 1 cup warm water for 20 minutes to soften them.
  Then drain the water and set aside)
Or if you use the sun-dried tomatoes in oil – use 6-7 pieces
2 TSP Organic Garlic – minced
1 of 14 Oz Package Organic Extra-Firm Tofu-drained
1½ Cup Organic Coconut Milk
1/2 Cup Filtered Water
1/2 TSP Himalayan Pink Salt (or adjust as per your taste since sun-dried tomatoes add a lot of flavor)
2 TSP Raw Sugar
1 TSP Dried Basil or 6 Fresh Basil Leaves
2 Heaping TB Organic Vegan Buttery Spread

Garnish
1/2 Cup Capers
Hot sauce (optional)

Suggested Shopping List:
- Tinkyada® Brown Rice Fettuccine Style Pasta
- Mediterranean Organic® Sun-dried Tomatoes in Oil
- Wildwood® Organic Sprouted Tofu
- So Delicious® Organic Coconut Milk (unsweetened)
- Earth Balance® Natural Buttery Spread (non-Soy version)
- Daiya® Vegan Cheese Shreds – Mozzarella
- Mediterranean Organic® Capers
- Tabasco® for hot sauce

To Make Fettuccine Alfredo:

1. Make long spaghetti strands out of the zucchini using a julienne peeler (see pg 115 for picture) or use a mandolin slicer (julienne blade).
2. Place zucchini strands in a large colander over a bowl, sprinkle with 1 TSP Himalayan pink salt and 1-2 TB olive oil, toss well. Let the zucchini noodles drain for 20-25 minutes, keep giving them a little squeeze every 5 minutes to drain excess liquid.
3. In the meantime, place all the ingredients shown above under the heading "Raw Alfredo Sauce" in a food processor or blender and process until the consistency is smooth and creamy.
4. In a large mixing bowl, toss the sauce in with the zucchini pasta. If you find the sauce too thick, you can add a little water to dilute it.
5. Garnish with capers.
6. Optional: Add a few drops of hot sauce and enjoy!

Garbanzo Bean Curry

A protein filled Indian dish also known as "Chana Masala" full of flavor and super easy to prepare

Serves 4

What You Will Need:

2 Medium Organic Tomatoes (about 2 cups) – quartered

1 Large Organic Onion (about 2 cups) – quartered

6 Sprigs Organic Cilantro (about 1/2 cup) – leaves and stems chopped up fine

1 TSP Organic Garlic – minced

1 TSP Organic Ginger – minced

1 of 15 Oz Can Organic Garbanzo Beans or Chick Peas – with 1/2 of the water drained

2 TSP Himalayan Pink Salt

1 TSP Raw Sugar

2 TB "Chole Masala" (or "Chana Masala") (see recipe below or store-bought)

Grapeseed Oil for cooking

> **Suggested Shopping List:**
> - Eden® Organic Garbanzo Can
> - Chole Masala also called Chana Masala can be found in Indian grocery stores.

To Make Garbanzo Bean Curry:

1. In a food processor or high pressure blender place tomatoes, onion, ginger, garlic, and cilantro, and process until completely puréed.
2. In a large pot, in three tablespoons of oil, pour the puréed mixture and sauté for 10 minutes on very low heat with the lid covered.
3. Season with "chole masala", salt and sugar, and mix well.
4. Open can and drain only half of the liquid the garbanzos are in.
5. Add garbanzos with half the liquid into the pot, stirring well to make sure the garbanzo beans are well coated with the spice mixture.
6. Cover the pot again, allowing the garbanzo beans to simmer on low heat for 20 minutes to blend flavors.
7. Serve over slices of bread or eat with Indian breads like "naan", "paratha" or "roti" or even rice.

If you're feeling adventurous, you can make your own chole masala by mixing:

1/8 TSP Cayenne Pepper

1/2 TSP Coriander Powder

1/4 TSP Ground Bay Leaves

1/4 TSP Ground Cumin

1/8 TSP Dry Mango Powder

1/4 TSP Ground Cinnamon

1/8 TSP Freshly Ground Black Pepper

1/8 TSP Ground Cloves

1/8 TSP Ground Cardamom

1/8 TSP Turmeric Powder

Toss all the spices in a bowl, mix well, and add to your dish.

>   Did you know that if use canned foods you should make sure that they come in a BPA-free (Bisphenol-A free) can because BPA is an endocrine disruptor and can contribute to many negative health effects? How can you tell if a can is BPA-free? Simple, if you aren't sure, in most cases, if the can is golden inside, it is BPA-free. If it is white or silver, it contains BPA (unless it says BPA-free on it) – because some cans are white and are still BPA free e.g. Eden® Food cans – but they do say "BPA-free" on the outside

Halloween Tamale Pie

Impress your friends on Halloween by creating this monster of a recipe or just make on any ordinary day minus the scary face, and you'll still enjoy its bold Tex-Mex flavors with sumptuous layers of vegan ground beef, refried beans, grits, and vegan cheese

Serves 6

What You Will Need:
1 Cup Organic Onions – diced
1 Cup Organic Green Bell Peppers – diced
1 TSP Organic Garlic – minced
1½ Cup Vegan Ground Beef (see page 161 for recipe or store-bought)
1 TSP Taco Seasoning
1 TSP Himalayan Pink Salt
Dash of Cayenne Pepper (optional)
1/2 TSP Dried Oregano
1 of 14.5 Oz Can Diced Tomatoes – undrained
1 of 15 Oz Can Refried Black Beans
1 Cup Organic Corn (frozen or canned)
2 Cups Vegan Cheese
Grapeseed Oil for cooking

What You Will Need for Cooking Grits:
1/4 Cup Organic Yellow Corn Grits
1 Cup Filtered Water
Dash of Himalayan Pink Salt

Suggested Shopping List:
-Trader Joe's® Beef-Less Ground Beef
-Bearitos® or Simply Organic® Southwest Taco Seasoning
- Eden® Organic Diced Tomatoes can
- Eden® Organic Refried Black Beans
- Daiya® Vegan Cheese Shreds – Pepper Jack
- Arrowhead Mills® Organic Gluten-free Yellow Corn Grits

What You Will Need for Creating the Monster's Face:
Note: These are mere suggestions; you can of course make your own creation

Option 1: Monster Man
Organic Carrots – shredded – for hair
Organic Green Bell Pepper – cut into short pieces – for eyebrows, mustache, and beard
Organic Dill Pickle slices – for eyes
Cherry/Grape Tomatoes – halved – for irises
Pretzels – for ears and nose

Option 2: Monster Woman
Organic Beet & Carrot Salad (see page 58) – for hair
Organic Tomato – sliced into rounds – for eyes
Sliced Green Olives – for irises and nostrils
Organic Tomato – shaped into lips
Organic Tomato – for hair barrettes
Small piece of Organic Romaine Lettuce – for nose
Short sprigs of Organic Rosemary – for eyelashes and earrings
Organic Shredded Carrots – to line her face

Continued…

Halloween Tamale Pie (Cont'd)

To Make Halloween Tamale Pie:

1. Preheat your oven to 350°F.
2. In a large skillet over medium heat in three tablespoons of oil, sauté the garlic, onions, and green bell peppers and cook until they are softened and onions are translucent.
3. Add the tomatoes and continue to sauté.
4. Season with taco seasoning, salt, cayenne pepper (optional), and oregano.
5. Add the vegan ground beef, corn, and refried black beans, stirring well to break up the refried beans and tossing well into the rest of the mixture.
6. Reduce heat to low, and allow the mixture to simmer for about 10 minutes to blend flavors.
7. In the meantime, prepare the grits. In a small saucepan, place yellow corn grits, 1 cup of filtered water, and a dash of salt. Bring to a rolling boil, stirring constantly.
8. Reduce heat and simmer for about 5 minutes until you get a thick consistency. Turn off the burner and set aside.
9. Return to large skillet, stir the mixture, and turn off the heat.
10. Transfer mixture to a lightly greased large glass ovenproof dish (13 x 9 inches – works well).
11. Top with shredded vegan cheese.
12. Spread the corn grits on top of the vegan cheese layer.
13. Place in pre-heated oven and bake at 350°F for 10 minutes.
14. Remove from oven and decorate with the assorted vegetables mentioned on previous page for creating the monster's face. Now you're ready to scare, I mean serve your guests!

Did you know the first Jack O' Lantern was actually made from a turnip and that "Halloween" is short for "Hallows' Eve", which was the evening before All Hallows Day (All Saints Day) on November 1st? Black and orange are typically associated with Halloween because orange symbolizes life, harvest, and autumn. Black is a symbol of death; thus Halloween marks the boundaries between life and death

Health: Corn is one of those foods which when combined with legumes helps our bodies to easily absorb minerals like zinc, calcium, and iron, and improves overall energy and protein absorption. So when you eat a meal with corn and beans it helps your body to boost the nutrients in the foods. Now we understand why most Mexican dishes have corn and beans in them!

Beauty: Corn is great for your skin, hair, and eyes due to its rich content of Vitamin C, antioxidants, and lycopene

Caution: Only eat corn if it is organic because all the corn sold in the USA is genetically modified (which comes with its own set of health issues – see page 18) unless it says "Organic Corn – non-GMO verified"

3-Lentil Stew

This is one of those dishes you can make when you don't have a lot of time. Put everything in your slow cooker, set to cook in the morning and come back to a yummy ready-to-eat stew that is filled with so many aromatic ingredients that your kitchen will smell delicious!

Serves 4

What You Will Need:

1 of 15 Oz Can Organic Crushed Tomatoes
3 Cups Filtered Water
1 TSP Organic Garlic – minced
1 TSP Organic Ginger – minced
1 Cup Organic Onions – diced
1 Vegetable Bouillon Cube
1 Cup Non-Alcoholic Red Wine
1 TSP Dried Basil
1 TSP Dried Thyme
1 TSP Coriander Powder
1 TSP Ground Cumin
2¼ Cups Dried Organic Lentils – 3/4 cup each of 3 of your favorites
    I use Green Mung, Masoor Dal (Split Red Lentils), and Brown Lentils
1 Cup Organic Carrots – shredded
1 Stalk Organic Celery – finely sliced
1 Cup Organic Potatoes – cubed
1 Cup Organic Spinach (frozen or fresh)
2 Vegan Sausages (optional) – thinly sliced

 Omit Vegan Sausages

2 TSP Himalayan Pink Salt
1 TSP Raw Sugar
Grapeseed Oil for cooking

Suggested Shopping List:
- Eden® Organic Crushed Tomatoes
- Edward & Sons® Not Chick'n Natural Bouillon Cubes
- Fre® Non-Alcoholic Red Wine
- Coriander and cumin can both be found in Indian grocery stores
- Tofurky® Kielbasa for Vegan Sausages

To Make Stew:

1. Soak lentils for about 15 minutes, then wash and drain. Set aside.
2. Grease a crockpot (slow cooker) with two tablespoons of oil. Plug in your crockpot and set to a low setting.
3. Add the garlic, ginger, and onions and mix well with the oil.
4. Season with basil, thyme, coriander, and cumin
5. Add the can of crushed tomatoes.
6. Heat three cups of filtered water in a small saucepan, and place 1 bouillon cube in water until it is completely dissolved to make vegetable broth.
7. Pour vegetable broth in crockpot. Mix well.
8. Add the non-alcoholic red wine.
9. Season with salt and sugar. Stir well.
10. Add the 3 types of lentils (washed), carrots, celery, potatoes, spinach, and vegan sausages (optional – please omit if you are making a gluten-free dish).
11. Stir all ingredients thoroughly.
12. Leave to cook in your crockpot on low for 6-7 hours or more. It doesn't affect the dish if you leave it cooking for longer.
13. You know the dish is done when the lentils are soft and the potatoes are tender.
 You can eat the stew as is, or serve over steamed brown or white rice

Ma Po Tofu

Minced tofu stewed with a blend of tomatoes, green peppers, and TVP (textured vegetable protein) in a succulent mildly spicy cilantro and scallion sauce
Serves 4-6

What You Will Need:

1 of 14 Oz Package Organic Silken or Medium Tofu – cut into cubes
1/2 Cup Organic Cilantro – leaves and stems chopped up fine
2-3 stalks Organic Scallions – chopped into pieces
1 Cup Organic Green Bell Peppers (1 medium sized pepper) – finely diced
1 Cup Organic Tomatoes (2 medium tomatoes) – finely diced
1 Cup Dry TVP – Textured Vegetable Protein
1 TSP Organic Garlic – minced
1 TSP Organic Ginger – minced
2 TB Chili Garlic Sauce (see page 154 for recipe or store-bought)
1 TSP Raw Sugar
1 TB Organic Shoyu Sauce

 Use Organic Tamari Sauce

2 TB Liquid Amino Acids
4 TB Organic Ketchup
1 Cube Vegetable Bouillon
2 Cups Filtered Water
Drizzle of Sesame Oil for garnish
Grapeseed Oil for cooking

Suggested Shopping List:
- Wildwood® Organic Sprouted Tofu
- Textured Vegetable Protein (TVP)
Suggested brands:
- Bob's Red Mill® TVP Granules
- VegeUSA® Vege Soy Chunks
- Lee Kum Kee® or Sriracha® for Chili Garlic Sauce
- San-J® Organic Shoyu (or Organic Tamari for gluten-free)
- Bragg® Liquid Amino Acids
- Tree of Life® Organic Ketchup
- Edward & Sons® Not Chick'n Natural Bouillon Cubes
- Wei-Chuan® 100% Black Sesame Oil

To Make Ma Po Tofu:

1. In a large skillet, in three tablespoons of oil on medium heat, sauté the ginger and garlic.
2. Add the chili garlic sauce and continue to stir.
3. Add the cilantro and scallions. Sauté on low heat to blend flavors.
4. Toss in the tomatoes and green bell peppers. Cover the pot and cook on low heat for 10 minutes or until tomatoes and green peppers are softened.
5. Add filtered water followed by the bouillon cube.
6. Increase heat to high to allow the bouillon cube to dissolve.
7. Add the ketchup, shoyu sauce (or tamari sauce for gluten-free), liquid amino acids, and sugar.
8. Add the diced tofu and the dry TVP (textured vegetable protein).
9. Lower the heat, and let the tofu and TVP simmer in the sauce for 5-10 minutes.
10. Turn off burner. Drizzle with sesame oil and enjoy over steamed white/brown rice.

 Health: Chili Peppers contain capsaicin which prevents sinusitis and relieves congestion hence when you have a cold, eat a spicy dish. They also contain Vitamin C which boosts immunity

Beauty: Chili Peppers help you burn fat and lose weight – come to think of it I haven't really seen any overweight Thai women! I wonder if eating chilies is their secret to staying slim...

Macaroni and Cheese

A creamy melted vegan cheese sauce made with caramelized onions and coconut milk, tossed with elbow macaroni. You actually might ditch the boxed macaroni cheese when you learn how quick, easy, and healthy it is to prepare this vegan version!

Serves 4-6

What You Will Need:

3 TB Organic Vegan Buttery Spread
1 Cup Organic Onions – diced
1 TSP Organic Garlic – minced
2½ Cups Coconut Milk
3 TB Organic Millet Flour
1 Cube Vegetable Bouillon
2 Cups Vegan Cheese Shreds
2 Cups Frozen Spinach (optional)
1 of 16 Oz package Brown Rice Elbow Pasta
12 cups Filtered Water for boiling pasta
1 TSP Himalayan Pink Salt for boiling pasta
1 TB Grapeseed Oil for boiling pasta
2-3 Vegan Sausages (optional) – sliced into thin rounds

Suggested Shopping List:
- Earth Balance® Natural Buttery Spread (non-Soy version)
- So Delicious® Organic Coconut Milk (unsweetened)
- Edward & Sons® Not Chick'n Natural Bouillon Cubes
- Daiya® Vegan Cheese Shreds – Cheddar
- Tinkyada® Brown Rice Elbow Pasta
- Tofurky® Italian Sausages (optional)

To Make Mac and Cheese:

1. Bring water to boil in a big pot, adding salt and oil before boiling. When the water comes to a rolling boil, add your pasta. Set the timer for cooking time. See pasta package for cooking time (15-16 minutes for brown rice pasta). Once pasta is done, drain and set aside.
2. You can pan-sear the vegan sausage rounds and set these aside. This gives them a crunchy texture. (Note: You can omit this step if you want, since vegan sausages are already pre-cooked. Or just eliminate the vegan sausages if you prefer a gluten-free dish.)
3. In a large pot, melt the vegan buttery spread.
4. Once the vegan buttery spread melts, add garlic and onions.
5. Lower heat, sauté onions and garlic until onions are translucent and limp.
6. Add 3 tablespoons of flour to the onion mixture. Mix thoroughly until it forms a lump.
7. Stir in the coconut milk, increase the heat to high, and keep stirring the mixture until there are no more lumps and the mixture thickens.
8. Lower heat, add the vegetable bouillon cube. Keep stirring until the cube dissolves.
9. Add the frozen spinach (optional) and the vegan sausages (optional).
10. Sprinkle in the vegan cheese and mix well until all the cheese is melted.
11. Toss the pasta into the sauce and mix thoroughly until it is completely coated with the sauce.

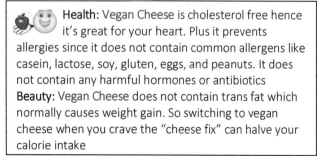 **Health:** Vegan Cheese is cholesterol free hence it's great for your heart. Plus it prevents allergies since it does not contain common allergens like casein, lactose, soy, gluten, eggs, and peanuts. It does not contain any harmful hormones or antibiotics
Beauty: Vegan Cheese does not contain trans fat which normally causes weight gain. So switching to vegan cheese when you crave the "cheese fix" can halve your calorie intake

 Did you know that the earliest Macaroni & Cheese was called "Makerouns" and was featured in a the famous medieval English cookbook The Forme of Cury in the 14th century?

Massaman Curry

Nothing can beat the warming flavors of curry on a cold day – learn to prepare this rich "Massaman" Malaysian curry sauce simmered in coconut milk and spices cooked with a medley of mixed veggies and tofu which can be eaten in two different ways

Serves 4

What You Will Need:

1 of 14 Oz package Organic Super Firm Tofu
1 Cup Organic Onions – diced
2 Cups Organic Cabbage – shredded
1 TSP Organic Garlic – minced
1 TSP Organic Ginger – minced
Cilantro – 2 to 3 sprigs – leaves and stems chopped up fine
1 of 4 Oz Can of Massaman Curry Paste
1/2 Cup Filtered Water
1 of 13.5 fl Oz Can Organic Coconut milk
1 Cube Vegetable Bouillon
1 TSP Himalayan Pink Salt
2 TSP Raw Sugar
Grapeseed Oil for cooking

Suggested Shopping List:
- Maesri® for Massaman Curry Paste
- Wildwood® Organic Sprouted Tofu
- Native Forest® Organic Coconut Milk
- Edward & Sons® Not Chick'n Natural Bouillon Cubes

In addition for Massaman Mash:
- Edward & Sons® Organic Mashed Potatoes
- So Delicious® Organic Coconut Milk (unsweetened)
- Earth Balance® Natural Buttery Spread (non-Soy version)

To Make Curry:

1. Drain the tofu, pat dry between paper towels, cut into cubes.
2. In a flat non-stick skillet, in 1-2 tablespoons of oil, shallow fry the tofu cubes until they are browned and crisp on both sides turning over often. Set aside.
3. In a large skillet, in 3 tablespoons of oil on medium heat, sauté the garlic, ginger, cilantro, onions, and cabbage for about 5-7 minutes or until the onions and cabbage are softened.
4. Add the Massaman curry paste and 1/2 cup filtered water to dilute the paste.
5. Season with salt and sugar. Mix thoroughly.
6. Pour in the coconut milk and refill empty can twice with distilled water, hence adding 2 cans of water.
7. Turn up the heat to high, and dissolve the cube of vegetable bouillon in the curry.
8. Toss in the fried tofu.
9. Mix well and bring the curry to a boil, then turn off heat.
10. Serve over steamed jasmine rice.

 Variation: you can enjoy this dish on with mashed potatoes instead of rice, see preparation below

What you will need for Massaman Mash:
4 Cups Organic Dried Potato Flakes
1½ Cup Organic Coconut Milk
3 Cups Filtered Water
4 TB Organic Vegan Buttery Spread
1 TSP Himalayan Pink Salt

To Make Massaman Curry for Mashed Potatoes:
Follow steps 3-9 above (omitting step 8) since we eliminate tofu for Massaman Mash.

To Make Mashed Potatoes

1. In a large pot, on high heat, place organic vegan buttery spread and water, and bring to boil.
2. Turn off the heat.
3. Remove pot from heat, and stir in the organic mashed potato flakes.
4. Add the coconut milk and stir the flakes in mixing vigorously to thoroughly mix in with the coconut milk.
5. Once the flakes are all mixed in well, make a small mound of mashed potatoes on a plate, make a little dip on top, pour curry into it, and enjoy! (see picture above)

Nasi Goreng–Indonesian Fried Rice

Come "eat, pray, and love" this dish as you get transported to exotic Bali! With this dish you can show off your culinary skills without spending lots of time in the kitchen! Pan-fried rice with chunks of tofu, carrots, tomatoes, and cucumbers, flavored with a thick aromatic sauce blended with garlic, scallions and zesty Indonesian spices

Serves 4

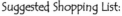

Suggested Shopping List:
- Wildwood® Organic Sprouted Tofu
- Bamboe® Indonesian Instant Spices "Nasi Goreng" found on amazon.com

What You Will Need:
1 of 14 Oz Package Organic Extra Firm or Super Firm Tofu
 – drained, dried, and cut into cubes
1 Cup Organic Carrots – shredded
1 Cup Organic Tomatoes – diced
1 Cup Organic Cucumbers – diced
1 TSP Organic Garlic – minced
4 Stalks Organic Scallions – thinly sliced
1 of 1.4 Oz Package Nasi Goreng Paste
1/4 Cup Filtered Water
Grapeseed Oil for cooking

For Rice:
4 Cups Cooked Left-Over Jasmine Rice
(Note: hot rice doesn't do well for making fried rice so if you make fresh rice, make sure it is cooled in the fridge before using in the recipe – otherwise you will end up with a mushy dish).
1½ TSP Himalayan Pink Salt
2 TB Grapeseed Oil

To Make Nasi Goreng:
1. In a rice cooker, cook 4 cups of rice with 4 cups water. Add 1½ teaspoons salt and 2 tablespoons oil. Once rice is cooked and completely cooled, put in the refrigerator to chill. Then use in the recipe on the same day after about 1 hour or the next day.
2. Drain the tofu, pat dry between paper towels, and cut into cubes.
3. In a flat non-stick skillet, in 1 tablespoon of oil, pan-fry the tofu cubes until they are browned on both sides, making sure to continuously flip them to prevent charring the tofu. Set aside.
4. In another large skillet, in 3 tablespoons of oil, sauté the garlic and scallions on low heat until you can smell the aroma of the garlic (about 2-3 minutes).
5. Add the Nasi Goreng spice packet. Stir in 1/4 Cup of filtered water, and mix well until scallions are well coated with spice mixture.
6. Increase the heat to medium, then add the tomatoes, cucumbers and, carrots and stir fry for 1-2 minutes.
7. Reduce heat to low, add the fried tofu cubes, and cover skillet and let the vegetables steam-cook for about 10 minutes.
8. Once the vegetables are cooked, lift the lid, and toss the cooked cooled rice in with the vegetable mixture until all the rice is completely coated.
9. Turn off burner and Enjoy!

Did you know that the scallion is known by many names: green onion (US and Canada), spring onion (UK, China, India, and New Zealand), salad onion (US), table onion (US), green shallot (Australia), onion stick (US), long onion (US), baby onion (US), chive (Caribbean), yard onion (US), gibbon (Wales), or syboe (France)?

 **Health:** Rice has high iron content and provides 8 percent of the daily suggested intake of iron in a 3/4 cup serving. It's great for boosting energy
Beauty: Rice is great for weight loss. Since it is low in fat and high in energy, it helps with workouts

Pad Thai

Flat rice noodles stir fried with seasoned tempeh, mung bean sprouts, and scallions in a tasty tamarind sauce, simmered with tempting Thai spices and garnished with crushed peanuts

Serves 4

What You Will Need:

1 of 14 Oz Package Brown Rice Pasta – "Fettuccine style"
1 Packet Organic Tempeh – sliced into short thin strips
10 Cups Filtered Water – for boiling noodles
1½ TSP Himalayan Pink Salt – for boiling noodles
Grapeseed Oil for cooking
1½ Cups Organic Onions – julienned
4 Stalks Organic Scallions – thinly sliced
1 Cup Organic Mung Bean Sprouts

What You Will Need For Seasoning the Tempeh:

2-3 Sprigs Organic Cilantro – leaves and stems chopped up fine
1 TSP Organic Garlic – minced
1 TSP Organic Ginger – minced
2 TB Organic Shoyu

 Use Organic Tamari Sauce

2 TSP Raw Sugar

What You Will Need For The Sauce:

1 TB Organic Shoyu Sauce

 Use Organic Tamari Sauce

1 TB Organic Fresh Lime Juice (juice of one lime)
8 TSP Raw Sugar
2 TB Organic Peanut Butter
1 TB Organic Tahini
1TSP Tamarind Paste
4 TSP Penang Curry Paste
1/2 Cup Filtered Water

What You Will Need For The Garnish:

1-2 Sprigs Organic Cilantro – leaves and stems chopped up
1/2 Cup Chopped Roasted Organic Blanched Peanuts
2 TSP Raw Sugar
2-3 Fresh lime wedges

Suggested Shopping List:
- Tinkyada® Brown Rice Fettuccine Style Pasta
- Lightlife® Organic Tempeh – flavor of your choice (For Gluten-free only use Soy, Wild Rice or Garden Veggie Tempeh flavor).
- San-J® Organic Shoyu (or Organic Tamari for gluten-free)
- Tamcon® Tamarind Paste available in Indian grocery stores
- Maesri® Penang Curry Paste

 Did you know that Pad Thai was made popular in the late 1930s in Thailand by its Prime Minister in the hope to increase export of domestic rice? Thai people were encouraged to sell rice noodles from street carts and in small restaurants. Pad Thai has since become one of Thailand's national dishes. According to a CNN poll in 2011, Pad Thai is listed at number 5 on the World's 50 most delicious foods

Continued...

Pad Thai (continued...)

To Prepare Seasoned Tempeh:

1. Bring 4 cups of water to boil in a pot. When the water starts to boil, place the tempeh slices in and boil for 10 minutes.
2. Remove Tempeh with a slotted spoon, pat dry with paper towels, and set aside.
3. Lightly grease a flat ceramic skillet and shallow fry tempeh strips until browned on both sides. Set aside.
4. In a small saucepan, in 1 tablespoon of oil, sauté garlic, ginger, and cilantro for 1 minute on low heat.
5. Add the Shoyu sauce (or Tamari) and sugar and mix well.
6. Add the fried tempeh strips and toss them in the sauce mixture until tempeh strips are well coated. Set seasoned tempeh aside.

To Prepare Peanuts for Garnish:

1. Grease a baking tray and place raw blanched peanuts (skins removed) on it.
2. Spray the surface of the peanuts with oil.
3. Roast in an oven at 350°F for10 minutes. (Note: do not pre-heat oven). Turn off oven and leave peanuts to crisp in the hot oven for 10 minutes ONLY.
4. Remove peanuts from oven. Allow them to cool. (Note you can omit steps 1-3 if you buy store-bought roasted peanuts).
5. When they are cooled, place roasted peanuts and 2 TSP sugar in a food chopper. Chop until roughly chopped. Set aside.

To Make Pad Thai:

1. Break fettuccine noodles in half. Bring 10 cups of water to boil in a big pot, adding salt and 2-3 TB of oil to the water before boiling. When the water comes to a rolling boil, add your pasta. Set your timer from this point for the cooking time. See pasta package for cooking time (16-17 minutes for brown rice pasta). Stir often to prevent noodles from sticking. Once pasta is done, drain the pasta and transfer back to the big pot. Toss with olive oil. Set aside.
2. In a small mixing bowl, make the sauce by mixing Shoyu (or Tamari for gluten-free), fresh lime juice, peanut butter, tahini, sugar, tamarind, Penang curry paste, and 1/2 cup of filtered water. Whisk thoroughly. Set aside.
3. In the same skillet in which you fried the tempeh, add 3 tablespoons of oil and sauté onions and scallions on medium heat for about 2 minutes.
4. Season with the sauce mixture, and cook for 2 minutes, stirring frequently.
5. Mix in the seasoned tempeh pieces and cook for another 2 minutes.
6. Turn off heat. Toss the noodles in with the sauce. Stir in bean sprouts and garnish with cilantro.
7. Sprinkle the roasted peanut and sugar mixture over the top of the Pad Thai dish and place fresh lime wedges on the side of the dish just before you serve it.

> **Health:** Tamarind with its sticky pulp is a rich source of non-starch polysaccharides (NSP) which is a dietary fiber which helps with better bowel movements. This fiber also binds to toxins and protects the colon from cancer-causing chemicals. Plus they also bind to bile salts (produced from cholesterol) and decrease their re-absorption in the colon; thereby help excretion of "bad" or LDL cholesterol from the body
> **Beauty:** Tamarind, when used topically, is great for your skin. It can reduce the appearance of scars or blemishes since it contains alpha-hydroxyl acids – a common ingredient in many skin beauty creams

Palak Tofu Paneer

Golden cubes of lightly fried tofu simmered in a creamy spinach and coconut cashew cream gravy flavored with aromatic cilantro, ginger, and garlic

Serves 4

Suggested Shopping List:
- Wildwood® Organic Sprouted Tofu
- Native Forest® Coconut Milk Can
- Garam Masala can be bought at Indian grocery stores

What You Will Need:

16 Cups of Organic Spinach – 3 pounds (fresh or frozen)
2 Organic Tomatoes – quartered
1 TSP Organic Garlic – minced
1 TSP Organic Ginger – minced
1 Cup Organic Cilantro – leaves and stems chopped fine
2 TSP Himalayan Pink Salt
1 TSP Raw Sugar
1 Cup Raw Organic Cashews
5 Cups Organic Super Firm Tofu (20 Oz package) – cut into cubes
1/2 TSP Himalayan Pink Salt – for sprinkling over tofu
1 of 13.5 fl Oz Organic Coconut Milk
Dash of Cayenne Pepper (optional)
1 TSP Garam Masala (see page 156 for recipe or store-bought)
Grapeseed Oil for cooking

To Make Palak Tofu Paneer:

1. Steam spinach for 10 minutes. Allow it to cool and set aside.
2. Drain the tofu, pat dry between paper towels, and cut into cubes.
3. Place tofu cubes in a bowl and sprinkle with 1/2 TSP of salt. Toss well to coat all the tofu cubes with salt.
4. In a flat non-stick skillet, in 2 tablespoons of oil, pan-fry the tofu cubes until they are browned on both sides, making sure to continuously flip them to prevent charring the tofu. Set aside.
5. Once the steamed spinach has cooled down sufficiently, place it in a food processor or high speed blender.
6. Place the tomatoes, cilantro, garlic, ginger, 1 TSP salt, sugar, and cashew nuts in the food processor or blender.
7. Process all the ingredients until you reach a smooth, creamy consistency.
8. Heat three tablespoons of oil in a large skillet.
9. Pour the processed mixture into the skillet. Reduce heat to low allowing the mixture to simmer.
10. Season with garam masala and 1 TSP salt.
11. Add the can of coconut milk.
12. Season with cayenne pepper if you like. You can omit this if you don't like spicy food.
13. Toss the fried tofu cubes into the spinach mixture making sure to coat them completely. Turn off your burner.

 You can serve palak tofu paneer with steamed rice or Indian breads like "naan", "paratha", or "roti"

 Did you know that Palak Paneer is a popular Indian dish usually made with spinach and cheese? The word "palak" means "spinach," and "paneer" is a type of Indian cottage cheese. The dish originated in the Punjab region. It is also known as saag paneer and saagwala. The word "saag" means "green". Aren't you glad we found a way to make this beauty vegan?

Pesto Pasta

Who can resist the fragrance of fresh basil leaves, pine nuts, and garlic? Here is my own super easy and quick-to-make version of this popular dish, made vegan with some additional ingredients like green peas to make the pesto even more delectable, plus also a delectable raw version (see next page)

Serves 4

What You Will Need:

2 Cups Fresh Organic Sweet Basil Leaves
3 TB Pine Nuts
1/2 Cup Vegan Parmesan Cheese
1 of 15 Oz Can Very Young Small Sweet Peas – drained
1/2 Cup Extra Virgin Olive Oil
3 TSP Organic Garlic – minced
1 TSP Himalayan Pink Salt
9 Organic Grape or Cherry Tomatoes – sliced into small rounds
1 of 16 Oz package Brown Rice Pasta (any kind)
12 Cups Filtered Water for boiling pasta
1 TSP Himalayan Pink Salt for boiling pasta
1 TB Grapeseed Oil for boiling pasta

> **Suggested Shopping List:**
> – Galaxy Nutritional Foods® Vegan Grated Topping – Parmesan flavor
> – LeSueur® English Peas Can
> – Tinkyada® Brown Rice Pasta

> Did you know that pine nuts are actually not nuts but edible seeds of certain pine cones?

To Make Pasta:

1. Bring 12 cups of water to boil in a big pot, adding salt and oil before boiling. When the water comes to a rolling boil, add your pasta. Set the timer for cooking time found on the pasta package (15-16 minutes for brown rice pasta). Once pasta is done, drain and transfer back into the big pot. Set aside.
2. In the meantime, you can make your pesto sauce. In a food processor or high powered blender, place basil leaves, pine nuts, vegan parmesan cheese, sweet peas, garlic, olive oil, and salt.
3. Process all the ingredients until you reach a smooth, creamy consistency.
4. Pour the sauce all over the boiled pasta in the big pot and toss well, making sure to coat the pasta thoroughly with the sauce.
5. Stir in the cut organic cherry or grape tomatoes and enjoy!

 You can stir in some capers to add extra flavor to your dish

> **Health:** Pine Nuts are a great food for when you are PMS'ing since they are high in iron which gets depleted when you menstruate. Plus they boost energy by providing protein and magnesium which help release tension and alleviate muscle cramps. They are also good for your heart since they lower cholesterol and are great for your eyes since they contain lutein and vitamin A
>
> **Beauty:** Pine Nuts slow down aging because of the presence of antioxidants which remove free radicals from the body. Plus they help boost your weight loss efforts since they contain pinoleic acid, which is an appetite suppressant. Pinoleic acid triggers the release of 2 hunger suppressant hormones: cholecystokinin (CCK) and glucagon-like peptide-1 (GLP-1)

Raw Pesto Pasta

Here's the raw version of this tasty dish!
Serves 4

Suggested Shopping List:
- Bragg® Organic Extra Virgin Oil

What You Will Need for the Sauce:
1 Cup Organic Cashew Nuts – soaked in filtered water for 2 hours
1/2 Cup Organic Pine Nuts
1/2 Cup Organic Fresh Parsley
 Or 1 TB Dried Parsley
1 Cup Fresh Organic Sweet Basil Leaves
1/4 Cup Organic Extra Virgin Olive Oil
1 TSP Italian Seasoning
2 Cloves Organic Garlic
 Or 2 TSP Organic Garlic – minced
1/2 TSP Himalayan Pink Salt
9 Organic Grape or Cherry tomatoes
- sliced into small rounds

What You Will Need for the Raw Pasta:
2 Organic Zucchinis (makes about 2 Cups)
1 TSP Himalayan Pink Salt
1-2 TB Extra Virgin Olive Oil

To Make Raw Pesto Pasta:

1. Make long spaghetti strands out of the zucchini using a julienne peeler (see pg 115 for picture) or use a mandolin slicer (julienne blade).
2. Place zucchini strands in a large colander over a bowl, sprinkle with 1 TSP Himalayan pink salt and 1-2 TB olive oil, toss well. Let the zucchini noodles drain for 20-25 minutes, keep giving them a little squeeze every 5 minutes to drain excess liquid.
3. In the meantime, prepare your raw pesto sauce.
4. Place soaked cashew nuts, pine nuts, parsley, basil leaves, olive oil, Italian seasoning, garlic, and salt in a food processor or high speed blender.
5. Process all the ingredients until you reach a smooth creamy consistency.
6. Once the zucchini strands are fairly dry, transfer to a large mixing bowl.
7. Pour the raw pesto sauce all over the zucchini noodles, and toss well, making sure to coat the zucchini pasta thoroughly with the sauce.
8. Stir in the cut organic cherry or grape tomatoes.

This is a great dish for when you don't have a lot of time to cook but want to eat something quick that is fragrant, healthy and delicious – both versions cooked and raw will serve this purpose!

Pineapple Fried Rice

Intoxicatingly fragrant jasmine rice stir fried with chunks of pineapple, tofu, cashew nuts, raisins, and a medley of mixed vegetables bursting with a rich curry flavor

Serves 6-8

What You Will Need:

2 Cups Organic Super Firm Tofu – cut into small cubes

1 Cup Organic Frozen Mixed Vegetables
  – beans, peas, carrots, and corn

1 TSP Organic Garlic – minced

1 TSP Organic Ginger – minced

4 Stalks Organic Scallions – thinly sliced

1 TB Madras Curry Powder

1 TB Organic Shoyu Sauce

 Use Organic Tamari Sauce

1 TB Liquid Amino Acids

1 TB Mirin <u>Or</u> Rice Vinegar

4 Cup Cooked Left-Over rice (I like Jasmine rice)
  (hot rice doesn't make good fried rice so if you want
  to use fresh rice, make sure it is refrigerated
  and cooled before using in this recipe)

1 of 14 Oz Can Organic Pineapple Chunks – drained

1 Cup Raw Organic Cashew Nuts

1/2 Cup Organic Raisins

Grapeseed Oil for cooking

What You Will Need for Tofu Marinade:

1 TB Organic Shoyu

 Use Organic Tamari Sauce

1 TSP Raw Sugar

1 TB Mirin or Rice Vinegar

Suggested Shopping List:
- Wildwood® Organic Sprouted Tofu
- Kim Thu Thap® Mild Madras Curry Powder
- San-J® Organic Shoyu or Organic Tamari Sauce (for gluten-free)
- Bragg® Liquid Amino Acids
- Eden® Foods® Mirin
- Native Forest® Organic Pineapple Chunks

 Did you know that pineapple fried rice originated in Thailand, and is called Khao Phat. In Thai, khao means "rice" and phat means "relating to being stir-fried". So next time you go to Thailand order in Thai, but remember to say "Ahaan Jai" – which means vegan!

To Make Pineapple Fried Rice:

1. Cook the jasmine rice and set aside (I generally cook mine in a rice cooker). Wash and rinse the rice well, place in the rice cooker, stir in 2 TB of oil and 1½ TSP of salt, and then press cook. You can cook it on the stove if you like. For white rice, the ratio is 1:1 so 4 cups of white rice to 4 cups of water. Once rice is cooked and cooled, refrigerate to use either the next day or later that day.

2. In a flat ceramic skillet, in 1-2 tablespoons of oil, shallow fry the tofu cubes until they are browned and crisp on both sides, turning over often.

3. Place fried tofu cubes in a small mixing bowl.

4. Toss cubes in tofu marinade ingredients, shoyu (or tamari), sugar, and Mirin. Set aside, leaving the tofu cubes in the marinade while you do the other steps.

5. In a large skillet, in 3 tablespoons of oil, sauté the ginger, garlic and scallions on low heat until you can smell the aroma of the garlic, and scallions. About 2-3 minutes.

6. Sprinkle in curry powder and mix well.

6. Increase the heat to medium, and add the pineapple chunks and cashew nuts and stir fry for 2 minutes.

7. Lower heat, add the organic mixed vegetables and raisins, and cover skillet allowing the vegetables to cook for about 10 minutes or until vegetables are softened.

8. Once the vegetables are cooked, lift the lid and add the marinated tofu cubes.

9. Season the dish with 1 TB Shoyu (or Tamari) sauce, 1 TB liquid amino acids and 1 TB Mirin. Mix thoroughly.

10. Toss the cooked left-over rice in with the vegetable mixture until all the rice is coated well.

 To make this dish even more fun, serve in half a hollow pineapple shell (see picture above)

Pommes De Terre Au Gratin

Scalloped potatoes covered in a rich white mornay sauce topped with melted vegan cheese and baked to excellence

Serves 6

What You Will Need:

8-10 Organic Yukon Gold Potatoes (about 3 cups)
3 TB Organic Vegan Buttery Spread
1 TSP Organic Garlic – minced
1-1½ cups Organic Onions – diced
3 TB Unbleached Organic Flour

 Use gluten-free flour or Arrowroot

1 of 8 Oz Container Vegan Cream Cheese
2 Cups Organic Coconut milk
1 Cube Vegetable Bouillon
1 TSP Himalayan Pink Salt
1 TSP Raw Sugar
1 TSP Italian Seasoning
2 Cups Vegan Cheese Shreds

Suggested Shopping List:
- Earth Balance® Natural Buttery Spread (non-Soy version)
- Bob's Red Mill® Organically Grown Unbromated Unbleached White Flour
- Follow Your Heart® Vegan Cream Cheese
- So Delicious® Organic Coconut Milk (unsweetened)
- Edward & Sons® Not Chick'n Natural Bouillon Cubes
- Daiya® Vegan Cheese Shreds – Mozzarella

To Make Pommes De Terre Au Gratin:

1. In a large pot, boil the potatoes for 30 minutes. Peel, slice into scallops, and set aside.
2. In a large skillet, on medium heat, melt 3 tablespoons of vegan buttery spread, and sauté onions and garlic until onions are limp and translucent (about 4-5 minutes). Lower heat.
3. Sprinkle 3 tablespoons of flour to the onion mixture. Mix thoroughly until it forms a lump.
4. Raise the heat to high, then add the coconut milk, and keep stirring the mixture until the flour mixture is all mixed in and there are no more lumps.
5. Add the vegetable bouillon cube, Italian seasoning, salt, and sugar. Keep stirring until the cube dissolves.
6. When the sauce thickens, lower heat.
7. Mix in the vegan cream cheese. You can use a wire whisk to break up the vegan cream cheese.
8. Let the sauce simmer on very low heat for about 5 minutes to bring out the flavors of the herbs and seasonings. Then turn off burner.
9. Lightly grease a glass baking dish (13 x 9 inch works well).
10. Layer the scalloped potatoes in a single layer.
11. Ladle the sauce over the potatoes, completely covering the potatoes.
12. Sprinkle some vegan cheese over the potatoes.
13. Repeat steps 10-12 until all the potato scallops are used up.
14. Bake in an oven at 400˚F for 20 minutes or until you see the dish start to bubble.
15. Remove from the oven and serve.

Did you know that potatoes are a "happy food" because they create an insulin response which has an effect on the movement of the amino acid tryptophan from your blood into your brain? Your body uses tryptophan to make serotonin. Serotonin is the brain chemical that makes you feel mellow and happy. That is why almost everyone young and old loves to eat potatoes!

Potato Hearty Casserole

Chunks of mashed potatoes and garden green peas smothered in a vegan creamy mixture – oh so delicious...oh so Irish!

Serves 4-6

What You Will Need:

4 Cups Homemade Organic Mashed Potatoes (about 8 potatoes)
<u>Or</u> 2 packets of store-bought Organic Mashed Potatoes
1 of 8 Oz Container Vegan Cream Cheese
1/2 Cup Organic Vegan Sour Cream
1/2 Cup Vegan Cheese Shreds
1/2 Cup Vegan Mayonnaise (see page 162 for recipe or store-bought)
1 Cup Organic Sweet Onions – finely chopped
1 of 15 Oz Can Organic Green Peas, drained
1 TSP Himalayan Pink Salt
1/4 TSP Pepper
1/4 TSP Paprika

Suggested Shopping List:
- Edward & Sons® Organic Mashed Potatoes
- Follow Your Heart® Organic Vegan Cream Cheese
- Follow Your Heart® Organic Vegan Sour Cream
- Daiya® Vegan Cheese Shreds – Cheddar
- Follow Your Heart® Vegenaise

To Make Homemade Mashed Potatoes:
1. Boil the potatoes with skins (see step 1 on page 47 for how to boil potatoes)
2. Place boiled potatoes in a large bowl and use a fork to mash the potatoes into a dough-like mixture.

<u>Or</u> To Make Store-Bought Mashed Potatoes
1. In a large pot, on high heat, place organic vegan buttery spread and water and bring to boil.
2. Turn off the heat. Remove pot from heat, and stir in the organic mashed potato flakes.
3. Add the coconut milk and stir in the flakes, mixing vigorously to thoroughly blend with the coconut milk.

To Make Potato Hearty Casserole:
1. In a large bowl, place mashed potatoes, vegan cream cheese, vegan mayonnaise, and vegan sour cream.
2. Using a wire whisk or electric mixer, whip everything together.
3. Season with salt, pepper, and paprika.
4. Fold in the onions and drained peas.
5. Pour into a greased casserole dish.
6. Generously sprinkle the top with vegan cheese shreds.
7. Bake at 350°F for 15 minutes.

This is a one of those dishes that you can make when you don't have a lot of time to cook but want to eat something filling and wholesome

Did you know that the reason why potatoes are so popular in Ireland is because in the 1800's, that's all the native Irish could afford to eat? The potato did well in their cool and damp climate and it provided more calories per acre than any other crop. Plus there were laws that forbade hunting, fishing, and foraging. Hence the Irish peasants became entirely dependent upon the potato

Ratatouille with a Curried Twist

Featured here is the traditional French vegetable stew with eggplant, tomatoes, zucchini, peppers, and onions, but untraditionally seasoned with Indian spices and herbs

Serves 4

What You Will Need:

1 Cup Organic Eggplant – cubed
2 Cups Organic Zucchini – cubed
1/2 Cup Organic Red Bell Pepper – diced
4 Medium Organic Tomatoes – finely chopped
1 Cup Organic Onions – diced
1/2 Cup Organic Cilantro – stems and leaves all chopped up
1 TSP Organic Garlic – minced
1 TSP Organic Ginger – minced
1 TSP Ground Cumin
1/2 TSP Black Mustard Seeds
1 TSP Turmeric
2 TSP Garam Masala (see page 156 for recipe or store-bought)
1 TSP Himalayan Pink Salt
1/2 TSP Cayenne Pepper
Grapeseed Oil for cooking

Suggested Shopping List:
– Cumin, Black Mustard Seeds, Turmeric, and Garam Masala can all be found in Indian grocery stores

To Make Ratatouille:

1. Heat three tablespoons of oil in a large skillet over medium-high heat until hot.
2. Carefully add the cumin and mustard seeds. Sauté the spices until they start to pop (be careful, the seeds do spatter). Cover the skillet. Lower heat.
3. When the popping stops, uncover the skillet, and add the garlic, ginger, garam masala, and turmeric, sautéing until you can smell the fragrance of the garlic (about 1 minute).
4. Add the onions, cilantro, and bell peppers and sauté over medium heat until onions are translucent and bell peppers are softened.
5. Stir in the zucchini, eggplant, tomatoes, and salt, mixing well to combine all the ingredients.
6. Turn the heat to low, cover with lid, and allow the stew to simmer for 20 minutes covered.

 Pour the stew into small bowls and enjoy with toasted garlic bread

 Did you know that the original Ratatouille was made only with zucchini, tomatoes, bell peppers, onions, and garlic, and that eggplants were only introduced later on when they were brought in from India in the 16th Century? It's interesting that most people think that the chief ingredient in Ratatouille is eggplant.
Also the word Ratatouille comes from French: "rata" a slang word for chunky stew and "touille' derived from the French verb "touiller" which means "to stir or toss"

Raw Marinara Zucchini Pasta

Zucchini Pasta mixed with a tangy and tasty raw marinara sauce, a classic Italian blend – quick, raw and absolutely delightful! No guilt yet all the flavor!

Serves 4

What You Will Need:
4 Medium Organic Tomatoes (about 1½ Cups)
1/2 Cup Organic Sun-dried Tomatoes in oil or dry
1 TB Dried Basil
<u>Or</u> 1/2 Cup Fresh Basil Leaves
1/4 Cup Organic Extra Virgin Olive Oil (omit if using sun-dried tomatoes in oil)
1 TB Organic Fresh Lemon Juice
1 Dried Date, pitted and roughly chopped
1 TSP Organic Garlic – minced
1/2 TSP Dried Thyme
1/2 TSP Dried Oregano
A few sprigs Organic Parsley – coarsely chopped
1/2 TSP Himalayan Pink Salt

What You Will Need for the Raw Pasta:
2 Cups Organic Zucchini – made into long spaghetti strands
using a julienne peeler or mandolin slicer (julienne blade) – see picture on right
1 TB Extra Virgin Olive Oil
1/2 TSP Himalayan Pink Salt

> **Suggested Shopping List:**
> – Mediterranean Organic® Sun-dried Tomatoes in oil or dried
> – Bragg® Organic Extra Virgin Olive Oil

To Make Raw Marinara Pasta:
1. Place zucchini strands in a large colander over a bowl.
2. Sprinkle with 1/2 TSP salt and 1TB olive oil and toss well.
3. Let the zucchini noodles drain for 20-25 minutes. Keep giving them a little squeeze every 5 minutes to drain excess liquid.
4. In the meantime, prepare your raw marinara sauce. Place tomatoes, sun-dried tomatoes, basil, olive oil, lemon juice, dried date, garlic, thyme, oregano, parsley, and salt in a food processor or high speed blender.
5. Process all the ingredients until you reach a smooth consistency.
6. Once the zucchini strands are fairly dry, transfer to a large mixing bowl.
7. Pour the raw marinara sauce all over the zucchini noodles, and toss well, making sure to coat the zucchini pasta thoroughly with the sauce.

 Health: Zucchini contains lutein and zeaxanthin which are both good for your eyes. It is also filled with anti-oxidants which stay with the vegetable even after steaming and freezing. Antioxidants protect your cells from free radicals, which are highly reactive compounds that oxidize your DNA, lipids, and proteins, and cause cell damage
Beauty: Zucchini is great for weight loss since it has very few calories and helps your body easily metabolize cholesterol. Plus, eating more zucchini erases wrinkles and fine lines because of the presence of manganese which helps the body produce collagen

Shepherd's Pie

Layers of tenderly cooked mixed vegetables, followed by seasoned vegan ground beef, and topped with vegan mashed potatoes and crunchy breadcrumbs, baked to perfection. This British staple makes a hearty meal and is a real party pleaser

Serves 4

What You Will Need for the Vegan Mashed Potatoes:

4 Organic Potatoes
1/4 Cup Organic Coconut Milk
1 TB Organic Vegan Buttery Spread
1/4 TSP Himalayan Pink Salt

What You Will Need for the Vegan Shepherd Pie Mixture:

1 TB Grapeseed Oil
1½ Cups Vegan Ground Beef (see page 161 for recipe or store-bought)
1 Cup Organic Onions – diced
1 TSP Coriander Powder
1 TSP Garam Masala (see page 156 for recipe or store-bought)
  Or 1 TSP Taco Seasoning instead of Indian spices
1 TSP Organic Garlic – minced
1 TSP Organic Ginger – minced
1/2 TSP Himalayan Pink Salt
1 Cup Organic Frozen Mixed Vegetables – steamed
  Or 1 Cup Organic Fresh Steamed Vegetables (beans, peas, carrots, corn etc)
Grapeseed Oil for cooking
1/2 Cup Breadcrumbs (Optional)

 Use Gluten-free breadcrumbs or Omit

> **Suggested Shopping List:**
> - So Delicious® Coconut Milk (unsweetened)
> - Earth Balance® Natural Buttery Spread (non-Soy version)
> - Trader Joe's® Beef-Less Ground Beef
> - Coriander Powder & Garam Masala can be found in Indian grocery stores
> - Bearitos® or Simply Organic® Southwest Taco Seasoning (if you choose Taco Seasoning)
> - Daiya® Vegan Cheese Shreds – Cheddar

 Instead of using Pam® spray, fill your own oil spray bottle with a higher grade of oil – it's cheaper and healthier. I use a Misto® oil spray bottle and fill it with grapeseed oil

To make Vegan mashed potatoes:

1. Boil the potatoes (see step 1 on page 47 to see how to boil potatoes)
2. Place boiled potatoes, vegan buttery spread, coconut milk, and salt in a food processor. Process until mixture is smooth and creamy and resembles mashed potatoes. Set aside.

To make Vegan Shepherd Pie mixture:

1. Sauté ginger, garlic, and onions in 3 tablespoons of oil until onions are slightly browned and you smell the aroma of roasted garlic. *(Note: if you are using your own vegan ground beef omit the ginger and garlic – and instead just sauté onions.)*
2. Stir in the vegan ground beef. Cook for about 5 minutes.
3. Add the steamed mixed vegetables.
4. Season the mixture with salt, coriander powder, and garam masala or taco seasoning *(your choice)* and mix thoroughly to blend in the flavors.

Now it's time to combine the two to complete making your Vegan Shepherd Pie:

1. Spray a large glass baking dish with oil.
2. Layer the bottom with the Vegan Shepherd pie mixture.
3. Layer the top with the mashed potato mixture.
4. Bake in the oven for about 10-15 minutes at 400°F until dish starts to bubble.

 Sprinkle Breadcrumbs on top in the last 5 minutes of baking for a crunchier dish

Singapore "Vegan Fish" Curry

Chunks of succulent soy protein, broccoli, and potatoes simmered in a mild yellow coconut curry
Serves 4-6

What You Will Need:

2 Slices "Vegan Fish fillets" – cut into small cubes

 Use Sophies Kitchen® Breaded Vegan Fish Fillets

2 Cups Organic Potatoes (about 3 potatoes) – cubed
2 Cups Organic Broccoli florets
1 Organic Onion – diced
1 of 14.5 fl Oz Can Singapore Curry Gravy
1 of 13.5 fl Oz Can Organic Coconut Milk
1 Cube Vegetable Bouillon
1 TSP Organic Garlic – minced
1 TSP Organic Ginger – minced
2 TSP Himalayan Pink Salt
3 TSP Raw Sugar
Grapeseed Oil for cooking

Suggested Shopping List:
- All Vegetarian Inc® Vegan Fish Ham or EcoVegan® Ocean's Delight for vegan fish fillets
- Sophie's Kitchen® (for gluten free) – Breaded Vegan Fish Fillets
- Yeo's® Singapore Curry Gravy sold in Oriental grocery stores
- Native Forest® Organic Coconut Milk
- Edward & Sons® Not Chick'n Natural Bouillon Cubes

To Make Curry:

1. Boil the potatoes with skins (see page 47 for how to boil potatoes). Set aside.
2. Optional step: In a flat ceramic skillet, shallow fry the vegan fish filet cubes in two tablespoons of oil until slightly browned on both sides.
3. In a large pot, on medium heat, sauté garlic, ginger, and onions until the onion are limp and translucent.
4. Add the curry paste. Dilute the curry paste by adding a few tablespoons of water to it.
5. Season with salt and sugar. Mix thoroughly.
6. Pour in the coconut milk and refill empty can twice with distilled water, thus adding 2 cans of water. Increase the heat to high.
7. Drop the vegetable bouillon cube into the curry stirring well to dissolve the cube.
8. Add the broccoli florets.
9. Mix well and bring the curry to a boil.
10. Add the boiled potatoes and cubes of vegan fish filets.
11. Simmer the curry on low heat for 15 minutes to blend flavors.
12. Turn off heat, and serve over steamed brown or white rice.

Spaghetti Bolognese

Spaghetti tossed in a rich tomato vegan-meaty sauce full of zest, flavor, and aroma

Serves 4

What You Will Need:

1 of 12 Oz Package of Brown Rice Spaghetti Noodles
1 Cup Organic Onions – finely diced
2 Cups Organic Tomatoes – diced
1 TSP Organic Ginger – minced
1 TSP Organic Garlic – minced
1/2 Cup Organic Ketchup
1/2 Cup of Organic Barbecue Sauce
1 TSP Himalayan Pink Salt
1 TSP Coriander Powder
1 TSP Garam Masala (see page 156 for recipe or store-bought)
1 TSP Dried Oregano
1 Cup Vegan Cheese Shreds
1½ Cups Vegan Ground Beef (see page 161 for recipe or store-bought)
Grapeseed Oil for cooking

Suggested Shopping List:
- Tinkyada® Brown Rice Pasta Spaghetti Style
- Tree of Life® Organic Ketchup
- Annie's® Organic BBQ Sauce
- Coriander Powder and Garam Masala can be found in Indian grocery stores
- Daiya® Vegan Cheese Shreds – Cheddar
- Trader Joe's® Beef-less Ground Beef

To Make Spaghetti Bolognese:

1. Fill a large pot of filtered water to boil and add salt and oil to the water. Bring the water to a rolling boil. Add the spaghetti style noodles, and cook for the amount of time noted on the pasta package instructions. Make sure to stir the pasta every so often to prevent sticking. Drain the pasta, then drizzle the surface of the cooked pasta with olive oil, and set aside.
2. In a large skillet on medium heat, in three tablespoons of oil, sauté the ginger, garlic, and onions until the onions are translucent and limp (about 5 minutes)
3. Add the tomatoes and cook on low heat for five minutes covered with the lid allowing the juice from the tomatoes to seep out into the dish.
4. Once the tomatoes seem softened, season with salt, coriander powder, garam masala, and oregano stirring thoroughly to mix everything in.
5. Season with tomato ketchup and barbecue sauce.
6. Sprinkle in the vegan ground beef and stir well into the mixture. Cook for 5-10 minutes on very low heat with the lid covered to blend flavors.
7. Remove the lid, and toss in the boiled spaghetti into the Bolognese mixture.
8. Mix in the vegan cheese shreds, and keep stirring, allowing the cheese to melt into the spaghetti Bolognese mixture.
9. Garnish with fresh tomato wedges and vegan parmesan cheese, and enjoy!

 This dish makes an excellent lunchbox filler. Even if you make it ahead of time and refrigerate it, this meal will still retain its delectability, and your family will love it!

Spinach & Corn in Cream Sauce

A quick delectable dish that has all the sweetness of corn and the hearty vitality of spinach

Serves 4

What You Will Need:

1 of 10 Oz Package Organic Frozen Chopped Spinach
  (thawed and drained)
<u>Or</u> 1 Pound Fresh Organic Spinach – chopped (6 cups)
2 Cups Organic Sweet Kernel Corn (canned or frozen)
1 of 13.5 fl Oz Can Organic Coconut Milk
1 Cube Vegetable Bouillon
1/2 Cup Filtered Water
3 TB Organic Vegan Buttery Spread
3 TB Millet Flour
1 Cup Organic Onions – finely diced
1 TSP Organic Garlic – minced
1 TSP Himalayan Pink Salt
1/4 TSP Freshly Ground Black Pepper
1/4 TSP Dried Oregano
1/4 TSP Dried Basil
1/2 Cup Vegan Cheese Shreds (optional)

> **Suggested Shopping List:**
> – Native Forest® for Organic Coconut Milk
> – Edward & Sons® Not Chick'n Natural Bouillon Cubes
> – Earth Balance® Natural Buttery Spread (non-Soy version)
> – Daiya® Vegan Cheese Shreds – Mozzarella

To Make Spinach & Corn in Cream Sauce:

1. In a large pot, melt 3 tablespoons of vegan buttery spread.
2. Once the vegan buttery spread melts, add garlic and onions.
3. Lower heat, sauté onions and garlic until onions are translucent and limp.
4. Add 3 tablespoons of the millet flour to the onion mixture. Mix thoroughly until it forms a lump.
5. Stir in the coconut milk, increase the heat to high, and keep stirring the mixture until there are no more lumps and the mixture thickens.
6. Season with salt, pepper, oregano, and basil.
7. Lower heat and add 1/2 cup of filtered water and the vegetable bouillon cube. Keep stirring until the cube dissolves.
8. Add the spinach and the corn (if using canned corn, make sure you drain the can) and cover the pot allowing the vegetables to cook for about 5-7 minutes on very low heat.
9. Enjoy the dish as is or for a variation see below.

 Variation: Pour into a greased casserole dish and sprinkle with vegan cheese shreds and bake in a preheated oven at 350°F for 5 minutes to allow the cheese to melt

Spinach Stuffed Shells

Jumbo brown rice pasta shells filled with a blend of tofu ricotta, spinach, and Italian herbs – who can resist stuffed shells that taste this good

Serves 4

What You Will Need For the Sauce:
1 of 13.5 fl Oz Can Organic Coconut Milk
1 Cube Vegetable Bouillon
1/2 Cup Filtered Water
3 TB Organic Vegan Buttery Spread
3 TB Millet Flour
1 Cup Organic Onions – finely diced
1 TSP Organic Garlic – minced
1 TSP Himalayan Pink Salt
1/4 TSP Freshly Ground Black Pepper
1/4 TSP Dried Oregano
1/4 TSP Dried Basil
1/2 Cup Vegan Cheese Shreds (optional)

Suggested Shopping List:
- Native Forest® for Organic Coconut Milk
- Edward & Sons® Not Chick'n Natural Bouillon Cubes
- Earth Balance® Natural Buttery Spread (non-Soy version)
- Wildwood® Organic Sprouted Tofu
- Follow Your Heart® Soy-Free Vegenaise
- Daiya® Vegan Cheese Shreds – Mozzarella
- Tinkyada® Brown Rice Pasta "Grand Shells"

What You Will Need For the Shells & the Stuffing:
3 Cups Tofu Ricotta (see page 88 for recipe)
1 of 10 Oz Package Organic Frozen Chopped Spinach (thawed and drained)
 Or 1 Pound Fresh Organic Spinach – chopped (6 cups)
1 TSP Himalayan Pink Salt
1 TSP Paprika
2 TB Vegan Mayonnaise (see page 162 for recipe or store-bought)
1 Cup Vegan Cheese Shreds
1 Package of Brown Rice Pasta Grand Shells

To Make the Sauce:
1. In a large pot, melt 3 tablespoons of vegan buttery spread.
2. Once the vegan buttery spread melts, add garlic and onions.
3. Lower heat and sauté onions and garlic until onions are translucent and limp.
4. Add 3 tablespoons of the millet flour to the onion mixture. Mix thoroughly until it forms a lump.
5. Stir in the coconut milk, increase the heat to high, and keep stirring the mixture until there are no more lumps and the mixture thickens.
6. Season with salt, pepper, oregano, and basil.
7. Lower heat and add 1/2 cup of filtered water and the vegetable bouillon cube. Keep stirring until the cube dissolves. Turn off burner and set aside.

To Make the Stuffed Shells:
1. Preheat oven at 350°F.
2. Fill a large pot of filtered water and add 2 teaspoons salt and 1 TB oil to the water. Bring the water to a rolling boil. Add the large shell pasta, and cook for the amount of time noted on the pasta package. Make sure to stir the pasta every so often to prevent sticking. Drain the pasta, then drizzle the surface of the cooked pasta with olive oil, and set aside.
3. Steam the spinach for 10 minutes and drain. Set aside.
4. In a mixing bowl, mix tofu ricotta, steamed spinach, salt, paprika, and vegan mayonnaise.
5. Stuff this mixture into the boiled pasta shells.
6. Arrange the stuffed shells on a greased oven-proof glass dish.
7. Pour the sauce over the stuffed shells.
8. Top with vegan cheese shreds.
9. Bake in the oven at 350°F for 10 minutes or until the cheese melts.

Stuffed Bell Peppers

Here I have showcased two different recipes of stuffed bell peppers – one with a hint of an Indian flavor and the other with a Tex-Mex twist…both of them equally delightful!

Serves 4

What You Will Need for Either Recipe:
1 Cup Organic Pasta Sauce – Tomato blend
6 Organic Bell Peppers (any color your choice)
  – tops cut off and deseeded – see instructions below
1 Cup Vegan Cheese Shreds
Grapeseed Oil for cooking
Tops of Bell Peppers – chopped

How to Prepare Bell Peppers for either recipe:
1. Cut around the top of each pepper in an even circle about 1 inch from the stem.
2. Pull out the stem and the seeds. Discard stem and seeds.
3. Wash the inside of the pepper to remove extra seeds that may not have gotten removed.
4. Save the top of the pepper, and chop up to add to the filling.
5. Boil empty bell peppers in a large pot for 20 minutes and then carefully remove from water, and set aside.

What You Will Need for Indian Stuffed Bell Peppers:
1 Cup Organic Quinoa
2 Cups Filtered Water
1/2 TSP Himalayan Pink Salt – for cooking quinoa
1 Cup Organic Onions – finely diced
1 Cup Organic Raisins
1/2 Cup Raw Blanched Almonds – chopped
1 TSP Organic Garlic – minced
1 TB Madras Curry Powder
1 TSP Himalayan Pink Salt
1 TSP Raw Sugar

> **Suggested Shopping List:**
> For Indian Stuffed Peppers:
> - Earthly Delight® or Ancient Harvest® for Organic Quinoa (just make sure whatever brand you buy the quinoa is pre-washed)
> - Kim Thu Thap® Mild Madras Curry Powder
> For Tex-Mex Stuffed Peppers:
> - Arrowhead Mills® Organic Gluten-free Yellow Corn Grits
> - Pace® Salsa
> - Bearitos® or Simply Organic® Southwest Taco Seasoning
> For Either Recipe You will need:
> - Bertolli® Organic Pasta Sauce – Tomato & Basil
> - Daiya® Vegan Cheese Shreds – Mozzarella

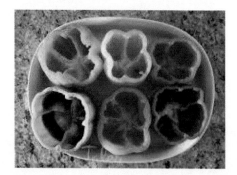

To Prepare the Filling for Indian Stuffed Peppers:
1. If using a rice cooker, place the quinoa with 2 cups water in the rice cooker. Mix in 1/2 teaspoon of salt and a tablespoon of oil. Stir the quinoa well before pressing the "cook" button on your cooker. If using a regular pot, mix the quinoa, water, oil, and salt together in a saucepan; bring to a boil. Cover, reduce heat, and simmer until quinoa is tender and water is absorbed (about 15 minutes).
2. In a large skillet over medium heat, in three tablespoons of oil, sauté the garlic, onions, and chopped up bell pepper tops, until the onions are limp and translucent (about 5 to 7 minutes).
3. Add the raisins and the almonds.
4. Season with curry powder, salt, and sugar. Stir well to mix in flavors.
5. Toss the cooked quinoa well into the curry mixture so that it is thoroughly coated with the curry mixture.
6. Fill the boiled bell peppers (see above on how to prepare bell peppers) with the quinoa mixture.
7. Place peppers in a greased glass baking dish.
8. Ladle tomato sauce over the filled peppers.
9. Top with vegan cheese shreds.
10. Bake in an oven for about 10 minutes or until the cheese melts.

Continued…

Stuffed Bell Peppers (Cont'd)

What You Will Need for Tex-Mex Stuffed Bell Peppers:

1/2 Cup Organic Yellow Corn Grits
2 Cups Filtered Water
1 TSP Organic Garlic – minced
1 Cup Organic Onions – finely diced
1/2 Cup Organic Cilantro – stems and leaves chopped fine
2 TB Salsa (see page 48 for recipe or store-bought)
1 TSP Himalayan Pink Salt
1 TSP Taco Seasoning
Grapeseed Oil for cooking

 Did you know that out of the three colors of Bell Peppers, "Red Bells" have the most nutrients?

To Prepare the Filling for Tex-Mex Stuffed Peppers:

1. Mix the grits and water together in a saucepan; bring to a boil. Reduce heat, and simmer until all the water is absorbed. Stir frequently to avoid sticking. Cooks in about 5-7 minutes.
2. In a large skillet, over medium heat in three tablespoons of oil, sauté the garlic, onions, cilantro, and chopped up bell pepper tops, until the onions are limp and translucent (about 5 to 7 minutes).
3. Add the salsa.
4. Season with salt and taco seasoning. Stir well to mix in flavors.
5. Toss the cooked grits well into the salsa mixture to thoroughly coat the grits.
6. Fill the boiled bell peppers (see previous page on how to prepare bell peppers) with the grits mixture.
7. Place peppers in a greased glass baking dish.
8. Ladle tomato sauce over the filled peppers.
9. Top with vegan cheese shreds.
10. Bake in an oven for about 10 minutes or until the cheese melts.

 Health: Bell Peppers remove free radicals because of their high content of Vitamin C & A. They also reduce the risk of heart disease because of the presence of Vitamin B6 & Folic Acid. Additionally, they help protect against rheumatism and arthritis (presence of Vitamin C). Red Bell Peppers are especially good for your eyes
Beauty: Bell Peppers prevent premature aging and beautify our skin cells because of their high Vitamin K content. They also help keep our joints and muscles supple

 Did you know that the stuffed pepper is a dish that is known by different names around the world? Spain – Pimientos Rellenos, India – Bharva Hari Mirch, Mediterranean – Dolma & Yemista, Mexico – Chile Relleno, Middle East – Filfil Mahshi, Denmark – Fyldte Peberfrugter, Finland – Täytetyt Paprika, Iceland – Fylltar Paprikur, Norway – Fylt Paprika, Sweden – Fyllda Paprikor . Lithuania – Kimšti Pipirai, Latvia – Pildīti Pipari, Estonia – Täidisega Paprika, Croatia/Serbia – Punjena Paprika , Albania – Speca Të Mbushur, Bosnia – Filovana Paprika, Slovenia – Polnjena Paprika, Macedonia – Polneti Piperki , Czechoslovakia – Plněná Paprika, Hungary – Töltött Paprika, Germany – Gefüllte Paprika/Pulnena Piperka, Bulgaria – Pulnena Chuska, and United States of America – Stuffed Bell Peppers

Sweet & Sour Tofu

Pan seared slabs of tofu drenched and simmered slowly in a sweet and sour sauce with pineapple chunks, bell peppers, and onions – A perfect balance of sweet and sour

Serves 4

What You Will Need:

1 of 14 Oz package Organic Extra Firm or Super Firm Tofu
 – cut into cubes
2-3 sprigs Organic Cilantro – leaves and stems chopped up fine
1 TSP Organic Garlic – minced
1 TSP Organic Ginger – minced
1 Cup Organic Onions – cut into rectangular wedges
1 Cup Organic Green Bell Peppers
 – cut into 1 inch rectangular pieces
1 cup Organic Bell Peppers – red, orange, yellow, green
 – cut into 1 inch rectangular pieces
1 of 20 Oz Can Pineapple Chunks in 100% pineapple juice
 – drained with pineapple juice reserved
1 Cube Vegetable Bouillon
2 Cups Filtered Water
1 TB Organic Raw Apple Cider Vinegar
1 TB Organic Shoyu Sauce

 Use Organic Tamari Sauce

3 TB Organic Tomato Ketchup
2 TSP Raw Sugar
3 TB Organic Cornstarch
 – mixed with 4 TB filtered water
Grapeseed Oil for cooking

Suggested Shopping List:
– Wildwood® Organic Sprouted Tofu
– Dole® Pineapple Chunks
– Edward & Sons® Not Chick'n Natural Bouillon Cubes
– Bragg® Raw Apple Cider Vinegar
– San-J® Organic Shoyu Sauce
<u>or</u> Organic Tamari (gluten-free)
– Tree of Life® Organic Ketchup

Health: Raw Apple Cider Vinegar promotes digestion and encourages the growth of friendly bacteria in the body. It also promotes cellular cleansing since it is high in minerals and potassium
Beauty: Raw Apple Cider Vinegar can help you lose weight because it actually cleans our digestive tract and promotes healthy bowel movements

To Make Sweet & Sour Tofu:

1. In a flat non-stick skillet on high heat, in 1 tablespoon of oil, pan-fry the tofu cubes until they are browned on both sides making sure to flip them often. Set aside.
2. In a large pot or skillet, on medium heat in three tablespoons of oil, sauté ginger and garlic until you can smell the aroma of the garlic.
3. Add the onions, bell peppers, and pineapple chunks, and stir fry on high heat for two minutes. Lower heat, cover the skillet, and let everything simmer for about 15 minutes or until onions, bell peppers, and pineapples are softened.
4. Add the vinegar and sugar and cook on low heat until the sugar has dissolved.
5. Increase the heat to high and add water and the vegetable bouillon cube. Reduce heat after the cube has dissolved.
6. Flavor with the reserved pineapple juice from the can, shoyu sauce (or tamari for gluten-free), and ketchup. Stir well.
7. Toss in the fried tofu cubes to the sauce.
8. In a small mixing bowl, whisk 3 tablespoons cornstarch with 4 tablespoons cold water, mix thoroughly. Add the cornstarch mixture to the dish to thicken the sauce. Increase heat, and keep stirring until the sauce is thickened. If the sauce gets too thick, you can add a little more water to dilute.
9. Serve the dish hot over steamed white or brown rice.

 Did you know that when you buy Apple Cider Vinegar you should always buy the "Raw" & "Unfiltered" kind? The pasteurized version does not have the same health benefits

Szechuan Shredded Faux Pork

Strips of marinated soy protein, tossed with bell peppers and onions, cooked in an aromatic garlic and scallions Szechuan sauce served over fluffy jasmine rice

Serves 6

What You Will Need:

1 Package Vegan Pork Shreds (made of TVP and wheat gluten)
1 Cup Organic Onions – julienned
1 Cup Organic Green Bell Peppers – julienned
1 Cup Organic Sweet Bell Peppers (red, orange, yellow) – julienned
1 TB White Sesame Seeds
3 TB Liquid Amino Acids
Grapeseed Oil for cooking
Drizzle of Chinese Sesame Oil as garnish
10 cups Hot Filtered Water for soaking the soy protein

What You Will Need for the Marinade:

2 TSP Organic Garlic – minced
2 TSP Organic Ginger – minced
2 Stalks Organic Scallions – chopped into small pieces
5 TB Organic Shoyu Sauce
4 TSP Raw Sugar
1 TB Chili Garlic Sauce (see page 154 for recipe
  or store-bought)
1/2 TSP Chinese Five Spice Powder

Suggested Shopping List:
- VegeUSA® Vegan Pork Shreds (Thit Soi Dai Loan available online at amazon.com
- Bragg® Liquid Amino Acids
- Wei-Chuan® 100% Black Sesame Oil
- San-J® Organic Shoyu Sauce
- Lee Kum Kee® or Sriracha® Chili Garlic Sauce
- Dynasty® Chinese Five Spice

To Make Szechuan Shredded Faux Pork:

1. Soak the soy protein shreds in a large bowl filled with 10 cups of hot water for 10 minutes.
2. Drain the water. Return the soy protein shreds to the large bowl.
3. Add all the marinade ingredients – garlic, ginger, scallions, shoyu sauce, chili garlic sauce, sugar, and Chinese five spice powder – to the drained vegan pork shreds.
4. Toss the strips in the marinade mixture and mix well so that the strips are well coated.
5. Let the strips marinate in this mixture for about 20 minutes. Set aside.
6. In a large wok or skillet on medium heat, in 3 tablespoons of oil, sauté the onions and bell peppers until the onions are limp and translucent.
7. Add the marinated tofu shreds to the onion and bell peppers and stir fry on high heat.
8. Add the sesame seeds and mix thoroughly into the mixture.
9. Add the liquid amino acids. Stir fry for about 5-7 minutes, letting the flavors blend. Keep tossing until all the liquid is absorbed.
10. Turn off burner. Drizzle with sesame oil. Serve over steamed brown or white rice.

 Unfortunately this dish cannot be made gluten-free – there is no gluten-free substitute for vegan pork shreds

Tandoori Tofu Biryani Rice

A tasty Indian version of fried rice – white fluffy rice cooked with cubes of tofu and fresh vegetables mixed in a creamy sauce infused with aromatic Indian spices and garnished with cashew nuts and raisins

Serves 4

What You Will Need:

1 Package Organic Extra Firm or Super Firm Tofu
  – cut into cubes
2 Cups Organic Fresh Tomatoes – diced
1/2 Cup Organic Carrots – shredded
1 Cup Organic Green Bell Peppers – diced
1 Cup Organic Onions – diced
1/4 Cup Organic Cilantro – leaves and stems
  chopped fine
1/2 Cup Raw Whole Cashews
1/2 Cup Organic Raisins
1 of 8 Oz Container of Vegan Cream Cheese
1 TB Tandoori Powder
1 TSP Turmeric Powder
1 TB Organic Lemon Juice
1 TB Organic Raw Apple Cider Vinegar
1½ TSP Himalayan Pink Salt
2 TSP Raw Sugar
1 TSP Organic Garlic – minced
1 TSP Organic Ginger – minced
3 Cups Steamed White Rice (I like Jasmine rice but you can use whatever kind you prefer)
Grapeseed Oil for cooking

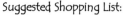

> **Suggested Shopping List:**
> – Wildwood® Organic Sprouted Tofu
> – Follow Your Heart® Vegan Cream Cheese
> – Tandoori Powder can be found in Indian grocery stores
> – Bragg® Raw Apple Cider Vinegar

To Make Tandoori Tofu Biryani:

1. Cook the white rice and set aside (I generally cook mine in a rice cooker). Wash and rinse the rice well, place in rice cooker, stir in 1 TB of oil and 1 TSP of salt, and then press cook. You can cook it on the stove if you like. For white rice, the ratio is 1:1 so 3 cups of white rice to 3 cups of water.
2. In a non-stick skillet place a few tablespoons of oil and pan-sear your tofu cubes until browned on both sides, making sure to flip the tofu cubes often to avoid charring. Set aside tofu cubes.
3. In a large pot, in three tablespoons of oil, and on medium heat, sauté ginger, garlic, onions, green peppers, cilantro, and cashew nuts until the onions and peppers are softened (about 5-7 minutes)
4. Add the carrots and tomatoes and stir fry for a few more minutes (1-2 minutes).
5. Season with tandoori powder, turmeric, lemon juice, vinegar, salt, sugar, and raisins. Mix thoroughly and cook on low heat for 10 minutes while covered with lid to blend flavors.
6. Add the tub of vegan cream cheese. Whisk in until the vegan cream cheese is well blended into the mixture.
7. Toss in the fried tofu cubes.
8. Stir in the steamed white rice. Toss well to thoroughly combine and coat the rice with the vegetable mixture. Enjoy!

 Did you know that Biryani was a dish created by royalty? There is an interesting story as to how Biryani first came to be: Mumtaz Mahal (Emperor Shah Jahan's queen who inspired the Taj Mahal) once visited the army barracks and found the army personnel under-nourished. She asked her Court Chef to prepare a special dish which provided balanced nutrition, and thus the "Biryani" was created

Thai Basil Not-Chik'N

Pan-seared chili peppers stir-fried with bell peppers, onions, and sliced spicy bits (seitan), aromatized with basil leaves and sautéed in a hot chili garlic sauce – Super hot but Super Tasty!

Serves 4

What You Will Need:

2 Packets Seasoned Seitan – thawed and sliced thin (about 4 Cups)
2 TSP Organic Garlic – minced
1 TSP Organic Ginger – minced
4-5 Organic Hot Green Chilies (preferably Thai Bird Chilies)
  – deseeded and chopped *(use gloves to do this)*
Note: adjust this to your taste please;
If you don't like it that hot, then use only 1 chili pepper)
1 Cup Organic Bell Peppers (yellow, red or green –
  your choice) – julienned
1 Cup Organic Onions – julienned
1 TB Organic Shoyu Sauce
1 TB Liquid Amino Acids
2 Cups Filtered Water
1 Cube Vegetable Bouillon
3 TB Organic Cornstarch mixed with 4 TB
  Filtered Water
2 TSP Raw Sugar
Drizzle of Sesame Oil for Garnish
Grapeseed Oil for cooking
40 Fresh Basil Leaves – torn into shreds

> **Suggested Shopping List:**
> - EcoVegan® Spicy Bits for seasoned seitan soy protein
> - San-J® for Shoyu Sauce
> - Bragg® Liquid Amino Acids
> - Edward & Sons® Not Chick'n Natural Bouillon Cubes
> - Wei-Chuan® 100% Black Sesame Oil

To Make Thai Basil Not-Chik'N:

1. In a large skillet or wok on a medium heat, in three tablespoons of oil, sauté the ginger and garlic for a few minutes, until you can smell the aroma of the garlic.
2. Lower the heat, add the Thai chilies, onions, and bell peppers, and stir fry for 5 minutes. Then cover the pot and cook for another 5 minutes until the onions and peppers are softened.
3. Toss in the sliced seasoned seitan.
4. Add 2 cups of filtered water and the bouillon cube.
5. Increase the heat to high to dissolve the bouillon cube.
6. Season with Shoyu sauce, liquid amino acids, and sugar. Mix thoroughly.
7. Sprinkle in the basil leaves. Stir the mixture until the basil leaves are wilted.
8. In a separate bowl, stir 3 tablespoons cornstarch with 4 tablespoons cold water, and mix thoroughly. Add the cornstarch mixture to the dish to thicken the sauce. Increase heat, and keep stirring until the sauce is thickened. If the sauce gets too thick, you can add a little more filtered water to dilute it.
9. Drizzle the dish with sesame oil.
10. Serve with steamed white or brown rice or steamed rice noodles.

 Unfortunately this dish cannot be made gluten-free – there is no gluten-free substitute for seasoned seitan

---

 Did you know that before the development of modern refrigeration, humans used chili peppers to preserve food? Chili peppers inhibited bacterial growth and thus delayed food decay

Thai Tempeh with Quinoa

A medley of marinated tempeh with sweet smelling cilantro, quinoa, broccoli, cabbage, and carrots sautéed in a savory peanut sauce

Serves 4-6

What You Will Need for Thai Tempeh with Quinoa:

2 Cups Organic Quinoa
4 Cups Filtered Water – for cooking quinoa
1 of 8 Oz Package Organic Tempeh – cut into cubes
2 to 3 Sprigs Organic Cilantro – leaves and stems chopped up fine
1 TSP Organic Garlic – minced
1 TSP Organic Ginger – minced
2 TB Organic Shoyu

 Use Organic Tamari Sauce

2 TSP Raw Sugar
2 Cups Organic Broccoli Florets
2 Cups Organic Carrots – shredded
2 Cups Organic Purple Cabbage – shredded
Grapeseed Oil for cooking
1/4 Cup Filtered Water

What You Will Need for Thai Peanut Sauce:

2 Cups Raw Organic Peanuts – with skins removed
2 TB Penang Curry Paste
1 Cup Organic Coconut Milk
1/2 TSP Himalayan Pink Salt
1 TSP Raw Sugar
1 TB Organic Canola or Sunflower Oil

Suggested Shopping List:
- Earthly Delight® or Ancient Harvest® Organic Quinoa (just make sure whatever brand you buy, the quinoa is pre-washed)
- Lightlife® Organic Tempeh – flavor of your choice (For Gluten-free only use Soy, Wild Rice or Garden Veggie Tempeh flavor)
- San-J® Shoyu Sauce (or gluten-free Tamari Sauce)
- Maesri® Penang Curry Paste
- Native Forest® Organic Coconut Milk

To Make Thai Peanut Sauce

1. Grease a baking tray and place raw blanched peanuts (skins removed) on it. Spray the surface of the peanuts with oil and roast in an oven at 350°F for 10 minutes. Turn off oven and leave peanuts to crisp in the hot oven for 10 minutes. Remove peanuts from oven and set aside to cool.
2. Once the peanuts are cooled, place in a food processor or powerful blender like a Vitamix.
3. Add all the remaining ingredients for Thai Peanut Sauce into the food processor or blender.
4. Process all the ingredients, until you reach a smooth, creamy, paste-like consistency.
5. Set aside the Thai Peanut Sauce. (You can even refrigerate this for up to a week or freeze it for up to a month).

To Make Thai Tempeh with Quinoa:

1. If using a rice cooker, place the quinoa and 4 cups water with 1 TSP salt and 1 TB oil into the rice cooker. Stir the quinoa well before pressing the "cook" button on your cooker. If using a regular pot, mix the quinoa, water, oil, and salt together in a saucepan; bring to a boil. Cover, reduce heat, and simmer until quinoa is tender and water is absorbed (about 15 minutes). Once it is cooked, set aside.
2. Bring 4 cups of water to boil in a pot. When the water starts to boil, place the tempeh cubes in and boil for 10 minutes.
3. Remove Tempeh with a slotted spoon, pat dry with paper towels, and set aside.
4. In a flat skillet in 1 to 2 TB oil, shallow fry the tempeh cubes until they are browned on both sides. Set aside.

5. In a separate pan, in 1 TB oil, sauté the garlic, ginger and cilantro for 1 minute on low heat. Add the Shoyu sauce (or Tamari for gluten-free) and Raw Sugar and mix well.
6. Add the fried tempeh cubes and toss them in the sauce mixture until tempeh cubes are well coated. Set seasoned tempeh aside.
7. In a large skillet, add 2 TB oil and stir fry broccoli, cabbage, and carrots for 2-3 minutes on high heat. Then cover the skillet, and allow the vegetables to cook on very low heat for 15-20 minutes.
8. Once the vegetables are crisp tender, add 2 cups of Thai peanut sauce and 1/4 cup water. (Note: If you like the dish to be saucier, you can add 1 cup of water instead of 1/4 cup to dilute the sauce further). Mix the sauce thoroughly into the vegetables.
9. Toss in the cubes of the marinated cooked tempeh.
10. Add the cooked quinoa and toss well into the saucy vegetable mixture until quinoa is well mixed in.

Tofu & Spinach Quiche

This vegan quiche is a wholesome, low-cholesterol breakfast, lunch, or brunch entrée made with protein-packing tofu and vitamin-rich spinach! This delicious eggless alternative to traditional quiche will please even the most devoted brunch aficionados

Serves 4-6

What You Will Need for the Tofu & Spinach Quiche:

1 Cup Organic Onions – diced

1 TSP Organic Garlic – minced

1½ Cups Organic Broccoli Florets (optional)
  – roughly chopped

2 Cups Organic Frozen Chopped Spinach (frozen or fresh)

1 of 14 Oz Package Organic Firm or Extra Firm Tofu – drained and patted dry

2 Cups Vegan Cheese Shreds – Cheddar Flavor

1/2 Cup Nutritional Yeast Flakes

1 TSP Himalayan Pink Salt

Pepper (to taste)

1 TSP Dried Basil

1/4 TSP Cayenne Powder (optional)

2 Organic Pie Crusts

 Use gluten-free Pie Crusts

Grapeseed Oil for cooking

To Make Tofu & Spinach Quiche:

1. Prick the inside of the empty pie crusts with a fork.
2. Then partially bake both empty pie crusts for 7 minutes at 350°F. Set aside.
3. In a large skillet, on medium heat, in three tablespoons of oil, sauté the garlic and onions until the onions are limp and translucent.
4. If you choose to use broccoli, add the broccoli and cover the skillet and allow the broccoli to steam on low heat for about 10 minutes. Otherwise omit this step.
5. In the meantime, place tofu, vegan cheese shreds, nutritional yeast, salt, pepper, and basil (optional: add cayenne pepper) in a food processor or blender and process until you reach a puréed consistency.
6. Pour the tofu mixture into the skillet with the cooked vegetables and mix well to combine the tofu mixture in with the vegetables.
7. Add the spinach, and cook on low heat for about 5 minutes until the spinach wilts. Turn off stove.
8. Pour the filling into both pie crusts.
9. Bake at 350°F for 20-30 minutes. You know it is done when the center is firm.
10. Wait about 5 minutes before cutting into wedges and enjoy!

 This dish makes a great lunchbox filler. You can make it ahead of time, but it will still taste just as delicious the next day and your family will love it!

Tofu Loaf

This vegan loaf is a great accompaniment to a compassionate Thanksgiving celebration – it is as chock-a-block full of flavor as it is hearty and filling

Makes 2 Loaves

What You Will Need for the Tofu Loaf:
1 of 10 Oz Package Frozen Organic Spinach, thawed
<u>Or</u> 6 Cups Fresh Organic Spinach Leaves
1 Organic Onion – diced
2 TSP Organic Garlic – minced
1 Vegetable Bouillon Cube
1¾ Cups Hot Filtered Water
2 Cups TVP (Textured Vegetable Protein)
1 Package Firm Organic Tofu
1 Cup Unbleached Organic Flour
1 TB Nutritional Yeast Flakes
1½ TSP Himalayan Pink Salt
Freshly Ground Pepper to taste
1 TSP Paprika Powder
1 TSP Raw Sugar
Grapeseed Oil for cooking

What You Will Need for the Balsamic Glaze:
1/4 Cup Organic Ketchup
1 TB Organic Maple Syrup (Grade B)
2 TB Organic Strawberry Preserves or Jam
2 TB Balsamic Vinegar

Suggested Shopping List:
- Edward & Sons® Not Chick'n Natural Bouillon Cubes
- Textured Vegetable Protein (TVP)
Suggested brands:
• Bob's Red Mill® TVP Granules
• VegeUSA® Vege Soy Chunks
- Wildwood® Organic Sprouted Tofu
- Bob's Red Mill® Organically Grown Unbromated Unbleached White Flour
- Bragg® Nutritional Yeast
- Tree of Life® Organic Ketchup
- Spectrum® Organic Balsamic Vinegar

 Unfortunately this dish cannot be made gluten-free – I tried making it with gluten-free flour, but it came out tasting pasty and gummy

To Make Tofu Loaf:
1. Preheat oven to 350°F.
2. Steam the spinach for about 10 minutes and set aside.
3. In a large skillet, on medium heat, in 3 TB of oil sauté the garlic and onions, stirring occasionally, until the onions are limp and translucent (about 5 minutes) then turn off burner and set aside.
4. In another small saucepan bring 2 Cups of water to a boil and dissolve the bouillon cube in water to make a vegetable broth. Turn off burner and set aside.
5. Stir the TVP (textured vegetable protein) into the vegetable broth and let stand for about 10 minutes.
6. Pat the tofu dry, and then mash with a fork in a mixing bowl.
7. Toss the steamed spinach into the mashed tofu.
8. Add the sautéed garlic and onions, TVP, nutritional yeast, salt, pepper, paprika, raw sugar, and flour. Mix thoroughly to combine all ingredients.
9. Pour the entire mixture into 2 lightly greased 8½ x 4½ inch loaf pans. Smooth the top and bake for 40 minutes, or until brown on top. *Note: If the loaf begins to get too brown on top, cover with aluminum foil.*
10. Optional: Mix all the ingredients together for Balsamic Glaze, and brush the tops of the loaves with the glaze. Bake for another 10 minutes.

 If you don't like the Balsamic Glaze, then this dish is paired perfectly with Vegan Gravy. (See page 94 for recipe)

Dessert

Raw Cookies/Donuts p. 132

Banana Cashew Pudding p. 134

Vegan French Toast p. 139

Brownies p.135

Chocolate Chip Cookies p.137

Mango Crumble p.140

Orange Glazed Muffins p.143

Trifle O'Chocolate p 145.

Chocolate Mousse p.133

Dear Gluten-Free Friends,

Here in the dessert section, I have tried my best to give you gluten-free options where I can, but unfortunately the selection is limited especially when it comes to baked desserts.

During my kitchen experiments, I quickly found out that gluten-free baking is a culinary art in itself!

I tried to substitute gluten-free flours in place of regular flours in some of the baked desserts but the results, let's say, were far from appetizing except for the Brownies!

So my gluten-free buds, until I have perfected this art, I have decided to exclude my "gluten-free" baked goods experimental recipes from this book. I am so sorry, maybe in my next recipe book?

Almond & Pecan Chocolate Raw Cookies/Donuts

Nutty, chewy, chocolaty morsels of delight rolled in decadent coconut and sweetened with organic maple syrup

Makes 54 Medium Sized Cookies

What You Will Need:

2 Cups Raw Blanched almonds
(Note: To blanch, soak almonds in filtered water for 1-2 hours, then slip off skins. Allow blanched almonds to air dry before using in the recipe, otherwise your mixture will be runny)
1/2 Cup Raw Pecans
1/2 Cup Organic Shredded Coconut
  (unsweetened)
1/4 Cup Raw Almond Butter or Peanut
  Butter
3/4 Cup Organic Maple Syrup (Grade B)
2 TB Organic Natural Cocoa Powder
  – full flavor and unsweetened
1/4 Cup Filtered Water
1 TB Organic Sunflower
  Or 1 TB Organic Canola oil

Suggested Shopping List:
- Let's Do Organic® Shredded Coconut
- Tree of Life® Almond Butter or Peanut Butter
- Coombs® Family Farms for Organic Maple Syrup (Grade B)
- Spectrum® Organic Sunflower/Canola Oil

To Make Raw Cookies/Donuts:

1. Combine the raw nuts, coconut, cocoa powder, nut butter, maple syrup, oil, and water all in a food processor with an S-blade.
2. Blend until all the ingredients are well-processed into a dough-like mixture (making sure all the nuts are well chopped up).
3. The dough should be fairly dry, but wet enough to hold together when rolled into balls.
4. Take a teaspoon of mixture into the palm of your hand and roll into a smooth ball. In the picture shown above, I decided to leave them as balls – like this they remind me of donuts – just as delicious. But if you want cookies, then flatten the ball into a flat cookie.
5. Steps 5-6 are optional if you want to make your dessert even more delicious and presentable. Pour out 4-5 tablespoons of shredded coconut in a small bowl.
6. Dress up your cookie by rolling each of them in the shredded coconut (see picture at right).
7. Lay out cookies in a container that can be refrigerated.
8. Refrigerate for several hours.
9. Indulge!

Apple Pie

This traditional favorite made vegan is a welcome addition to any Thanksgiving or Christmas meal – even your non-vegan friends and family will love it as much as mine do!

What You Will Need:

3 Cups Organic Apples – peeled, cored, and diced
1/4 Cup Raw Sugar
1/4 Cup Unbleached Organic Flour
 Use gluten-free flour or Arrowroot

2 TB Organic Vegan Buttery Spread
1/4 TSP Cinnamon
Dash of Himalayan Pink Salt
2 Organic Pie Crusts
 Use gluten-free Pie Crusts

Suggested Shopping List:
- Bob's Red Mill® Organically Grown Unbromated Unbleached White Flour
- Earth Balance® Natural Buttery Spread (non-Soy version)
- Wholly Wholesome® Organic Pie Crusts

To Make Apple Pie:

1. Bake one empty pie crust for 7 minutes at 350°F. Set aside.
2. In a large mixing bowl, mix the cut up apples, raw sugar, flour, vegan buttery spread, cinnamon, and salt with a wooden spoon.
3. Fill the baked pie crust with the apple mixture.
4. Bake the other empty pie crust in the oven for 2 minutes at 350°F then remove pie crust.
5. Position the empty pie crust over the filled pie crust. The foil pan holding the pie crust should easily lift off. Discard foil pan.
6. Using your fingers, fold and press the edges to seal the apple mixture in.
7. Carefully prick holes in the top shell with a fork.
8. Bake in the oven for 35-40 minutes at 350°F.

You can serve the apple pie à la mode with a scoop of your favorite flavor of non-dairy ice cream

Avocado Chocolate Mousse

Moderately sweet creamy chocolaty smooth indulgence topped with fresh organic strawberries and bananas
Serves 10

Suggested Shopping List:
- Coombs® Family Farms Organic Maple Syrup (Grade B)

What You Will Need:

5 Very Ripe Avocados
3/4 Cup Organic Maple Syrup (Grade B)
2 Dried Pitted Dates
1/2 Cup Organic Natural Cocoa Powder- full flavor and unsweetened
2 TSP Organic Vanilla Extract
1/4 TSP Himalayan Pink Salt
1 Cup Pecans

To Make Chocolate Mousse:

1. Combine all the above ingredients in a food processor with an S-blade or in a high powered blender.
2. Process all the ingredients until a smooth paste is formed. (about 5-7 minutes)
3. Refrigerate for several hours.
4. Serve mousse by topping with sliced bananas, strawberries, or blueberries.

 Variation: You can freeze the vegan chocolate mousse to make a delicious chocolate gelato! Or use in a Trifle dessert (see page 145)

Banana & Cashew Cream Pudding

Creamy banana and cashew nuts with a tinge of orange – a tasty combination blended into a smooth delightful concoction

Serves 4

Suggested Shopping List:
- Sunspire® Vegan Carob Chips or Fair Trade® Organic 42% Cacao Chips

What You Will Need:

1 Cup Raw Cashews – soaked in water for at least 30 minutes
1/2 Cup Organic Orange Juice
1 Ripe Organic Banana
Optional for Garnish:
Sliced Organic Berries of your choice
Sliced Organic Bananas
Vegan Carob Chips or Vegan Chocolate Chips

To Make Pudding:

1. Drain the water from the cashews.
2. Blend the cashews and orange juice in a blender or food processor until the mixture is super smooth.
3. Add the banana. Blend or process again until the banana is mashed in.
4. Top with sliced bananas or fresh berries of your choice.
5. Sprinkle with carob chips. Enjoy!

Health: Bananas help with depression and stress. They contain tryptophan, an amino acid that the body converts into serotonin – known to make you relax, improve your mood, and generally make you feel happier
Beauty: Bananas support workouts since they give an instant, sustained and substantial boost of energy. Research has shown that just 2 bananas provide enough energy for a strenuous 90-minute workout

Note: If you are using a blender, you might have to use a spatula to scrape the sides a few times during blending.

Banana Nut Bread

A moist and delicious treat with loads of banana flavor and the crunch of pecans and walnuts – Plus it's wonderful toasted with a dab of melted vegan butter...Mmm...

Makes 2 Loaves

Suggested Shopping List:
- Bob's Red Mill® Organically Grown Unbromated Unbleached White Flour
- Bob's Red Mill® Aluminum-Free Baking Soda
- Ener-G® Egg Replacer

What You Will Need:

1¾ Cups Unbleached Organic Flour
2 TSP Baking powder
1/4 TSP Aluminum-free Baking Soda
1/2 TSP Himalayan Pink Salt
3/4 Cup Raw Sugar
1/2 Cup Chopped Pecans or Walnuts
3 TSP Egg Replacer mixed with 4 TB Warm Filtered Water
3 Overripe Bananas (unripe bananas don't make good banana bread)
1/2 Cup Organic Sunflower Oil or Organic Canola Oil
1 TSP Organic Vanilla Extract

Did you know that ripe bananas are alkaline-forming in your body? So don't shy away from your spotted bananas. The spottier the banana, the riper it is, and the more alkaline it is. Unripe fruit on the other hand is acid-forming.

To Make Banana Nut Bread:

1. Preheat oven to 350°F
2. Mash the bananas in a separate mixing bowl and set aside.
3. Chop the nuts and set aside.
4. Mix the egg replacer with warm water in a small bowl making a smooth paste, and set aside.
5. Sift together all the dry ingredients: the flour, baking powder, baking soda, salt, and sugar.
6. Stir in the egg replacer paste, bananas, oil, and vanilla. Mix well using an electric hand blender.
7. Pour into 2 greased 8-inch glass rectangular loaf pan dishes.
8. Bake for 40 minutes (or until your knife comes out clean).

 When cooled, slice the banana nut bread and enjoy with vegan butter

Brownies – Fudgy & Gluten-free

What can be better than fudgy rich dense nutty chocolate chip brownies with a crispy crust? Not only is this recipe vegan but it's gluten-free too! Nobody will ever know these are vegan – that's how moist and yummy they are!

Makes 12-16 Squares

What You Will Need:

3/4 Cup + 2 TB Gluten-free Flour

 <u>Or</u> Unbleached Organic Flour (if you don't want gluten-free)

1/2 Cup Organic Natural Cocoa Powder- full flavor and unsweetened

1 Cup Whole Blanched Almonds – ground

1/4 TSP Aluminum-free Baking Soda

2 TB Organic Cornstarch

1/2 TSP Himalayan Pink Salt

3/4 Cup Raw Sugar

1/4 Cup + 3 TB Vegan Buttery Spread

1½ TB Ground Flax Seeds + 3 TB Filtered Water

1/2 Cup Vegan Dark Chocolate Chips – for melting

1/4 Cup Organic Coconut Milk

1/4 Cup Agave Nectar

1/4 Cup Vegan Chocolate Chips – whole

1/2 Cup Walnuts – finely chopped

1/4 Cup Organic Sunflower <u>or</u> Organic Canola Oil

1 TSP Organic Vanilla Extract

Suggested Shopping List:
- *Bob's Red Mill® Organically Grown Unbromated Unbleached White Flour*
- *Bob's Red Mill® Aluminum-Free Baking Soda*
- *Rapunzel® Organic Corn Starch*
- *Earth Balance® Vegan Buttery Spread (non-Soy version)*
- *Sunspire® "Fair Trade" Organic 42% Cacao Chips*
- *So Delicious® Unsweetened Organic Coconut Milk*

To Make Brownies:

1. Preheat oven to 350°F
2. Lightly grease an 8x8 inch square glass Pyrex® dish, and set aside
3. Chop the walnuts and set aside.
4. In a food processor or blender – process the almonds until they resemble coarse flour. Set aside.
5. Make your flax egg replacer, by mixing the ground flax seeds and filtered water in a small bowl. Mix thoroughly using a fork or a small wire whisk, until the mixture resembles a thick gooey paste.
6. In a large bowl, sift together all the dry ingredients: flour, cocoa, baking soda, cornstarch, and salt.
7. In a small saucepan on low heat, melt 1/2 cup of chocolate chips in the vegan buttery spread for about 1 minute or until the chocolate is completed melted. Keep stirring to prevent sticking. Turn off burner.
8. Add the flax egg replacer mixture into the melted chocolate, and mix well.
9. Sprinkle in the raw sugar, and pour in the coconut milk.
10. Flavor with vanilla extract, giving the mixture a good final whisk.
11. Pour this wet mixture over the dry ingredients in the large bowl.
12. Add the agave nectar and sunflower <u>or</u> canola oil.
13. Mix well with a wooden spoon. The mixture will resemble wet cookie dough; keep mixing until you have all the ingredients well mixed in.
14. Sprinkle in the chopped walnuts and the 1/4 cup of whole chocolate chips, and fold them into the mixture.
15. When you have everything well mixed in, scoop your thick batter into the greased square glass dish
16. Using a metal spoon, flatten the batter until it is smooth and even in the pan.
17. Bake at 350°F for 35 minutes or until your knife comes out clean.
18. Take the glass pan out of the oven, leaving the brownies in the dish to cool. Once cooled, cover, and place the entire pan in the refrigerator. *Note: Do not attempt to slice the brownies while hot (since they will crumble.*
19. After 1 hour or so, remove the glass dish from the refrigerator, cut the brownies into squares, and indulge!
20. Brownies will keep in the refrigerator for up to 2 weeks.

Brownies can be enjoyed with a scoop of vegan ice cream or used in Trifle dessert (see page 145)

Butterscotch Pecan Bars

These melt-in-your-mouth bars are little morsels of delight – they're quick to prepare and always the first to disappear at a party

Makes 24 Little Bars

What You Will Need:
1/3 Cup Organic Vegan Buttery Spread
3/4 Cup + 2 TB Raw Sugar
1 Cup Unbleached Organic Flour
1/2 TSP Baking Powder
1/8 TSP Aluminum-Free Baking Soda
1/2 TSP Himalayan Pink Salt
1/3 Cup Pecan – chopped into bits
1½ TSP Egg Replacer mixed with 2 TB warm filtered water
1 TSP Organic Vanilla Extract
1/3 Cup Vegan Chocolate Chips

Suggested Shopping List:
- Earth Balance® Natural Buttery Spread (non-Soy version)
- Bob's Red Mill® Organically Grown Unbromated Unbleached White Flour
- Bob's Red Mill® Aluminum-Free Baking Soda
- Ener-G® Egg Replacer
- Sunspire® "Fair Trade" Organic 42% Cacao Chips

To Make Butterscotch Pecan Bars:
1. Preheat oven to 350°F, grease an 8×8 inch square ovenproof dish. Set aside.
2. In a small bowl, vigorously whisk together egg replacer powder and warm water to make a paste. Set aside.
3. In a small saucepan, on low heat, melt vegan buttery spread.
4. Add the raw sugar, and keep stirring to dissolve the sugar. Once it is completely dissolved, turn off stove, and remove pan from heat and allow mixture to cool. Set aside.
5. In a large bowl, sift together the dry ingredients: flour, baking powder, baking soda, and salt. Stir in the pecan bits and vanilla extract.
6. Add the cooled down vegan buttery sugar mixture to the dry ingredients in the large bowl.
7. Sprinkle in the vegan chocolate chips.
8. Combine all the ingredients together by stirring thoroughly with a wooden spoon until well blended into a thick batter.
9. Pour batter into the square greased ovenproof dish.
10. Bake in the oven for 20 minutes.
11. Allow it to cool before placing in the fridge for about 1-2 hours.
12. Remove from fridge, cut into small bars, and serve.

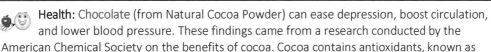

Health: Chocolate (from Natural Cocoa Powder) can ease depression, boost circulation, and lower blood pressure. These findings came from a research conducted by the American Chemical Society on the benefits of cocoa. Cocoa contains antioxidants, known as polyphenols, which is an ideal fuel for friendly bacteria in your digestive system
Beauty: Chocolate (Dark) helps reduce stress hormones, which means less collagen breakdown in the skin, and fewer wrinkles. (but to reap the benefits of Chocolate it must be natural cocoa minus the added sugar – some of my dessert recipes call for natural cocoa powder – so go ahead, indulge, and still be healthy!)

Chocolate Chip Cookies

I was always in search for the perfect vegan chocolate chip cookie – the ones I bought in the store were either too sweet and the rest had eggs or lots of preservatives in them! So I decided to make them myself and finally discovered the "Perfect Chocolate Chip Cookie"! Moist and delicious with just the right amount of sweetness...Plus they're organic without any baddies!

Makes 56 Cookies

What You Will Need:

2 Cups Unbleached Organic Flour
2 TSP Baking Powder
1/2 TSP Himalayan Pink Salt
1/4 Cup Vegan Chocolate Chips or Vegan Carob Chips
3/4 Cup Raw Sugar
3/4 Cup Organic Sunflower Oil <u>or</u> Organic Canola Oil
1 TSP Organic Vanilla Extract
1/4 Cup Filtered Water

Suggested Shopping List:
- Bob's Red Mill® Organically Grown Unbromated Unbleached White Flour
- Sunspire® Vegan Chocolate Chips

To Make Cookies:

1. Preheat oven to 350°F.
2. In a large bowl, sift together flour, baking powder, and salt. Stir in chips. Make a well in the center of the mixture, and set aside.
3. In a medium sized mixing bowl, mix the sugar, oil, vanilla, and water thoroughly.
4. Pour the wet ingredients into the well made in the dry ingredients. Once poured in, stir consistently making sure not to overwork the mixture so as not to break up the chocolate chips.
5. Spoon the cookie mixture onto ungreased cookie sheets.
6. Place the cookie sheets into the oven.
7. Bake at 350°F for 12 minutes.
8. The cookies are done when they seem a little bit softer than you want them to be. They will harden as they cool.
9. Allow the cookies to cool for about 10 minutes. Then slide them off with a flat spatula, and store in your favorite cookie jar.

Variation: You can add 1/4 to 1/2 cup of chopped pecans or walnuts for a nuttier cookie, just add them in step 2 after you stir in the chocolate chips

Chocolate Mousse Cake

I've made this cake for several birthdays and people always wow at its moist, delicious texture. It's not heavy like traditional birthday cake. In fact it's light, fluffy and oooh...so delicious! I want a piece of vegan chocolate cake right now!

What You Will Need for the Cake:

3 Cups Unbleached Organic Flour
1 Cup Organic Natural Cocoa Powder – full flavor and unsweetened
2 TSP Egg Replacer Powder
1 TSP Aluminum-Free Baking Soda
1/4 TSP Himalayan Pink Salt
8 Oz Organic Silken Tofu (or Firm Tofu – if you don't have Silken)
1½ Cup Organic Coconut Milk
1½ Cup Organic Maple Syrup (Grade B)
1 Cup Organic Canola Oil **or** Organic Sunflower Oil
4 TSP Organic Vanilla Extract
1/2 TSP Organic Lemon Juice
1 Cup Organic Vegan Chocolate Chips
1/2 Cup Chopped Pecans

> **Suggested Shopping List:**
> - Bob's Red Mill® Organically Grown Unbromated Unbleached White Flour
> - Ener-G® Egg Replacer Powder
> - Wildwood® Organic Sprouted Tofu
> - So Delicious® Organic Coconut Milk (Unsweetened)
> - Coombs® Family Farms for Organic Maple Syrup (Grade B)
> - Sunspire® Vegan Chocolate Chips
> - Follow Your Heart® Vegan Cream Cheese
> - Earth Balance® Soy-Free Vegan Buttery Spread

What You Will Need for the Icing:

1 of 8 Oz Carton Vegan Cream Cheese
1 Cup Organic Vegan Buttery Spread
1/2 Cup Raw Sugar
2 TB Peanut Butter (Optional)
 Or 2 TB Cocoa Powder (Optional)

To Make Cake:

1. Preheat the oven to 350°F.
2. In a large bowl, sift the flour, cocoa powder, egg replacer, and baking soda together.
3. In a blender or food processor, combine the tofu, coconut milk, maple syrup, oil, vanilla essence, and lemon juice.
4. Process until the mixture is smooth and creamy. If you are not using silken tofu but regular tofu, then make sure the tofu is well puréed.
5. Add this wet mixture to the dry mixture and using a hand electric blender, mix these together to form a smooth cake batter.
6. Pour the cake batter into a large well-greased baking dish (15x10 inch glass baking dish).
7. Bake the cake for 35 minutes.
8. Prick the middle of the cake with a bamboo or stainless steel skewer and if it comes out clean, the cake is done.
9. Allow the cake to completely cool, before icing it.

To Make Icing:

1. Place the vegan cream cheese, vegan buttery spread, raw sugar, and peanut butter (optional) or cocoa powder (optional) in a food processor with an S-blade or a high powered blender, and process until creamy and smooth.
2. Apply the icing over the cake with a rubber spatula.
   Note: make sure the baked cake has been cooled before applying icing
3. Decorate with sprinkles.
4. Place iced cake in refrigerator for the icing to set.

French Toast – made Vegan

Although French toast is traditionally not a dessert item, I have decided to put it in the dessert section because this version is so yummy – it almost has the sumptuousness of doughnuts! Thick slices of bread dipped in a tropically flavored batter made of bananas and coconut milk with a touch of sweetness and a hint of cinnamon and nutmeg, then pan-fried to perfection – completely egg-free, relatively low in both calories and cholesterol

Makes 10 large pieces

What You Will Need:
2 Organic <u>Ripe</u> Bananas (unripe bananas don't work)
1/2 Cup Unsweetened Coconut Milk
2 TB Organic Canola <u>or</u> Organic Sunflower Oil
1/4 TSP Himalayan Pink Salt
3 TSP Raw Sugar
1/4 TSP Aluminum-Free Baking Soda
1 TB Chickpea Flour
2 TB Organic Cornstarch
1 TB Nutritional Yeast
1 TSP Ground Cinnamon
1/2 TSP Ground Nutmeg
1 TSP Organic Vanilla Extract
10 Thick Slices of Organic Bread
 (only hearty bread works e.g. French bread, Italian bread
 (but they must be a few days old – soft bread doesn't work)
For frying: Vegan Coconut Spread
 <u>or</u> Organic Coconut oil

What You will Need For Serving:
Organic Maple Syrup (Grade B)
Organic Powdered Sugar

Suggested Shopping List:
- So Delicious® Organic Coconut Milk (unsweetened)
- Spectrum® Organic Canola or Sunflower Oil
- Chickpea flour can be found in Indian grocery stores
- Rapunzel® Organic Cornstarch
- Bragg® Nutritional Yeast
- Frontier® Organic Vanilla Extract
- Earth Balance® Coconut Buttery Spread
 <u>or</u> Dr Bronner's® Organic Virgin Coconut Oil
- Coombs® Family Farms for Organic Maple Syrup (Grade B)
- Wholesome Sweeteners® Organic Powdered Sugar

To Make French Toast:
1. Place bananas, coconut milk, canola <u>or</u> sunflower oil, salt, sugar, baking soda, chickpea flour, cornstarch, nutritional yeast, cinnamon, nutmeg, and vanilla extract in a food processor or blender, and process until mixture is smooth.
2. Dip both sides of a piece of bread in the mixture. Note: Don't dunk the bread, just lightly coat it on both sides – otherwise your toast will be soggy).
3. In a <u>non-stick*</u> skillet, melt 2 TB coconut vegan butter, gently place the dipped bread onto the flat skillet, and lightly fry it over medium heat for 2 minutes on one side – it will be light brown.
4. Then flip the bread over to the other side and cook for another 1-2 minutes until light brown.
5. Note: bread should turn easily when done.
6. Sprinkle with powdered sugar and enjoy with organic maple syrup!

Did you notice I mentioned to use a *non-stick skillet to fry the toast instead of a ceramic one? I usually don't like to use non-stick skillets but in this recipe the ceramic skillet didn't work well for the French toast – the same goes for frying tofu – so I sometimes resort to a non-stick skillet (make sure the one you use is PFOA-free though). I use Ecolution® brand – their products are PFOA-free

Mango Very Berry Crumble

This tropical dessert is low in calories, filled with anti-oxidants, yet you can still satisfy your sweet tooth and pack in a sugary punch! Layers of sweet mangoes, strawberries, and blueberries covered in a crumbly, crunchy oat mixture

Serves 6

What You Will Need:
3 Cups Organic Ripe Mangoes – peeled and diced
2 Cups Organic Strawberries – sliced with stems removed
1 Cup Organic Blueberries
1/4 Cup Organic Powdered Sugar
1/4 Cup Unbleached Organic Flour

 Use gluten-free flour or Arrowroot

2 TSP Organic Cornstarch

For the Crumbly Topping:
1 Cup Unbleached Organic Flour

 Use gluten-free flour

1/2 Cup Rolled Oats

 Use gluten-free oats

1 Cup Raw Sugar
1/2 Cup Vegan Buttery Spread

Suggested Shopping List:
- Bob's Red Mill® Organically Grown Unbromated Unbleached White Flour
- Rapunzel® Organic Cornstarch
- Wholesome Sweeteners® Organic Powdered Sugar
- Earth Balance® Soy-Free Vegan Buttery Spread

To Make Mango Very Berry Crumble:

1. Preheat oven to 400°F.
2. In a large mixing bowl, combine the powdered sugar, flour, and cornstarch.
3. Toss the mangoes, strawberries, and blueberries into the flour-sugar mixture.
4. Transfer the fruit mixture into a lightly greased 8-inch square baking dish. Set aside.
5. In another mixing bowl, mix the ingredients for the topping, flour, oats, and raw sugar and stir well to combine. Cut in vegan butter spread with 2 knives until the mixture resembles coarse meal.
6. Spread the mixture evenly over the mango/berry mixture.
7. Bake at 400°F for 35-40 minutes or until brown and bubbly.

 Serve the Mango Very Berry Crumble warm with your favorite non-dairy ice cream – I recommend So Delicious® Coconut Ice Cream – vanilla flavor

Health: Mangoes contain antioxidant compounds that protect against colon, breast, leukemia, and prostate cancers. These compounds include quercetin, isoquercitrin, astragalin, fisetin, gallic acid, and methylgallat, as well as abundant enzymes
Beauty: Mangoes can be used both internally and externally to give healthy looking skin – plus they are low in fat and can contribute to weight loss

Morning Must-Have Bars – Recipe 1

These breakfast bars are truly a breakfast of the champions! They are filled with healthy "must-haves" that will keep you satiated all the way until lunchtime. Plus they make an awesome snack too! They are very economical and quick to make (no cooking at all) and will save you a ton of time, money, and your health instead of store-bought granola bars. In the next few pages I show you how to make 2 different kinds

Makes 20 bars

What You Will Need:

2 Cups Gluten-Free Granola (your favorite flavor)
  Or Gluten-Free Rolled Oats
1 Cup Puffed Rice Cereal
1 Cup Puffed Millet Cereal
1/2 Cup Sunflower Seeds
1/2 Cup Pumpkin Seeds
1 Cup Raw Blanched Almonds
1/2 Cup Dried Cranberries or Raisins
1 TB Psyllium Husk
1 TB Dulse Flakes
1 TB Chia Seeds
1 TB Hemp Seeds
1 TB Ground Flax Seeds
1 TB Black Sesame Seeds
1/2 Cup Organic Coconut Oil
1 Cup Peanut, Almond, or Any Seed or Nut Butter (your choice)
1/2 Cup Organic Maple Syrup (Grade B)
1/4 Cup Vegan Chocolate Chips (optional) for garnish

Suggested Shopping List:
- Nature's Path° or Bakery on Main° Gluten-free Granola (some of their blends are not vegan e.g. "Summer Berries" so check the ingredients carefully)
- Arrowhead Mills° Puffed Rice Cereal and Puffed Millet Cereal
- Buy Dried Cranberries that are fruit juice sweetened rather than sugar sweetened I use Eden° Dried Cranberries which are apple juice sweetened
- Dr Bronner's° Organic Virgin Coconut Oil
- Coombs° Family Farms for Organic Maple Syrup
- Sunspire° Vegan Chocolate Chips

To Make Bars:

1. In a small mixing bowl whisk together, the coconut oil, nut butter and maple syrup until well blended. To aid blending, place mixing bowl in a shallow tub of boiled water. This will warm the mixture and make it easier to blend.
2. In a large mixing bowl, stir together gluten-free granola (or rolled oats), puffed rice cereal, puffed millet cereal, sunflower seeds, pumpkin seeds, almonds, dried cranberries (or raisins), psyllium husk, dulse flakes, chia seeds, hemp seeds, ground flax, and black sesame seeds with a wooden spoon.
3. Add the whisked mixture from the small bowl to the dry ingredients to bind everything together.
4. Keep mixing until the whole mixture resembles a large lump. Mixture should hold together when pressed into a ball. If your mixture is too dry and not holding together, add a little more maple syrup until the mixture sticks together.
5. Press this mixture firmly into 2 rectangular 6 cup glass baking dishes (8 x 6 x 2 inch). It is important to press it firmly into the dishes; otherwise your bars will fall apart.
6. Cover your dish with a plastic lid.
7. Place in the refrigerator for a few hours (preferably 24 hours) before cutting the bars and eating.

8. My bars can keep in the refrigerator for up to 3 weeks. I cut each batch into 10 rectangles and enjoy one little bar for breakfast.
9. Sometimes I make a double batch (by doubling the recipe) since they keep a long time (up to 3 weeks).
10. The bars taste great just as they are, but if you are feeling adventurous and wish to garnish them with chocolate, then once they have set, you can drizzle them with chocolate. See process below.

To Garnish the bars with Chocolate (Optional):

1. In a small saucepan, on low heat, melt the chocolate chips.
2. Drizzle the melted chocolate over the bars by dipping a fork into the chocolate.
3. You could also place cooled chocolate into a Ziploc bag. Snip one tip off, and then drizzle the melted chocolate over the bars.
4. Store granola bars in the refrigerator, covered.

Morning Must-Have Bars – Recipe 2

These bars can be eaten at any time of the day because they make a great dessert too! They are not as health-packed as Recipe 1 but are still very nutritious and make a dessert worth waiting for! Again, these too are very quick to make. This recipe is filled with chocolaty goodness for all you chocoholics out there!

Makes 12 bars

What You Will Need:
3 Cups Puffed Rice Cereal
1 Cup Puffed Millet Cereal
1/4 Cup Raisins (optional)
1/2 Cup Roasted Peanuts (optional)
1/2 Cup Vegan Chocolate Chips
1 TB Dulse Flakes
1/2 Cup Organic Maple Syrup (Grade B)
1/2 Cup Brown Rice Syrup
1/2 Cup Any Organic Nut Butter e.g.
  Peanut, Hazelnut, Almond
A Pinch of Himalayan Pink Salt
2 TSP Coconut Flakes
2 TSP Sesame Seeds
Organic Canola oil for greasing pan

Suggested Shopping List:
- Arrowhead Mills® Puffed Rice Cereal
- Dr Bronner's® Organic Virgin Coconut Oil
- Coombs® Family Farms for Organic Maple Syrup
- Sunspire® Vegan Chocolate Chips

To Make Bars:
1. In a large saucepan, on low heat, mix together maple syrup, brown rice syrup, nut butter, and salt.
2. Mix well until the mixture is smooth and creamy.
3. Add the chocolate chips and keep stirring on low heat until the chocolate is melted. Remove the saucepan from the heat.
4. In the chocolaty mixture, toss in the puffed rice, puffed millet, raisins (optional), roasted peanuts (optional), and dulse flakes.
5. Mix well until everything is well blended and the puffed cereals are well coated with the chocolate mixture.
6. Lightly grease a square glass baking dish.
7. <u>Firmly</u> press the crispy mixture into the glass dish.
8. Place the covered dish in the refrigerator for a few hours, until it has hardened and is firm.
9. Once the mixture has hardened, cut into squares and serve.

 So why are these bars so good for you? These bars are choc-o-bloc full of healthy ingredients; you will never find so many healthy ingredients in one single store-bought granola bar

1. **Low in Fat: Puffed Cereals & Raisins, Cranberries** – have very few calories e.g. 1 cup of puffed rice cereal is only 60 calories and 0 calories from fat. 1 cup Raisins has 0.2 g of fat and 1 cup Cranberries 0.6 g of fat. Plus these are gluten-free. Eating a diet that is gluten-free helps you lose weight quickly
2. **Beautify You: Sunflower Seeds, Pumpkin Seeds, Black Sesame, Raisins & Cranberries, Maple Syrup** – These ingredients are loaded with zinc, calcium, potassium, magnesium, and Vitamins C & E. All of which are great for healthy skin and hair
3. **Happy Foods: Sunflower Seeds, Pumpkin Seeds, Black Sesame, Maple Syrup, and Raisins** – They are filled with B vitamins which boost your serotonin and improve your mood and general feeling of well being
4. **Improves Your Immune System: Sunflower Seeds, Pumpkin Seeds, Black Sesame, Maple Syrup** – They are filled with Vitamin C and essential Amino Acids – all of which help you to prevent coughs, colds, and common infections
5. **You get Omega-3 & Omega-6 Fatty Acids: Raw Seeds, Nuts, Flax, Chia, and Hemp Seeds** – These are all a healthy form of fatty acids that help prevent heart attacks and provide vitamins, minerals, and fiber. Omega-3 and Omega-6 fatty acids are usually found in fish so if you are vegan, then eating nuts, flax, and chia seeds are a good source of these beneficial fatty acids
6. **Prevents Constipation and Keeps you Regular – Psyllium Husk and Flax Seed Powder** – Both are high in fiber and help you lose weight efficiently
7. **High in Protein, Calcium, and Vitamin B12 – Black Sesame, Dulse, Nuts & Nut butter** – plus since the bars are sweet, the dulse with its high mineral content helps to balance the sugar in our body
8. **Detox You Everyday – Flax Seeds, Chia, Hemp Seeds, and Psyllium Husk** – eliminating unhealthy toxins from your body everyday to help you lose weight, have healthy skin, and feel energetic
9. **You get the many Benefits of Coconut Oil –** easily digestible; doesn't put a heavy burden on your liver or gallbladder; restores your thyroid function, thus improves metabolism; lowers cholesterol; is an antibacterial and antifungal agent, hence helps prevent infections; and improves your brain power and memory, preventing Alzheimer's and Parkinson's

And now you know why I make my own granola bars!

Orange Glazed Muffins

When you are craving something sweet, these light and fluffy treats with their citrusy flavor and aroma will hit the spot. Plus your kitchen will smell like heaven when you're baking! Take them to a party and nobody will detect "no dairy" in these little cuties!

Makes 30 Mini Muffins

What You Will Need for the Muffins:
2 Cups Unbleached Organic Flour
1½ TSP Aluminum-Free Baking Soda
1/2 TSP Himalayan Pink Salt
2 TB Orange Zest *(Note: Be careful when grating the orange zest it's very easy to injure your fingers)*
3/4 Cup Raw Sugar
1/2 Cup Organic Orange Juice
1/2 Cup Organic Coconut Milk
1/3 Cup Organic Sunflower
<u>or</u> Organic Canola Oil
1 TSP Organic Orange Extract
1/4 TSP Organic Vanilla Extract
1 TB Organic Raw Apple Cider Vinegar

What You Will Need for the Glaze:
1/4 Cup Organic Orange Juice
2 TSP Orange Zest
1/2 Cup Organic Powdered Sugar

Did you know an orange is actually a type of berry called a hesperidium?

To Make Muffins:
1. Preheat oven to 350°F.
2. Lightly grease mini muffin trays or place mini cupcake paper wrappers on a baking tray. Set aside.
3. In a large mixing bowl, sift the flour and baking soda.
4. Add the salt, grated orange zest, and sugar and mix well.
5. Stir in the orange juice, coconut milk, organic oil, orange and vanilla extracts, and apple cider vinegar. You will notice the mixture fizzing up when you add the vinegar – this is normal.
6. Using an electric hand blender, thoroughly whisk all the ingredients together to create a smooth cake batter.
7. Pour the cake batter into the greased muffin trays or cupcake wrappers making sure to only <u>half fill</u> each slot or wrapper with the cake batter.
8. Bake at 350°F for 15 minutes. The muffins are done when a toothpick comes out clean after being inserted into the muffins. Make sure not to pull them out of the oven until completely done.
9. Allow the muffins to cool before glazing.

To Make Glaze:
1. Place orange juice, grated orange zest, and powdered sugar in a food processor or high powered blender.
2. If you like, you may want to add more sugar or orange juice depending on your desired consistency – the more sugar, the thicker the glaze; the more orange juice, the lighter the glaze.

 These muffins are yummy even without the glaze. You can eliminate it if you want to save on calories

 Health: Oranges contain high Vitamin C content, which helps prevent infections. They also support teeth and bone health because of the presence of calcium. They aid with constipation – an orange a day will literally keep "irritable bowel syndrome" away
Beauty: Orange's high content of Vitamin C helps your body to stimulate collagen which gives you younger looking skin; plus its Vitamin A content helps with acne prevention

Scones

English bread-like treats with a lovely crisp crust and a rich buttery flavor, light and mildly sweet – sliced in half and served with vegan butter and jam – perfect for high tea. So delicious that even the Queen of England won't be able to resist these vegan treasures!

Makes 12 Scones

What You Will Need for the Scones:
2 Cups Unbleached Organic Flour
2 TSP Aluminum-Free Baking Powder
1/4 Cup Raw Sugar
1/2 TSP Himalayan Pink Salt
4 TB Organic Canola Oil <u>or</u> Organic Sunflower Oil
2/3 Cup Organic Coconut Milk
1/2 Cup Organic Raisins (optional)

To Make Scones:
1. In a large mixing bowl, sift together all the dry ingredients – the flour, baking powder, raw sugar, and salt.
2. Add the canola <u>or</u> sunflower oil, and mix well with your fingers to create a crumbly mixture.
3. Pour in the coconut milk and sprinkle in raisins.
4. Knead the mixture with your hands to create a soft dough.
5. Roll the dough onto a lightly floured board to about 1/2 inch thick.
6. Cut the dough into large rounds or triangles.
7. Lightly grease a large cookie sheet.
8. Bake the rounds or triangles on a cookie sheet at 475˚F for 10-12 minutes.
9. The scones are ready when they look golden brown.
10. Eat them hot, cold, or reheated.

 Slice the scones in half, and serve with vegan butter and jam or marmalade of your choice and enjoy with a hot cup of your favorite brewed tea – I recommend Earl Grey Tea or Orange Pekoe Tea

Trifle o'Chocolate Fantasy

These little cups o'fantasy are easy to make and they are a real crowd pleaser. As soon as your guests lay their eyes on them they'll be ooh'ing and aah'ing. Make an impression with these beauties! Indulge in layers of chocolate orange cake, rice whipped cream, and chocolate mousse topped with crushed roasted peanuts

Makes 14 Mini Cups or 10 Larger Cups

What You Will Need for the Chocolate Mousse:

3 Very Ripe Avocados
1/2 Cup Organic Maple Syrup (Grade B)
1 Dried Pitted Date
2 TB Organic Natural Cocoa Powder – full flavor and unsweetened
1 TSP Organic Vanilla Extract
1/8 TSP Himalayan Pink Salt
1/2 Cup Pecans

To Make Chocolate Mousse:
1. Combine all the above ingredients in a food processor with an S-blade or a high powered blender.
2. Process all the ingredients until a smooth paste is formed. (about 5-7 minutes). Set aside.

What You Will Need for the Chocolate Orange Cake:

1 Cup Unbleached Organic Flour
3/4 TSP Aluminum-Free Baking Soda
1/4 Cup Organic Natural Cocoa Powder
- full flavor and unsweetened
1/4 TSP Himalayan Pink Salt
1/2 Cup Raw Sugar
1/4 Cup Organic Orange Juice
1/4 Cup Organic Coconut Milk
2½ TB Organic Sunflower
<u>or</u> Organic Canola Oil
1/2 TSP Organic Orange Extract
1/8 TSP Organic Vanilla Extract
1/2 TB Organic Raw Apple Cider Vinegar

What You Will Need for the Garnish:
1/2 Cup Roasted Crushed Peanuts
Rice Whipping Cream

To Make Cake:
1. Preheat oven to 350°F.
2. Lightly grease an 8-inch glass rectangular loaf pan. Set aside.
3. In a large mixing bowl, sift the flour, baking soda, and cocoa powder.
4. Add the salt and sugar and mix well.
5. Allow the cake to cool before slicing into small cubes.

Continued…

6. Stir in the orange juice, coconut milk, organic oil, orange and vanilla extracts, and apple cider vinegar. You will notice the mixture fizzing up when you add the vinegar – this is normal.
7. Using an electric hand blender, thoroughly whisk all the ingredients together to create a smooth cake batter.
8. Pour the cake batter into the greased loaf pan.
9. Bake at 350°F for 30 to 40 minutes. The cake is done when a toothpick comes out clean when inserted into the center of the cake. Make sure not to remove cake from the oven until completely done.

To Put the Trifle Together:
1. In a small glass, first place a couple of chocolate cake cubes.
2. Next squirt some rice whip on top of the cake cubes.
3. Top with a tablespoon of chocolate mousse.
4. Refrigerate the trifles for a few hours.
5. When you're ready to serve. Remove the trifle cups from the fridge.
6. Squirt the top with some rice whip.
7. Garnish the top by sprinkling with crushed roasted peanuts
8. Indulge!

 Instead of chocolate orange cake, you can use brownie cubes if you prefer (see page 135 for brownie recipe)

Sips & Slurps

Smoothies & Shakes

This next section is filled with yummy juices and smoothies; beverages that you can blend together in your own kitchen so you can enjoy delicious, healthy drinks without the extra calories and baddies of store-bought processed ones

To make any of the smoothies and shakes below: Place each recipe's ingredients in a high powered blender, and blend until smooth; you can add crushed ice to each of the recipes during the blending process to make your drink cold and delectable or enjoy as is!

Apple Pie Smoothie
Craving a slice of apple pie? Drink this instead and save yourself 100s of calories

What You Will Need:
1 Organic Apple – peeled, cored, and roughly chopped up with seeds removed
  Or 1 cup Unsweetened Organic Applesauce (if you don't have a high powered blender)
2 TB Ground Chia Seeds or Ground Flaxseeds
1 Cup Unsweetened Organic Coconut Milk
1 TSP Organic Vanilla Extract
1/2 TSP Ground Cinnamon
1 TB Organic Maple Syrup (Grade B)
Dash of Nutmeg
Dash of Himalayan Pink Salt

Pumpkin Pie Smoothie
Have a hankering for a slice of pumpkin pie? Drink this and take in all the holiday flavors without compromising your waist line

What You Will Need:
1/2 Cup Grated Organic Pumpkin
1/2 Frozen Organic Banana (peeled)
1/2 Cup Unsweetened Organic Coconut Milk
1 TSP Ground Cinnamon
1/4 TSP Ground Ginger
Dash of Ground Nutmeg
1 TB Organic Maple Syrup (Grade B)
  Or 2 Dried Pitted Dates

Orange & Kale Creamsicle
With this one you will be licking your glass clean – plus it's a powerhouse filled with Vitamins A & C

What You Will Need:
1 Organic Orange – peeled with seeds removed
1 Cup Kale leaves – with stems removed and leaves roughly chopped
1 Cup Unsweetened Organic Coconut Milk
2 TB Ground Chia Seeds or Ground flaxseeds
1/2 TSP Organic Vanilla Extract
1 TB Organic Maple Syrup (Grade B)

Continued...

Smoothies & Shakes (Cont'd)

Strawberry Dream Shake
This drink will take you back to the 40's the time of Malt Shoppes and jukeboxes

1 Cup Organic Coconut Water or Filtered Water
1/2 Cup Organic Strawberries – stems removed
1 Cup Crushed Ice
1/2 Organic Banana – peeled
1/4 Cup Raw Cashew Nuts (soaked for 2 hours before use)
4 pieces Dried Pitted Dates
1 TB Beetroot – peeled and grated
1 TB Organic Maple Syrup (Grade B)
2 TSP Organic Vanilla Extract

Caribbean Cooler
When you sip on this smoothie, it will transport you to island breezes and ocean waves…
Go on, take a vacation now!

What You Will Need:
1/2 Cup Organic Pineapple – cut into chunks
1 Organic Orange – peeled with seeds removed
1 TB Organic Maple Syrup (Grade B)
2 TB Raw Cashew Nuts (soaked for 2 hours before use)

Cure a Cold Charm
If you feel like you're coming down with something or are slightly under the weather, drink this concoction and feel reenergized

What You Will Need:
1 Small Organic Carrot – peeled
1 Small Organic Apple – peeled, cored, and roughly chopped up with seeds removed
1/4 TSP Grated Ginger
1 TSP Organic Lemon Juice
2 TB Organic Maple Syrup (Grade B)

Continued…

Hawaiian Fun in the Sun
If you like Piña Coladas, then you'll definitely like this mixture which will send you a-surfin'!

What You Will Need:
1/2 Cup Organic Strawberries – stems removed
1 Organic Orange – peeled with seeds removed
1 Cup Unsweetened Organic Coconut Milk
1/4 Cup Organic Pineapple – cut into chunks
1/2 Organic Banana – peeled
1 TB Maple Syrup

Mango Magic
It was once written that mangoes are the fruit of the Gods – give this one a try and transform into a God yourself

What You Will Need:
1/2 Cup Organic Mango – peeled and cut into chunks with seed removed
1 Organic Banana – peeled
1 Organic Orange – peeled with seeds removed
1 TB Maple Syrup

PBJ Sandwich Drink
Yearning for a treat from your childhood, a peanut butter and jelly sandwich? Well why not give this one a try and again save yourself the calories and fat from childhood indulgence

What You Will Need:
1/2 Cup Organic Peanut Butter
1/4 Cup Raw Cashew Nuts (soaked for 2 hours before use)
1 TB Organic Flax Seed Oil
2 TB Organic Maple Syrup (Grade B)
1/2 Cup Organic Strawberries – stems removed
1 Cup Unsweetened Organic Coconut Milk

Pom-Cherry Blast
Nothing quite like the tangy taste of berries and cherries tantalizing your tongue – uplifting you and blasting you with energy and happiness

What You Will Need:
1 Cup Unsweetened Coconut Milk
1/4 Cup Pomegranate Seeds
5 Organic Cherries – pit and stems removed
1/4 Cup Maple Syrup

Kombucha

Here's a health tonic filled with antioxidants, B-vitamins and Probiotics. This drink will bring vitality and energy to your life. Start with 1/2 cup everyday and then slowly work up to 1/2 cup 3 times a day for maximum benefits

What You Will Need:

1 Gallon Filtered Water

1 Cup Organic Raw Sugar

8-10 Organic Black or Green Teabags – my personal favorites are
   jasmine and oolong
   (Note: don't use any teas with added flavorings and oils e.g. Orange
   Spice, Earl Grey, etc – these will interfere with maintaining a consistent
   pH level)
   (Note 2: Mild tea e.g. jasmine, oolong, green tea give milder flavored
   kombucha and black tea e.g. English breakfast tea gives a stronger
   flavored kombucha

Large Coffee "Basket" Filters (#4 size – fit 8-12 cup coffee makers)

Large Rubber Band or String

1/2 Cup Starter Tea (Mature Acidic Kombucha from previous batch)

Kombucha mother or SCOBY (Symbiotic Colony Of Bacteria and Yeast)

To Make Kombucha:

1. In a large pot, mix the water and sugar, and bring to a boil.
2. Turn off the heat; Steep the tea bags in the sugar water mixture for about 10-15 minutes.
3. Remove the tea bags. Allow the tea to cool.
4. Once the tea is cooled to body temperature, pour the tea into a glass container. (Note: it's best to use something wide; kombucha needs adequate surface area and works best if the diameter of the container is greater than the depth of the liquid).
5. Add the starter tea to the cooled tea.
6. Gently place the kombucha mother or Scoby into the liquid.
7. Cover the jar with a coffee filter and secure with a large rubber band, and store in a warm spot (ideally 70°F to 85°F – on top of the refrigerator is a good place). Leave undisturbed to ferment for 3-14 days (depending on how strong you want the flavor to be – the longer you leave it, the stronger and more acidic the flavor).
8. After a few days to 1 week, depending on the temperature, you will notice a haze or white film that will form on the surface – this is another scoby forming. (Note: if you see green, black, or orange forming – this is mold – please throw away your kombucha. If you see a brownish color this is fine.)
9. Once it reaches the acidity that you like, you can flavor it with fruit or fruit juice.
10. Option A for flavoring: Add fresh fruit – slice up pear or peaches into your kombucha or add fresh mashed berries or pieces of crystallized ginger.
11. Note: If you are using fresh fruit, then you may want to let it sit on your counter bottled for another 2 days. A gas will build up, so be careful when opening your bottle after 2 days it may pop. Open slowly to carefully let the gas out.
12. Option B for flavoring: – Add store-bought organic juice to the kombucha – If you are using fruit juice, then a 20% fruit juice: 80% kombucha is a good ratio, i.e. 1 to 4 parts. You don't need to ferment any longer if you're using this option, and can drink it right away or you can let it ferment (if you want a more alcoholic taste). Then you can cover it with an airtight lid, and store in your fridge to enjoy. (Note: storing in the refrigerator stops the fermentation process – if you leave it out – it will continue to ferment and sour).
13. You can start a new batch and store your mature kombucha in the refrigerator. You will now have 2 mothers – the original you started with and a new one. You can use the old or new one in your new batch or you can leave the two together to fuse together to become a fatter mother.

 Before making this drink, you will need to obtain a SCOBY and starter tea from a friend or you can purchase it on the internet

Ancient Elixirs & Their Benefits – my Mother's Wisdom

Here's some wisdom of the ages that was handed down to me by my mother who learned these treasures from my grandmother, who was given this precious knowledge by her mother. So I am sharing with you recipes that have remained in my family for ages. I hope you will benefit from these as much as I

Carrot	+ Ginger	+ Apple	= Boosts and cleanses our system
Apple	+ Cucumber	+ Celery	= Prevents cancer, reduces cholesterol, and eliminates stomach upsets and headaches
Tomato	+ Carrot	+ Apple	= Improves skin complexion and eliminates bad breath
Bitter gourd	+ Apple	+ Any Non-Dairy Milk	= Prevents bad breath and reduces body heat
Orange	+ Ginger	+ Cucumber	= Improves skin texture and moisture and reduces body heat
Pineapple	+ Apple	+ Watermelon	= Helps dispel excess salts, nourishes the bladder and the kidneys
Apple	+ Cucumber	+ Kiwi	= Improves skin complexion
Pear	+ Banana		= regulates sugar in body

Carrot + Apple + Pear + Mango

= Reduces body heat, counteracts toxicity, decreases blood pressure, and fights oxidization of cells

Honeydew + Grapes + Watermelon + Any Non-Dairy Milk

= Rich in Vitamin C and Vitamin B2 that increase cell activity and strengthen immune system

Papaya	+ Pineapple	+ Any Non-Dairy Milk = Rich in Vitamins C & E, iron, Improves skin
Banana	+ Pineapple	+ Any Non-Dairy Milk = Full of Vitamins and prevents constipation

Bits & Bobs

Green Goddess Chutney p. 156

Vegan Mayonnaise p.162

Homemade Bread p.155

Tomato Chutney p. 159

Bits & Bobs

This is the section of the book where I have put recipes of things that I couldn't for the life of me find a place to put them in any other section. Here you will find recipes for homemade bread, sauces, fillers and many other miscellaneous things that don't belong anywhere else but here!

Coconut Chutney

This is a delicious condiment from South India which compliments anything with lentils. It also makes a delicious dipping sauce for any of the Indian appetizers in this book and you get the added health benefit of coconut!

Suggested Shopping List:
- Let's Do Organic® Shredded Coconut
- Bengal Gram Dal (Chana Dal) and Mustard seeds can be found in Indian grocery stores

What You Will Need:
1 Cup Organic Shredded Coconut (unsweetened)
1/4 Cup Organic Peanuts <u>or</u> Bengal Gram Dal (Chana Dal)
2 or 3 Fresh Cayenne Peppers
1 TSP Himalayan Pink Salt
1/4 Cup Filtered Water
1/4 TSP Black Mustard Seeds
Grapeseed Oil for cooking

 If you like a slightly tangy flavor, you can mix in 1/2 TSP of Organic lemon juice to the chutney

To Make The Chutney:

1. In a ceramic skillet on medium heat, in 2 TB of oil, roast the peanuts <u>or</u> Bengal gram dal until slightly browned and crisp (about 5-7 minutes).
2. In a food processor with an S-blade, place the coconut, chilies, roasted peanuts <u>or</u> dal, salt, and filtered water, and pulse the ingredients until you reach a thick paste-like consistency.
3. Heat the oil in a pan, add the mustard seeds, and cover with a lid until they stop spattering.
4. Season the chutney with the mustard seeds and oil. You can store this chutney in an airtight container for up to 1 week.

Chili Garlic Sauce

A work of spice that can be used in several dishes to create zesty creations or as a spicy condiment to add flavor to most any dish
Makes about 1 cup

Suggested Shopping List:
- Eden® Organic Brown Rice Vinegar

What You Will Need:
15 fresh red hot chili peppers (e.g. Cayenne or Thai)
  (if you don't want your sauce to be too spicy, then substitute a few red peppers with red bell peppers instead)
4-6 Garlic Cloves (depending on how garlicky you want the flavor) – peeled
1 teaspoon Himalayan Pink Salt
2 TB Raw Sugar
1/4 Cup Brown Rice Vinegar

 If you forgot to wear gloves and got pepper juice on your hands, use rubbing alcohol and dish soap on your hands to stop the burning

To Make The Sauce:

1. Make sure you wear gloves before handling peppers. Wash the peppers.
2. Trim off the stems and roughly chop the peppers. If you are using some bell peppers – remove the core and the seeds.
3. Put peppers, garlic cloves, salt, sugar, and brown rice vinegar in a food processor or blender, and process all ingredients until they are completely puréed.
4. Transfer the sauce to a clean sterilized glass jar for storage in the refrigerator. Will keep for up to 6 months.

Easy Peasy Home Made Bread

A very easy homemade bread which requires no bread maker or kneading

What You Will Need:

3 Cups Unbleached Organic Flour
1/4 TSP Instant Yeast
3/4 TB Himalayan Pink Salt
1½ Cups Warm Filtered Water
5 Quart or Larger Covered Pot
  Must be a big pot without plastic handles that can go into a 450°F oven: stainless steel, cast iron, glass, ceramic, or enamel

To Make Bread:

1. Place flour, yeast, salt, and warm distilled water in a large bowl.
2. Mix all the ingredients using a wooden spoon until the dough comes together. The dough will resemble an ooey, gooey, saggy blob.
3. Cover your dough with plastic wrap and let it sit for 12-18 hours. The longer the dough sits, the yummier your bread will be.
4. When you return to your dough the next day, it will be wet and bubbly.
5. Fold the dough a few times with a wet rubber spatula and form it into a circular ball.
6. Place parchment paper in the bottom of baking pot with sides of paper coming up slightly so you can later grab the paper to slide out your bread.
7. Carefully slide your dough ball into the pot.
8. Cover the pot and let the dough ball sleep for another 2 hours or more.
9. Place covered pot in cold oven and bake at 450°F for 30-35 minutes.
10. After 30 minutes, very carefully remove the hot lid with oven mitts.
11. Bake for another 15-20 minutes until crust is golden brown.
12. Carefully remove the pot from oven.
13. Either lift up the bread using the paper (caution: hot) or turn the pot over and the bread should fall out pretty easily.
14. Allow the bread to cool on a wire rack before cutting.

 You can re-crisp the bread in the oven at 300°F before serving
Store leftover bread in a glass container or a paper bag (not a plastic bag)

Garam Masala

An array of Indian spices that give flavor and festivity to many Indian dishes – several recipes in this book call for this spice mixture

What You Will Need:
4 TB Cumin Seeds
4 TB Caraway Seeds
2 TB Split Cardamoms (only the seeds with the skins removed)
2 Cinnamon Sticks
8-10 Whole Black Peppercorns

To Make Garam Masala:
1. In a ceramic skillet, in 3 TB of oil, on medium heat, roast the cumin seeds, caraway seeds, cardamom seeds, cinnamon sticks, and black peppercorns until slightly brown (about 5-7 minutes).
2. In a grinder, pulse the roasted ingredients into a fine powder.
3. Store in an airtight jar in the pantry.

Green Goddess Chutney

If Indians had a version of Green Goddess Dressing this would be it! A delicious blend of cilantro and mint to create a sweet and sour condiment that can accompany many Indian dishes

What You Will Need:
1 Cup Fresh Organic Cilantro – leaves chopped and stems discarded
1 Sprig Fresh Organic Mint – leaves chopped and stem discarded
1/4 Cup Organic Onions – roughly chopped
1/2 TSP Organic Ginger – minced
2 TSP Organic Garlic – minced
2 TSP Raw Sugar
1/2 TSP Himalayan Pink Salt
1 TSP Tamarind Paste
1/4 Cup Warm Filtered Water

> Suggested Shopping List:
> – Tamicon® Tamarind Paste available in Indian grocery

To Make Chutney:
1. In a small bowl, dilute 1 TSP tamarind paste with 1/4 Cup warm distilled water. Stir well until all of the paste is well blended with the water.
2. In a food processor, place cilantro, mint, onions, ginger, garlic, sugar, salt, and the tamarind juice that you just mixed, and pulse all the ingredients until you reach a smooth green paste-like consistency.
3. You can refrigerate this chutney for up to 1 week in an airtight jar.

This chutney makes a great dipping sauce for appetizers or can even be used as a sandwich spread

Health: Cilantro: has a detox property. It can aid your body to extract heavy metals and other toxins. It also can minimize or relieve the symptoms of some cases of autism which may have been caused by immunizations and heavy metal toxicity in the brain. Juicing 1 cup of cilantro everyday with other sweet fruits and veggies like apples and carrots can give the person suffering from autism improvements in 3 months (I learned this from a Chinese Herbalist in Hong Kong). *Note, any kind of detox should be done carefully and only on advice of your physician (see page 160 for a detox protocol)*
Beauty: Cilantro gives you healthy, young looking skin because of its content of Vitamins A & C which fight free radicals, preventing the visible signs of aging such as wrinkles, sagging skin, and skin spots

Sauerkraut – Raw

I cannot stop singing the praises of this precious recipe. It will bring health and vitality into your life – it can be used on your salad, and you won't even need salad dressing! For maximum benefits eat 1/2 cup to 1 cup with dinner at least 5 nights a week

Makes enough to go into 2 (64 Oz) half gallon glass Mason® jars

What You Will Need:

2 Small Head Organic Green Cabbages <u>or</u>
  1 Large Head Organic Green Cabbage
  – shredded in a food processor
  (pull off 2-4 of the larger outer leaves and set aside
  the whole leaves)
3 Heaping TSP Himalayan Pink Salt
2 Jalapeno Peppers (finely chopped) – Optional

To Make Sauerkraut:

1. Run the glass jars in your dishwasher. Use heat dry, and leave in the clean dishwasher until ready for use. Hand-wash the rings and lids and dry well to prevent from rusting – set aside.
2. Using your food processor shred your cabbage and place in a large mixing bowl.
3. Sprinkle the salt all over the shredded cabbage as you go. The salt pulls water out of the cabbage (through osmosis), and this creates the brine in which the cabbage can ferment and sour without rotting. The salt also has the effect of keeping the cabbage crunchy, by inhibiting organisms and enzymes that soften it.
4. Using your hands knead the cabbage to squeeze out as much water as you can.
5. Once the cabbage is all slushy looking, stir in the sliced jalapenos (optional) with a wooden spoon.
6. Remove the glass jars from your dishwasher and place on kitchen counter.
7. Using a pair of tongs fill the wide-mouthed jars with your cabbage mixture, tamping and packing down as much as you can allowing the water to submerge the cabbage. The tamping packs the kraut tight in the jar and helps force water out of the cabbage. (Recipe continued on next page)

 Health & Beauty: Sauerkraut

1. When eaten with healthy greens it is highly beneficial. The greens feed the healthy bacteria, so that they can flourish and build more probiotic colonies in your gut
2. You get the beneficial lactobacilli and enzymes that are naturally present in the vegetables, giving you a food that is rich in probiotics, enzymes, and minerals
3. When you eat grains or a dish high in protein or starches, the raw sauerkraut actually helps you digest it better, giving you more energy!
4. It is loaded with enzymes so it helps maintain our body's enzyme reserves. The more enzymes we have, the more our bodies have energy to rebuild our skin and hair and help us lose excess weight
5. Helps us feel full and reduce the cravings for sweets
6. Gives us healthy radiant looking skin

Continued...

Sauerkraut – Raw (Cont'd)

8. Fold the larger outer leaves into a tight roll or a wad, and place them on top of the mixture to fill that 2-inch space or gap.
9. Loosely close the lid. (Note: don't tighten lid or your kraut will explode!)
10. Place on paper towel or kitchen rag (since the liquid bubbles over and makes a mess on your counter) in a dark unobtrusive spot in your kitchen for one week – making sure to cover the jars with a towel so that gnats won't get to them. You could also store it in a cool basement if you want a slower fermentation that will preserve for longer – here the kraut can keep improving for months.
11. Check the kraut every day or two. The volume reduces as the fermentation proceeds.
12. You will see the fermentation process in 1-2 days as you see the mixture bubbling (good sign) which means that the healthy probiotics are teeming. Sometimes mold appears on the surface. This is called "scum". Skim what you can off of the surface; it will break up and you will probably not be able to remove all of it. Don't worry about this. It's just a surface phenomenon, a result of contact with the air. The kraut itself is under the anaerobic protection of the brine. Rinse off the lid. Taste the kraut. Generally it starts to be tangy after a few days, and the taste gets stronger as time passes.
13. I like it best after a week. Once you are happy with your kraut, open the jars, remove the outer cabbage leaves, and discard.
14. Tighten your lids, and place sauerkraut in the refrigerator (this slows down the fermentation process).
15. The sauerkraut will keep in your refrigerator for up to 6 months.

For your next batch:
We try to start a new batch before the previous batch runs out. You can remove the remaining kraut, pack the jars with fresh salted cabbage, and then pour the old kraut and its juices over the new kraut. This gives the new batch a boost with an active culture starter.

 Add other vegetables to your sauerkraut. Grate carrots for a coleslaw-like kraut. Other vegetables you can ferment e.g. garlic, seaweed, bell peppers, Brussels sprouts, turnips, beets, and burdock roots all do well – My mother-in-law says that if you put pieces of horseradish in your vegetable ferments they keep the vegetables crunchy and prevent them from going limp

 The good bacteria attack toxic sludge and loosen hard and encrusted fecal matter in your gut. Hence, when you first start eating fermented foods, you might experience more gas and bloating as you detox and the sludge becomes dislodged. This is temporary and it will pass

Tasty Tomato Chutney

When I first tasted this chutney at my friend's house, I was hooked. Not only did it taste great as a condiment but I was happy eating it as a main dish with rice, bread or anything so I went home recreated and revamped my friend's recipe, added a few things of my own and voilà – a new masterpiece!

Makes 3 Cups

What You Will Need:
3 Medium Organic Onions – diced
3 Stalks Organic Celery – diced
3 Organic Tomatoes
1 TSP Organic Ginger – minced
1 TSP Organic Garlic – minced
1 TB Raw Sugar
Juice of 2 Organic Lemons
2 TB Organic Dijon Mustard
1 Cup Organic Ketchup
2 TB Organic Shoyu Sauce

 Use Organic Tamari Sauce

1/4 Cup Raw Apple Cider Vinegar
Dash of Cayenne Pepper
2 TSP Himalayan Pink Salt
Grapeseed Oil for cooking

Suggested Shopping List:
- Organic Dijon Mustard
- Tree of Life® Organic Ketchup
- San-J® Organic Shoyu Sauce (Organic Tamari for gluten-free)
- Bragg® Raw Apple Cider Vinegar

To Make Tomato Chutney:

1. Blanch the tomatoes by placing them whole in boiling water for 1 minute or as soon as you see the skins start to detach themselves.
2. Immediately plunge the tomatoes in a large bowl of icy cold water with a spoon. (*Note: Be careful when handling tomatoes, they will be extremely hot*)
3. Remove tomatoes with a slotted spoon. The skins should come off pretty easily.
4. Sprinkle blanched tomatoes with sugar.
5. In a large skillet on medium heat, in 3 tablespoons of oil, sauté the garlic, ginger, onions, and celery until onions are translucent and limp.
6. Add the blanched tomatoes, lemon juice, mustard, ketchup, shoyu sauce (or tamari sauce), apple cider vinegar, cayenne pepper, and salt.
7. Mix thoroughly, then allow the mixture to simmer on a low heat for 15 minutes, stirring occasionally.
8. Remove the mixture from burner. Allow it to cool.
9. Pour the cooled cooked mixture into a food processor and pulse until all ingredients are pulverized into a smooth purée.
10. This chutney can be stored in the refrigerator in an airtight container for 1 week.

A Simple Detox Protocol using Cilantro

If you have been trying to detox for a while, but don't know how to start, here's a simple protocol you can follow. <u>Remember if and when you start a detox regimen, do it slowly, and never rush in.</u>
Note, any kind of detox should be done carefully and only on advice of your physician

What You Will Need:
Chlorella:
The Chlorella MUST be the kind where **"the cell wall has been pulverized"**. If you get a cheaper quality, it won't work and you'll risk your health and waste your money. If the packaging doesn't say so, then it isn't the right kind. Chlorella manufacturers who have taken quality to that level will state this on the package.

Raw Organic Cilantro:
The cilantro must be raw and organic. If it hasn't been grown organically i.e. *without* pesticides, fertilizers, etc., then it will not be potent enough to achieve the goal of detox. Organic cilantro is more fragrant and nutrient-rich.

Fresh Organic Garlic:
Garlic strengthens the body for the detox process. It should be fresh, and in clove form. You'll want to use a small clove if you're just making for 1-2 people otherwise it will be very strong. In the pesto, the garlic should be noticeable but tasty.

Salt:
Himalayan Pink Salt is preferred but Sea Salt is okay to use. Standard table salt should never be used in general as it scours the arteries, raises blood pressure, and offers little, if any nutritional value. With Himalayan pink salt, the body can detox without having any reaction to the salt.

The Process:
Start taking Chlorella for a few days – at least 3000mg before starting the detox regimen. Take it for a week before you start the cilantro detox. At this phase, chlorella can get heavy metals like mercury out of the easy to reach places – get the "low-hanging fruit" as it were. After a week, move to the cilantro/chlorella detox in the following paragraph.

1. Take Chlorella 30 minutes before dinner.
2. After 30 minutes, make a pesto of raw organic cilantro, garlic, olive oil, and salt (to taste) in a mini food processor. Eat right away. Start with about a tablespoon of the pesto per day and take for 3 weeks.
3. After eating the pesto you can follow it up with dinner.

Why this works:
The chlorella binds to heavy metals & keeps them moving out. Without chlorella the heavy metals may be re-absorbed into the body via the colon's enteric nervous system. The 30 minute lead time ensures that chlorella is in the right place to be effective when the toxins start to dump. Toxins can find their way to more dangerous places than where they came from, so it is important to ease into a detox protocol slowly.

Note: If you detox too quickly you may feel nauseous or even have diarrhea so be sure to take it slowly at first. After a few days of detox, you can begin to gradually increase the cilantro and chlorella dosage.

We adapted this from Dr. Klinghardt's Neurotoxin protocol which has all the details (http://www.klinghardtacademy.com/images/stories/neurotoxin/NeurotoxinProtocol_Jan06.pdf) Please read the protocol prior to performing the detox to ensure your full understanding.

Vegan Ground Beef

This recipe teaches you how to season and prepare delicious TVP crumbles – making your own vegan ground beef. It helps you to avoid the added preservatives and artificial flavoring that comes with store-bought vegan ground beef crumbles

Suggested Shopping List:
- Textured Vegetable Protein (TVP)
Suggested brands:
• Bob's Red Mill® TVP Granules
• VegeUSA® Vege Soy Chunks
- San-J Organic Shoyu Sauce
  Or Organic Tamari Sauce (gluten-free)

What You Will Need:

1½ Cups of Textured Vegetable Protein (TVP) Granules
Filtered Water (enough to cover all granules)
1 TSP Garlic – minced
1 TSP Ginger – minced
3 TB Organic Shoyu Sauce

 Use Organic Tamari Sauce

1 TSP Raw Sugar

To Make Vegan Ground Beef – ready to use in recipes:

1. Soak the textured vegetable protein (TVP) granules in warm water for 10 minutes.
2. Drain the water.
3. Add garlic, ginger, shoyu (or tamari) sauce, and sugar to the soaked TVP granules. Mix thoroughly until the granules are well coated.
4. Let the granules marinate in this mixture for at least 20 minutes. The longer they marinate the better they will taste.

 Did you know that textured soy protein (TVP) is made from soy flour hence it is a gluten-free food but if you buy store-bought vegan ground beef, do check to see whether they have added wheat ingredients

 Health: TVP lowers bad cholesterol and decreases thrombosis which reduces the risk of heart attack and stroke. It also prevents the body from free radical damage and boosts the immune system
Beauty: TVP has very few calories compared to ground beef. So it helps you stay slim.
Let's do a quick comparison:
1/2 cup cooked lean ground beef (90% lean) equals: 178 calories, 9 g fat, 4 g saturated fat, 70 mg cholesterol, 22 g protein
1/2 cup rehydrated TVP equals: 80 calories, 0 g fat, 0 g saturated fat, 0 mg cholesterol, 12 g protein

Vegan Mayonnaise

Here is a recipe for making your very own vegan mayonnaise – plus I have given you seven different variations for making new concoctions

Makes 1 half gallon sized jar

What You Will Need:
1/2 Cup Organic Soy Milk (unsweetened)
1/8 TSP Organic Mustard
1/4 TSP Maple Syrup (Grade B)
3/4 TSP Himalayan Pink Salt
1 Cup + 2 TB Organic Canola Oil
1/4 TSP Organic Raw Apple Cider Vinegar
1/2 TB Fresh Organic Lemon juice
1 TSP Zest from Organic Lemon

Suggested Shopping List:
– Eden® Organic Soy Milk
– Bragg® Organic Raw Apple Cider Vinegar

To Make Vegan Mayonnaise:
1. Place soy milk, mustard, maple syrup, and salt in a high powered blender and slowly mix all the ingredients on a low speed.
2. Gradually pour in the oil until the mixture thickens.
3. Add the vinegar, lemon juice, and lemon zest, and blend again.
4. Refrigerate before using.
5. Vegan Mayonnaise can keep in the refrigerator for up to 1 month.

Here are some tasty variations to just plain ol' vegan mayonnaise:

- Curry Mayo – Add 1 TB curry paste or curry powder to the mixture during the blending process
- Herb Mayo – Add 1 TSP of fresh or dry herbs e.g. parley, rosemary, basil, thyme, and oregano during the blending process
- Tartar Sauce – Add 3 TB of capers, 3 TB of gherkins, and chopped parsley during the blending process
- Quick Tartar Sauce – Add 1-2 TB of store-bought organic sweet relish during the blending process
- Thousand Island Dressing – Add 1/2 Cup organic tomato ketchup and 2 TB sweet relish during the blending process
- Garlic Mayo – Add 1 TB minced garlic to the mixture during the blending process
- Barbecue Mayo – Add 1/4 Cup organic store-bought barbecue sauce during the blending process

Dear Readers,

In the next section, I am going to share some information and recipes on how you can use food to cure simple ailments and how you can beautify yourself using things you will find in your own kitchen!

This treasure-trove of information has been in my family for generations. My great grandmother passed these tips down to my grandmother, who then imparted this knowledge onto my mother. I am so honored that my mother took the time to teach me her food secrets and precious family recipes. I have benefitted a lot from these home remedies, and so now I am continuing the tradition of passing these recipes on to whomever they can help. They are truly tried and tested but not scientifically proven to work. But I can definitely vouch for them since I have used them on myself and my family and have seen the results!

Health

Remedies

Health Remedies for Everyday Ailments

Note: Under each ailment there may be more than one remedy. You can choose any <u>one</u> option.

Bruises

- Apply a hot pack for the first day and then switch to an ice pack for the next few days if the swelling persists.
- **Option 1:** Drink an 8 oz glass of filtered water with 1 TSP ground turmeric mixed in to heal the internal bleeding.
- **Option 2:** Make your own turmeric capsules by buying empty capsules at your local health food store and filling with ground turmeric, and take 2 capsules per day until the bruising and swelling starts to subside.

Burns

- Apply toothpaste to the burn (this only works if it is a slight scald – do not use this method if the burn is oozing)

Congestion from Sore Throat, Colds, and Coughs

- **Option 1:** Dissolve 1 TSP Himalayan pink salt in 8 Oz of lukewarm filtered water. Gargle with warm salt water, making sure to hold mixture in your throat for 10 seconds with each gargle.
- **Option 2:** In a small pot, heat 8 Oz of any non-dairy milk (e.g. coconut milk, soy milk, almond milk etc.) until it starts to simmer. Once heated, turn off stove. Stir in 2 TSP maple syrup and 1/2 TSP ground turmeric. Drink this warm beverage for a few days to find relief.
- **Option 3:** Boil 8 Oz of filtered water with 1 TSP of freshly grated ginger, 1 TSP of black tea leaves, and bring to a boil. Once boiled, turn off stove. Stir in 2 TSP maple syrup to sweeten, and drink.

Crusty Eyes

- Soak 1/2 Cup of coriander seeds *(Dhanya in Indian)* in 1/2 Cup filtered water overnight. In the morning, put a few drops of the water in the infected eyes.

Cuts & Wounds

If a cut or wound won't stop bleeding:
- **Option 1:** Cover with ground turmeric and bandage it up. Within a few minutes the bleeding should stop.
- **Option 2:** Apply coffee grounds to the wound.
- **Option 3:** Apply a cut potato to the wound.

Diarrhea

- **Option 1:** Grate 1 TSP of fresh ginger, mix it with 2 Oz of filtered water and 1/2 TSP Himalayan pink salt, and drink it.
- **Option 2:** Drink at least 5 glasses of apple juice.
- **Option 3:** In a large saucepan, boil 1/2 Cup of white rice with 6 Cups of filtered water. Once the mixture comes to a rolling boil, turn off the stove. Allow the mixture to cool, and then drink this water.

Ear Ache

- Grate an onion in a small bowl. Retain the juice. In a small pot, heat the onion juice until slightly warm but not boiling. Place a few drops of warm onion juice into the infected ear.

Gall stones

- Prepare 1 Pint of extra virgin olive oil (no other kind will do).
- Prepare 1 Cup of freshly squeezed lemon juice (no bottled kind).
- Don't eat after 12 noon.
- Don't drink anything after 2 pm.
- At about 6 pm – get into bed (you can't get up once you start the process).
- Have someone help you measure and give you the liquids otherwise you will feel sick. Lie still or you will become nauseous. Don't mix the oil and lemon juice. Drink 1/4 Cup olive oil chasing it down with 2 TB of lemon juice. If you swish the lemon juice in your mouth, it helps to remove the flavor of oil.
- Wait 15 minutes, drink 1/4 Cup of oil followed by 2 TB of lemon juice, wait 15 minutes, then repeat.
- Continue this every 15 minutes until all liquids are consumed. At the end, if you have run out of oil but still have lemon juice, drink the rest of the lemon juice.
- Go to sleep. In the morning gallstones will pass out painlessly with your bowel movements. They can actually be seen in the water.

Indigestion

- **Option 1:** Chew on a few carom seeds *(Ajwain – Indian name)*
- **Option 2:** Place 8 Oz filtered water, 1 TSP cumin, 1 TSP freshly grated ginger, and 5 curry leaves in a small pot. Allow mixture to boil making a tea. Sip this tea slowly.

Kidney stones

- A bottle of Magnesium Oxide 500 mg tablets (60 pills) – taking one tablet a day will dissolve the stones.

Mosquito Bite Itch Relief

- **Option 1:** Rub a bar of soap or liquid soap on the bite – this will stop the itching.
- **Option 2:** Apply rubbing alcohol to the bite.

Nausea

- **Option 1:** Chew on a few carom seeds *(Ajwain – Indian name)*.
- **Option 2:** Chew on 1 clove.
- **Option 3:** Chew on 1 cardamom.
- **Option 4:** Chew on a few anise seeds *(Saunf – Indian name)*.
- **Option 5:** Suck on an ice cube.
- **Option 6:** This one is especially good for car sickness: Cut a wedge of fresh lemon, sprinkle it with a dash of Himalayan pink salt and freshly ground pepper, and then suck on it.

Ticks

- Soak a cotton ball with any cooking oil. Then hold the soaked cotton ball on the embedded tick for about 1 minute. This will loosen the tick's grip on your skin. Then carefully remove tick with tweezers.

Tooth or Gum Infection

- Dissolve 1 level teaspoon of Himalayan pink salt in an 8 Oz glass of warm (not hot) water. Allow the water to remain in your mouth, swish around your mouth for 30 seconds, then spit. Use the entire glass of salt water solution. If the infection is in the lower jaw, tilt your head back and to one side allowing the salt water to penetrate the sore. If in the upper jaw, use gentle force and hold it for at least 30 seconds. Rinse your mouth 3 times a day. The sore or ulcer will soon disappear.

Urinary Tract Infection

- Dissolve 1 level scoop of D-Mannose powder in a glass of filtered water. Mix well and drink.

Beauty

Remedies

Here are several recipes for skin care and beauty. From homemade beauty masks to facials and creams, all using leaves, grains, fresh fruits, and vegetables – each recipe passed down from my Great Grandmother

Almond Age Defying Cream

Almond oil prevents sagging skin and wrinkles if used daily. Mix almond oil with gram flour (chick pea/garbanzo bean flour), lemon juice, and coconut milk to make a creamy paste. Apply to your face and neck and leave it to dry for 20 minutes. Once dry, carefully massage your face and neck in circular motions to gently rub the paste off. Then wash your face with warm water followed by a splash of cold water.

What You Will Need:
1/2 TSP Almond Oil
1 TB Gram Flour (Chickpea Flour/Garbanzo Bean Flour)
1 TSP Organic Coconut Milk

Carrot Face Wash

Use this concoction to revive your skin – apply onto dry skin and wash off with cold water

What You Will Need:
2 Organic Carrots – finely grated
1/4 Cup Organic Coconut Milk

Lentil Mask

If you want to soften your skin, and remove blemishes, then use this – Grind the lentils into a powder, mix in the turmeric, add a few drops of lemon juice and coconut milk, and mix well to make a paste. Massage onto skin using small circular movements. Leave onto the skin until the mask feels dry. Then wash it off with cool water.

What You Will Need:
1/4 Cup Lentils (Turkish split red or yellow lentils work best) – ground into powder
1/2 TSP Ground Turmeric
3 Drops Organic Lemon Juice
1/4 Cup Organic Coconut Milk

Lettuce-Rose Astringent

If you have greasy skin, then this astringent is exactly what you need – Grate lettuce, soak the grated lettuce in rose water for 12 hours. Strain the grated lettuce through fine muslin or a strainer, and pour the liquid into a bottle with a tight-fitting lid. Apply to face with a cotton ball.

What You Will Need:
3 Leaves Organic Romaine Lettuce – grated
1/2 Cup Rose Water

Continued…

Beauty Recipes (Cont'd)

Melon Moisturizer
If you need some moisturizing and softening to your skin, then look no further – apply onto dry skin and wash off with cold water

What You Will Need:
1/2 Cup Juice of Melon (Honeydew, Cantaloupe, or Watermelon)

Oatmeal Mask
This mask softens and refines your skin. Make oatmeal, then mix in cultured coconut milk, and apply onto dry face. Leave it on for about 20 minutes and wash off with warm water.

What You Will Need:
1/3 Cup Instant Oatmeal
1/2 Cup Hot Filtered Water
2 TB Cultured Coconut Milk

Orange Peel Moisturizer
If you suffer from dry skin in the winter, and would like to keep it moisturized, then rub the inside and outside of an orange peel onto your skin

What You Will Need:
1 Organic Orange – peels

Papaya Antioxidant Mask
Papaya is rich in antioxidants, and its enzymes help to rejuvenate old, dry skin cells to give a glowing, healthy complexion – in a food processor or blender, purée the papaya into a paste and mix in the lemon juice. Slather the papaya mask all over your face, avoiding your eyes, and let it sit for 10-15 minutes. Wash your face with cool water.

What You Will Need:
1/2 Ripe Papaya—peeled, seeded, and sliced
1/4 TSP Lemon Juice

Rice Cleansing Milk
This mixture cleanses your pores and removes makeup – mix rice flour and cultured coconut milk, apply onto dry face, and wash off with cool water.

What You Will Need:
1 TB Rice Flour
2 TB Cultured Coconut Milk

Tomato Juice Skin Enhancer
Tomato juice taken both internally and externally improves our complexion. It cleanses our skin and closes our pores. Apply onto dry skin and allow it to dry on the skin for at least 5 minutes, then wash off with cool water.

What You Will Need: 2 TB Organic Tomato Juice

Other Quick Beauty Tips

Weight Loss

Avoid drinking cold water

- **Option 1:** Drink 1-2 TSP apple cider vinegar mixed in 8 Oz warm filtered water first thing in the morning.
- **Option 2:** Drink 1 Cup hot filtered water with 1-2 slices of fresh lemon slices squeezed in it after every meal.

Foot Care

Dry Cracked Heels:

- Mix 1 TB warm castor oil with 1 TSP ground turmeric to make a thick paste. Apply this with a cotton ball to the affected heels. Put some old socks on, and leave this paste on for about 1/2 hour. Then wash it off. Repeat this process for a few days and your heels will be smooth.

Hair Care

Falling and Thinning Hair:

- **Option 1:** Massage scalp with almond oil, leave it in for a few hours, then shampoo.
- **Option 2:** Massage scalp with olive oil, leave it in for a few hours, then shampoo.

Dandruff:

- **Option 1:** Massage scalp with olive oil leave it in for a few hours, then shampoo.
- **Option 2:** Cut a fresh lemon in half, and rub one half into your scalp making sure to squeeze the lemon half allowing the juice to squeeze out as you move around your scalp.

Skin Care

Pimple Cure:

- When you wake up in the morning, before brushing your teeth, apply your own saliva to any pimple that is just starting to form, and it will dry up very quickly. Smaller pimples just disappear!

Let's Talk A Little About Ayurveda

Dear Readers,

In the next section, I am going to touch on an Ancient Form of Healing called Ayurveda. Modern medicine is known as Allopathy, and is based on external knowledge and experimentation, while Ayurveda is based on inner knowledge and experience.

I am by no means an expert on this very diverse subject. I do have some important tidbits that I wanted to share with you which may help you in your day to day eating habits.

Let's call it a casual conversation on Ayurveda. Imagine that you and I are having a very interesting chat on Ayurveda while we sip our tea and munch on vegan snacks.

Satwic, Rajasic, and Tamasic Foods

Did you know that according to Ayurveda, all foods can be categorized into 3 types?
Note: non-vegan foods are listed here for information purposes only. We are not encouraging non-vegan food consumption.

Satwic Foods: are the balanced and moderate foods which are neither too hot nor too spicy. They sit lightly in the stomach, do not cause digestive disorders and enable easy elimination. They do not affect the mind adversely. On the contrary, they induce a state of peace and tranquility which are very essential for meditation and spiritual practices.

> **Satwic Foods** include: Some dairy, curd, ghee, sweet fruit, vegetables, dried fruit and nuts, wheat, rice, barley, millet, jaggery (raw sugar), green gram, Bengal gram, ginger, honey, coconut, coconut water, sprouting pulses, uncooked or half-cooked vegetables, greens.

Rajasic foods are those which are too hot, too spicy and too rich. They increase the rajasic nature of man and produce qualities like extreme anger, pride, conceit, egoism, arrogance etc.

> **Rajasic Foods** include: fish, eggs, meat, chilies, pickles, tamarind, mustard, sour things, hot things, tea, coffee, cocoa, white sugar, spices.

Tamasic foods are those which are stale, colorless, too salty, too sour, too bitter and twice cooked food. They aggravate the tamasic qualities like sleep, dullness and laziness and the baser qualities like desire, craving, etc.

> **Tamasic Foods** include: beef, pork, mutton, wine, onions, garlic, tobacco, rotten things, twice cooked food, stale things, unclean things, all alcoholic beverages, sodas and all drugs.

Greed – is fueled by leftover or overripe food
Attachment – is fueled by meat, eggs, dairy, pickles or very pungent foods
Anger – is fueled by chilies and spicy food
Lust – is fueled by fish, seafood, garlic & onions, dairy products, fried foods, sweets, eggplants, caffeine, tobacco
Pride – is fueled by meat especially pork, wine, tobacco
Jealousy – is fueled by stale, leftover food, garlic, onions

One should learn to eat in moderation. One should eat to live and not live to eat. Ideally the stomach should be only 3/4 full after eating; 1/2 with solid, 1/4 with water, and 1/4 empty. Such a habit of eating will not lead to health problems.

According to Ayurveda, the human body is a prey to 386 types of diseases. These are caused by 3 main factors that are related to physical health called Doshas. They are Vata (wind), Pitta (bile), and Kapha (phlegm). Wind is the cause of 80 diseases, while 84 diseases arise from bile disorders, and 222 from phlegm.

The Three Doshas:
In general Vata people have too much gas/wind/air in their systems, the Pitta people have too much heat/bile, and the Kapha people have too much phlegm. This is a vast topic and cannot be covered very extensively here but in the following pages I have formulated a quiz to find out what type of dosha you have, so that you can incorporate into your diet what foods to eat based on what type of dosha you have. Of course you could also be a combination of any three in which case you would read the description of all the relevant types.

Ayurvedic Quiz – What is Your Dosha?

1. Are you:
a. Of large build, prone to weight gain
b. Thin built, lower weight
c. Moderate built, moderate weight, muscular

2. Is your skin:
a. Cool and moist
b. Cold, dry, and rough
c. Warm and soft

3. Is your mind:
a. Calm, slow, and receptive
b. Active, restless, and curious
c. Intelligent and aggressive

4. When in balance, are you:
a. Loving and stable
b. Adaptable and creative
c. Courageous and clear-sighted

5. When not in balance, are you:
a. Unmotivated, lazy, and depressed
b. Anxious, nervous, and insecure
c. Frustrated, angry, and impatient

6. Are your finger nails:
a. Wide, white, and thick
b. Cracking or thin
c. Pink, medium, and soft

7. Is your stool movement:
a. Moderate or solid
b. Small, hard, lots of gas
c. Loose and sometimes burning

8. Is your forehead:
a: Large
b. Small
c. Medium

9. Is your appetite:
a. Constant or low
b. Variable
c. Strong or sharp

10. Are your eyes:
a. Wide or white
b. Small or unsteady
c. Reddish or focused

11. Is your voice:
a. Quiet or silent
b. Low or weak
c. High or sharp

12. Are your lips:
a. Large or smooth
b. Cracking, thin or dry
c. Medium or soft

13. Which bothers you the most:
a. Cold and damp
b. Cold and dry
c. Heat and sun

14. Do you talk:
a. Slowly or silently
b. Quickly and a lot
c. Moderately and argue a lot

15. How do you sleep:
a. Like a log; long and deep
b. Pretty lightly; I wake up easily and am quite restless
c. Pretty soundly, but usually less than 8 hrs

16. You've won a one-week vacation. Which of these options will you choose:
a. A relaxing getaway to a quiet, gorgeous tropical island.
b. A whirlwind tour of Europe. You like the idea of seeing and doing lots of different things.
c. Road trip, with camp equipment, backpacks the works to wherever you please. The roaming around is the fun part.

17. How good is your memory:
a. I'm a bit slow on the uptake, but once I get something, it sticks with me.
b. I'm a fast learner, but I forget stuff pretty easily.
c. I learn fast and I remember stuff (but only if I want to).

18. How deeply do you believe in things:
a. I have steady, long held beliefs and values; not much is going to change those because they are a big part of who I am.
b. I change my mind fairly easily; I don't think it's a good idea to be stuck in one mindset.
c. I'm very passionate about what I believe in and don't mind arguing with people who disagree with me.

19. How many dreams do you have & what type:
a. few
b. moderate
c. a lot

Ayurvedic Quiz Analysis

Kapha

If you chose mostly a's, you are a Kapha person:
Kapha people tend to have the most stable and grounded natures of the three dosha types. When balanced, they are as solid and centered as a mountain – consistent, calm, patient, and thorough. Good listeners and caregivers, balanced Kaphas are loving, peaceful, compassionate, and supportive. If out of balance, Kapha people may become controlling, greedy, and materialistic. When completely out of balance they become lethargic and lazy. Although Kapha people are slow to anger, their explosive rage is uncontainable when finally provoked. Kaphas make great friends and they feel depressed when nobody seems to need or want their nurturing nature.

Kapha types gain weight easily and are usually well-nourished and healthy. Once they learn something, they seldom forget it. Their friendly, open dispositions make them excellent managers, but their stable natures can lead to mental and emotional dullness.

Kapha people make good doctors, nurses, social workers, and teachers. Their patience, determination, and understanding make them excel at teaching and helping people.

Vata

If you chose mostly b's, you are a Vata person:
Vata people are like the wind. Their moods change quickly, and they often move on to new pursuits before finishing old projects. Generally, imaginative, exciting, and excitable, Vatas move at a hectic pace. When balanced, Vata types are often artistic visionaries. Idealistic and spiritual, they have a strong sense of unity and are often healers and teachers. A Vata out of balance may be indecisive, unreliable, restless, overly talkative, superficial, and anxious. If completely out of balance, Vata people can be fearful, secretive, depressed, mentally disturbed, and even suicidal.

The Vata body may be thin due to inefficient methods of expending energy. Vatas prefer warm climates, food and drink, and may become especially moody and anxious if they miss a meal. Lacking endurance, Vatas often need time to recuperate; they thrive on healing massage and total relaxation. A regular schedule can help dispel their anxieties and promote inner harmony.

Pitta

If you chose mostly c's, you are a Pitta person:
Like fire, Pitta people are energetic, dynamic and passionate – but destructive when out of control. They are known for their keen intellect, perfectionist tendencies and sharp anger. When balanced, they are the most intelligent, perceptive, and courageous of the doshas. Warm, friendly, competitive, determined and independent, they make good leaders, but may pursue their strengths single-mindedly at the cost of holistic balance and compromise. Out of balance, Pittas can be impulsive, ambitious, aggressive, dominating, manipulative, angry, and frustrated. When completely out of balance they can be hateful and vindictive – even psychopathic or criminal.

The Pitta body is usually of average build and good proportion. Pittas usually prefer cool climates, food and drink, and often have hearty appetites. When well fed and content, their natural heat creates courage and clarity.

General Ayurvedic Guidelines

1. Have your heaviest meal at lunch: between 10 am to 2 pm. This is the best time of the day for good digestion.
2. Eat light meals in the evening and never after 7 pm. Allow at least 3 hours between your last evening meal and the time you go to bed.
3. Eat only when you feel hungry – not when you are nervous or bored.
4. Do not drink cold water or iced drinks while eating. This reduces your agni (digestive fire) in your stomach which is essential for healthy digestion.
5. Be seated while eating and if possible face the eastern direction.
6. While eating do not watch television, read, do work, or talk about business. If you can, eat silently, and be as relaxed as possible.
7. Take a short walk after eating your heaviest meal.

Bad Food Combinations for all types Kapha, Pitta, and Vata:

1. Milk should never be ingested with bananas, melons, or yogurt
2. Yogurt should not be eaten with melons, hot drinks, starches, cheese, or banana
3. Melons should not be eaten with starches, grains, fried food, or cheese
4. Starches should not be eaten with bananas
5. Honey should not be eaten with ghee
6. Corn should not be eaten with bananas, raisins, or dates
7. Potatoes, tomatoes, and eggplants should not be eaten with yogurt, milk, melons, or cucumber

Kapha People - Foods You Can Eat

Fruit/Nuts	Vegetables	Grains	Beans, Legumes	Condiments /Spices	Oil	Drinks/Tea
Apples	Artichoke	Barley	Aduki Beans	Black Pepper	Corn	Juices From
Apricots	Asparagus	Basmati Rice	Black Beans	Chili Pepper	Canola	Allowed
Berries	Beets	(White Or	Black-eyed	Cilantro		Fruit
Cherries	Bell Pepper	Brown)	Peas	Garlic		Cinnamon
Cranberries	Broccoli	Buckwheat	Chick Peas	Lime Juice		Tea
Dried Figs	Brussels Sprouts	Granola	Red Lentils	Rock Salt		Cloves Tea
Peaches	Cabbage	Corn	Lima Beans	Sea Salt		Dandelion
Pears	Cauliflower	Millet	Navy Beans	Himalayan		Tea
Pomegranates	Celery	Muesli	Pinto Beans	Pink Salt		Ginger
Prunes	Hot Chili Peppers	Oat Bran	Split Peas	Herbal		Tea
Raisins	Collards	Dry Oats	(Green Or	Vinegar		
NO NUTS	Fresh Corn	Rye	Yellow)	All Spices		
	Dandelion		White Beans			
	Greens					
	Eggplants					
	Garlic					
	Green Beans					
	Green Chilies					
	Kale					
	Leeks					
	Leafy Greens					
	Mushrooms					
	Okra					
	Onion					
	Parsley					
	Peas					
	Sweet & Hot					
	Peppers					
	White Potatoes					
	Spinach					
	Watercress					

Summary: Kapha people should minimize dairy products, especially butter, buttermilk, cheese, ice cream, yogurt, sour cream

Also avoid food that is cold, salty, too sweet, or too oily

Kapha People - Foods You Should Avoid

Fruit/Nuts	Vegetables	Grains	Beans, Legumes	Condiments /Spices	Oil	Drinks/Tea
Avocado Bananas Coconut Dates Fresh Figs Grapefruit Kiwi Melons Oranges Papaya Pineapple Plums Watermelon All Nuts	Cucumber Black & Green Olives Pumpkin Sweet Potatoes Tomatoes Turnips Zucchini	Bread With Yeast Brown Rice Oats (Whole Or Cooked) Pancakes White Rice Rice Flour Tapioca Wheat Flour Wheat Bran	Kidney Beans Brown Lentils Miso Soy Beans Tempeh	Almond Extract Coconut Milk Mayonnaise Tamari Sauce Shoyu Sauce Apple Cider Vinegar Salt In Moderation	Coconut Olive Soy	Avoid Juices of all fruits on the "Avoid List" Too Much of any Juice Excess Fluid Dairy Drinks Alcohol Caffeinated Drinks Licorice Tea Comfrey Tea

Vata People - Foods You Can Eat

Fruit/Nuts	Vegetables	Grains	Beans, Legumes	Condiments /Spices	Oil	Drinks/Tea
Apricots	Asparagus	Basmati	Mung Dhal	Mayonnaise	Sesame	Juices Of
Avocado	Beets	Rice	Cooked	Mustard	Olive	Allowed Fruit
Bananas	Black Olives	(White Or	Tofu	Pickles		Chamomile
Berries	Carrots	Brown)	Cooked	Rock Salt		Cinnamon
Cherries	Cooked Garlic	Brown	Black	Sea Salt		Ginger
Fresh Dates	Green Beans	Rice	Chickpeas	Himallayan		Lavender
Fresh Figs	Okra	Whole	(Not Yellow)	Pink Salt		
Grapes	Cooked	Cooked		Yogurt		
Grapefruit	Onions	Oats		All Spices		
Kiwi	Pumpkin	Pancakes		Except		
Lemons	Sweet	Wheat		Caraway		
Limes	Potatoes					
Mango	Zucchini					
Melons (No	Cooked Leeks					
Watermelon)	Cooked					
Oranges	Tomatoes					
Papaya	Watercress					
Peaches						
Pineapple						
Plums						
Strawberries						
Tangerines						
All Nuts						

Summary: Vata people should avoid food that is dry, crispy, cold, frozen, raw, or stale.

Vata People - Foods You Should Avoid

Fruit/Nuts

Dried Fruit
Cranberries
Pears
Promengranates
Prunes
Watermelon

Vegetables

Artichokes
Bell Peppers
Broccoli
Brussels
Sprouts
Raw Cabbage
Raw
Cauliflower
Celery
Eggplant
Mushrooms
Raw Onion
Sweet Peas
White
Potatoes Raw
Tomatoes
Turnips

Grains

Barley
Bread
Made
With Yeast
Dry
Crackers
Corn
Pasta Or
Spaghetti
Dry Puffed
And Crispy
Cereals
Granola
Dry Oats
Oat Bran
Rye
Millet
Bran

Beans, Legumes

Avoid
Beans
Especially:
Black Beans
Black-eyed
Peas
Brown
Lentils
Lima Beans
Navy Beans
Peas
Pinto Beans
Soy Beans
Split Peas
(Green Or
Yellow)
White
Beans

Condiments/Spices

Raw Garlic
Green
Olives
Ketchup
Iodized
Salt
Caraway

Oil

Corn
Flax Seed

Drinks/Tea

Alcohol
Caffeinated
Drinks
Blackberry
Tea
Dandelion
Tea

Pitta People - Foods You Can Eat

Fruit/Nuts	Vegetables	Grains	Beans, Legumes	Condiments /Spices	Oil	Drinks/Tea
Apples	Asparagus	Barley	Aduki Beans	Cilantro	Coconut	Aloe Vera Juice
Apricots	Broccoli	Rice (White	Black Beans	Coriander Leaves	Flax Seed	Rice Milk
Avocado	Cauliflower	Or Brown)	Black-eyed	Coconut	Ghee	Juice From
Berries	Carrots	Peas	Peas	Curry	Olive	Fruits That Are
Cherries	Cilantro	Chick Peas	Chick Peas	Mint Leaves	Sunflower	On The "Can
Coconuts	Cucumbers	Brown Lentils	Brown Lentils	Basil		Eat" List
Fresh Dates	Brussels Sprouts	Dry Cereal	Kidney Beans	Cinnamon		Coconut Milk
Fresh Figs	Fennel	Granola	Lima Beans	Cumin		Cool Cow's Milk
Grapes	Green Beans	Oat Bran	Mung Dhal	Fennel		Milk Shakes
Mango	Kale	Cooked Oats	Navy Beans	Mint		Chamomile Tea
Melons	Cooked Leeks	Pancakes	Pinto Beans	Peppermint		Comfrey Tea
Oranges	Lettuce	Pasta	Soy Beans	Saffron		Dandelion Tea
Pears	Mushrooms	Rice Cakes	Split Peas	Spearmint		Hops
Pineapple	Okra	Tapioca	(Green Or	Turmeric		Jasmine Tea
Plums	Black Olives	Wheat	Yellow)	Wintergreen		Passionflower
Prunes	Cooked Onions	Wheat Bran	Tempeh			Tea
Raisins	Parsley		Tofu			Peppermint Tea
Watermelon	Sweet Potatoes		White Beans			Spearmint Tea
All Nuts	White Potatoes					Wintergreen
	Pumpkins					Tea
	Zucchini					Licorice Tea

Summary: Pitta people should avoid food that is too hot (in both temperature and spice)

Pitta People - Foods You Should Avoid

Fruit/Nuts
Bananas
Grapefruit
Lemons
Papaya
Peaches
Strawberries

Vegetables
Beets
Green Chilies
Eggplants
Raw Leeks
Horseradish
Hot Peppers
Green Olives
Raw Onion
Radish
Tomatoes
Turnips
Raw Spinach

Grains
Bread
With Yeast
Buckwheat
Corn
Millet
Quinoa
Rye
Too Much
Rice

Beans, Legumes
Red Lentils
Thoor Dhal
Soy Sauce
Soy Meats
Urad Dhal

Condiments /Spices
Garlic
Kelp
Ketchup
Lemon
Mayonnaise
Mustard
Miso
Pickles
Scallions
Seaweed
Vinegar
Allpice
Dry Basil
Bay Leaf
Cayenne
Cloves
Fenugreek
Marjoram
Mustard
Seeds
Nutmeg
Oregano
Paprika
Sage
Thyme

Oil
Almond
Corn
Sesame

Drinks/Tea
Alcohol
Banana
Shakes
Caffeinated
Drinks
Carbonated
Drinks
Chocolate
Drinks
Juices Of All
Fruits On The
"Foods To
Avoid" List
Ginger Tea
Ginseng Tea

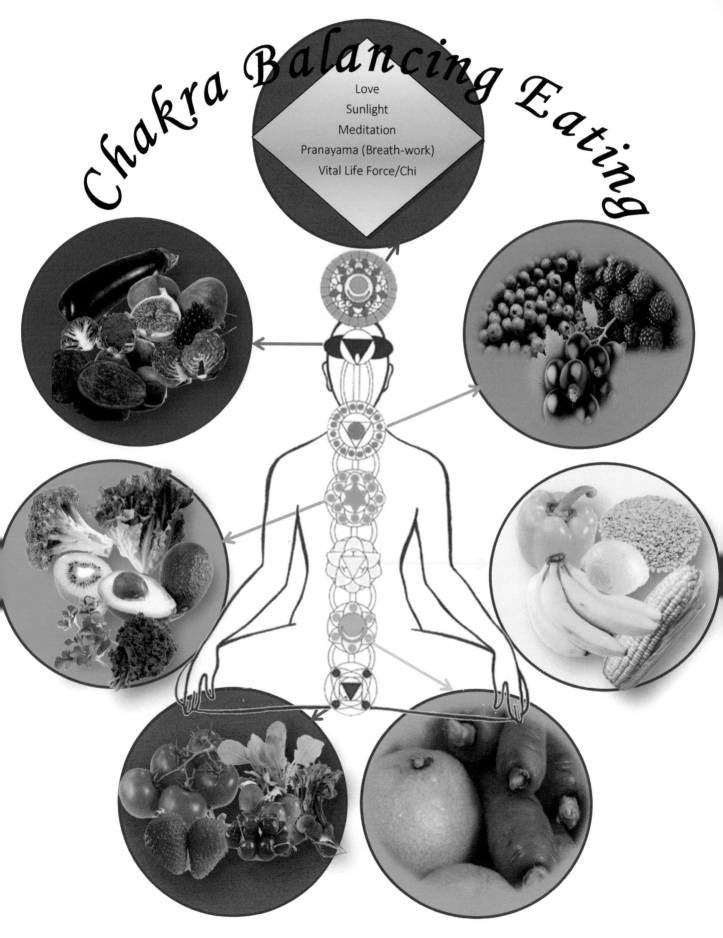

Chakra Balancing Eating

Love
Sunlight
Meditation
Pranayama (Breath-work)
Vital Life Force/Chi

What are Chakras?

Chakra (*pronounced chuck-rah*) is a Sanskrit word that comes from Ancient Hindu Scriptural Texts called the Upanishads. The direct translation of chakra in English is "Wheel". Chakras are located at the physical counterparts of the major plexuses of arteries, veins, and nerves. They are part of the subtle body, not the physical body, and are also the meeting points of the subtle energy channels, called nadis (*pronounced nuh-dees*). These nadis are channels through which prana or vital energies flow. They are not nerves, arteries or veins. Rather they are subtle and belong to the astral or mental body, and therefore cannot be seen with the physical eye. They can only be perceived through our finer senses. In most people some of the nadis may be blocked like windows in a room of a house that may not have been opened in a long time because that room has not been visited. As soon as you open the windows, the cool zephyr blows in and the musty smell and bacteria all disappear. When nadis are blocked, then chakras are also blocked.

One method of purifying the nadis is chakra balancing through the use of pranayama, or yogic breath exercises. This involves breathing exercises, repetition of bij-aksharas or root letters, and visualizing the colors of each corresponding chakra or energy center. You can find this method on our "Healing Meditations – You May Never Have to Visit the Doctor Again" audio CD available for sale on our website: http://www.soul2souleducare.org or on http://www.amazon.com

Another way to purify the chakras and create balance is through eating the right color foods that correspond to the relevant chakra. We are beings of color and light. The sun's rays fall onto the ground, and its energy is expressed through the color of the fruits or vegetables that grow in the soil. Each color holds an energy that nourishes our individual chakras.

Chakras interact with the physical body through two major vehicles, the endocrine system and the nervous system. Hence, each Chakra can be associated and govern particular parts of the body and its particular bodily functions.

Our endocrine system greatly affects our health and wellbeing. By adjusting the hormone levels, the endocrine system works to maintain the body in a state of optimum health.

Chakras are linked with the glands responsible for creating hormones. Each chakra's position thus corresponds to the positions of the glands in the endocrine system and hence affects their functioning.

This link between the chakras and our glands demonstrates to us that one needs to balance one's emotional, mental, and physical bodies (diet and exercise) to enjoy optimal health.

If a chakra is "open", then it is considered to be functioning normally. If a chakra is "out of balance" or "blocked", then it is not operating at its optimum, and thus can create health and emotional problems for us. In the Chakra Chart on the following page, you will see a column that reads "if the chakra is open", which states the personality traits related to an "open chakra", so you can clearly identify if your chakra is open. Similarly there is a column that reads "If this chakra is out of balance" and lists the personality traits of an under-active or over-active chakra, plus the health problems that can ensue from an unbalanced chakra.

By doing chakra balancing meditation and eating the right kinds of foods your chakras can start functioning normally so that you can live a life of optimum health and happiness! Start by referring to the chart on the next page to be able to identify what's going on and where you stand with your "chakras" and then refer to the menu to easily find recipes in this book to incorporate the different colored foods into your diet.

Chakra Balancing Chart

Name	Sanskrit Name	Location	Body Part it Governs	If this Chakra is Out of Balance:
Root Chakra	Muladhara	Base of Spine	Skeletal System	Under-Active: You feel insecure, ungrounded, fearful, nervous
			Back, Feet, Hips, Spine and Legs	unwelcome, and lost
				Over-Active: You will feel materialistic and greedy
				and obsessed with building security. You also resist change
				Health Problems: Anorexia, Obesity, Osteoarthritis
				Auto-Immune Disease, Arthritis, Cancer, AIDS
				Chronic fatigue, Spinal Column problems
Sacral Chakra	Swadhishthana	3 Inches below the Navel	Reproductive System; Excretory	Under-Active: You will feel stiff and unemotional, frigid; not very
			System; Sexual Organs, Testes,	open to people
			Ovaries, Urinary Tract, Bladder,	Over-Active: You will feel overly emotional all the time, emotionally
			Kidneys, Bowel and Lower Intestine	attached to people, oversexed, craving sensual and worldly desires
				Health Problems: Bladder problems, Frigidity,
				Gall and Kidney stones, Reproductive Organ problems e.g. Vaginal
				Cancer, Prostate Cancer, Pelvic Disease
Solar Plexus Chakra	Manipura	Behind the Naval	Digestive System;	Under-Active: You tend to be passive and indecisive; timid and don't
			Stomach, Liver, Gall Bladder, Spleen,	get what you want
			Pancreas, Upper Intestine, Upper	Over-Active: You are domineering and sometimes aggressive
			Back and Upper Spine	Constantly seeking power and control; egocentric and self-centered;
				Lack willpower; Overly ambitious
				Health Problems: Diabetes, Digestive / Adrenal organ illness,
				Hypoglycaemia; Upper back pain, Upper spine pain, Indigestion
Heart Chakra	Anahata	Heart Region	Circulatory System and	Under-Active: You tend to be cold and distant
			Thymus Gland; Heart, Lungs, Blood	Over-Active: You suffocate people with your love and you are clingy
				and overattached, smothering and demonstrate selfish love
				Health Problems: Cancer, High Blood Pressure, Heart Problems,
				Thymus, Blood, Circulatory System issues, Involuntary Muscles.
Throat Chakra	Vishuddi	Throat	Respiratory System and Thyroid Gland	Under-Active: You tend to not speak as much; probably introverted
		(Adam's Apple Region)	Throat, Thyroid, Mouth, Teeth,	and shy;
			Tongue, Jaw, Ears, Larynx,	Over-Active: You tend to talk too much; You are domineering and
			Pharynx	keep people at a distance. You are a bad listener
				Health Problems: Asthma, Neck Problems, Lung problems
				Hypoactive Thyroid, Throat issues, Jaw problems, Alimentary Canal,
				Teeth problems, Vocal Cord problems eg laryngitis, Ear issues
				Note: lying too much blocks this chakra
Third-Eye Chakra	Ajna	Middle of Brow between	Autonomic Nervous System and	Under-Active: You are not good at thinking for yourself and you
		Two Eyes	Pituitary Gland; Skull,	tend to rely on authoritive people. You may be rigid in your thinking,
			Eyes, Brain, Nervous System and	relying on belief systems and doctrines too much. You get confused
			the Senses	easily
				Over-Active: You may live in a world of fantasy too much. In
				excessive cases, you may be prone to hallucinations
				Health Problems: Glaucoma, Headaches, Neurological problems,
				Cerebellum issues, Nose issues, Pituitary problems, Issues with
				Central Nervous System and issues with Left Eye
Crown Chakra	Sahasrara	Top of the Head	Central Nervous System and	Under-Active: Not very aware "spiritually"; rigid in your thinking
			Pineal Gland; Top of Spinal cord,	Over-Active: You tend to intellectualize things too much. Addicted
			Brain Stem, Pain center and Nerves	to spirituality, while ignoring your own bodily and world-survival needs
				Health Problems: Exhaustion, Epilepsy, Cerebrum, Pineal Gland
				problems, issues with Right Eye

If this Chakra is Open	Color	Foods to Help Balance this Chakra
You will feel at home in situations, grounded, stable, secure. You trust people. You feel present here and now and connected to your physical body	Red	Root Vegetables, Eg Radishes, Red Beets, Parsnips, Red Potatoes, Red Onions, Rutabaga; Red Foods Red Apples, Blood Oranges, Cherries, Cranberries, Red Grapes, Pink/Red Grapefruit, Red Pears, Pomegranates, Rasberries, Strawberries, Watermelons, Red Peppers, Radicchios, Rhubarb, Tomatoes; All Dairy Products
Your feelings flow freely and are expressed without you being over emotional. You are open to intimacy and can be passionate and lively. You have no problems dealing with your sexuality.	Orange	All Seeds And Nuts; Orange Foods Eg Apricots, Canteloupe, Mangoes, Nectarines, Oranges, Papayas, Peaches, Persimmons, Tangerines, Butternut Squash, Carrots, Orange Bell Peppers, Pumpkins, Sweet Potatoes; Drink Lots Of Water
You feel in control, self-confident and have sufficient self esteem; You are constructively creative	Yellow	Yellow Foods Eg Lemons, Yellow Pears, Pineapples, Yellow Bell Peppers, Summer Squash, Corn, Acorn Squash, Bananas, Yellow Lentils Avoid Processed White Sugar For This Chakra. Eat More Complex Carbohydrates Like Oats, Spelt, Millet Or Brown Rice.
You are loving, kind, affectionate, compassionate and friendly. You work at harmonious relationships You practice unconditional love	Green	Green Foods like Artichokes, Asparagus, Arugula, Avocados Broccoli, Brussel Sprouts, Cabbage, Celery, Chard, Cilantro Collards, Cucumber, Green Beans, Kale, Lettuce, Parsley, Zucchini, Green Apples, Green Grapes, Green Pears, Honeydew Melon, Kiwi, Limes Cook with love, and infuse the food with this vibration
You have no problem expressing yourself; self-confident, You tend to be creative and express yourself in creative ways. You express yourself in a way that is authentic and true	Light Blue	Blue Foods eg Blueberries, Blackberries, Black Currants, Elderberries, Blue Corn, Sea Vegetables
You have good intuition, are clairvoyant, psychic, and spiritually inclined; You understand spiritual guidance and inspiration	Indigo Purplish blue)	Purple Foods eg Figs, Purple Grapes, Plums, Prunes, Raisins, Purple Cabbage, Eggplants, Purple Bell Peppers, Purple Potatoes, Purple Cauliflower,
You are unprejudiced and aware of the world and yourself, you are wise, and understand that you are one with the world. You have self-less love for all beings. You feel connected with your "Higher Self"	Violet	This chakra can only be balanced through Love, Sunlight, Meditation, Prana (breath work - Vital Life Force, Chi) and not through physical food

References

Appliances pg 10 – Cuisinart® Food processor, Vitaclay® Rice Cooker, Excalibur Dehydrator available at http://www.amazon.com
Vitamix® Blender available at Costco
Farberware® Mandolin Slicer and Proctor & Silex® Mini Food Chopper available at Walmart
Cooking Utensils pg 10 – Fagor® Pressure Cooker and Tools of the Trade®
Belgique® Stainless Steel Pots and Pans and Zwilling J.A. Henckels® 12 inch ceramic frying pan (Non-Stick Skillet) available at Macy's
Oxo® Julienne Peeler available at Whole Foods
Misto® Stainless Steel Oil Sprayer available at Bed Bath and Beyond or http://www.amazon.com

Health Food Suppliers pg 12
Himalayan Pink Salt – http://www.saltworks.us
http://www.vitacost.com
http://www.veganessentials.com
http:// www.amazon.com

Organic Whole Cane Sugar (Panela) – pg 13
Paper in Scientific Journal (1999) *Food Chain (UK) no. 25, p. 11-13,* Authors: Veldhuyzen van Zanten, C.
Paper in Scientific Journal (April 17 2012) *Health Effects of Non-Centrifugal Sugar (Panela),*
Author Walter R. Jaffé (Institution: Innovaciones Alimentarias INNOVAL, Caracas, Venezuela

Sucanat – pg 13
Journal of the American Dietetic Association (Jan 2009): *Total Antioxidant Alternatives to Refined Sugar*Authors: Phillips KM, Carlsen MH, Blomhoff R.

Himalayan Pink Salt – pg 13
Global Healing Center (May 15 2009) *The Benefits of Himalayan Salt,* Author: Dr Edward Group III DC, ND, DACBN, DCBCN, DABFM

Grapeseed Oil – pg 14
http://healthyeating.sfgate.com/grape-seed-oil-health-benefits-6827.html .Article: *Grape See Oil Health Benefits*, Author: Joanne Marie

Coconut Oil and Coconut Milk – pg 14
Book: *Alzheimer's Disease: What If There Was a Cure?* (Oct 31 2011), Author: Mary T. Newport

Flour should be Unbleached, Unbromated Flour – pg 14
Book: *The Staying Healthy Shopper's Guide,* USA (1999), Author: Dr. Elson M. Haas, MD.
Food Standards Agency, UK (1998) *The Bread and Flour Regulations*, p 6.
Scientific Paper: Department of Chemistry (2003) – Office of Science and Society, McGill University *Alloxan* , Author: Joe Schwarcz

Why is it important to eat Seaweed when on a vegan diet? – pg 15
Sea Vegetables retrieved from World's Healthiest Foods http://www.whfoods.com

What is the difference between all the Soy Sauces out there? – pg 16
Information retrieved from http://www.nal.usda.gov/fnic/foodcomp/search/

Water – pg 17
Book: *Ayurveda, The Science of Self-Healing* (1984), Author: Dr. Vasant Lad
Book: *Ayurvedic Yoga Therapy" (2007),* Author: Mukunda Stiles
Rhino Whole House Water Filtration system: http://www.aquasana.com
A good resource for understanding common water filter technologies is retrieved from http://www.foodmatters.tv/articles-1/what-water-filter-should-I-be-using

Organic Foods & Pesticides – pg 17
Organic Center State of Science Review: *Minimizing Pesticide Dietary Exposure Through the Consumption of Organic Food* (May 2004), Author: Dr Charles M. Benbrook PhD
The Organic Trade Association's 2004 All Things Organic™ Conference and Trade Show: *Organic Agriculture as Good Prenatal Care: Pesticides and Children's Health* (May 4 2004), Author: Dr Sandra Steingraber, PhD

What are GMOs and why should I avoid them – pg 18
Book: *Genetic Roulette: The Documented Health Risks of Genetically Engineered Foods* (Jan 31 2007) Author: Jeffrey M Smith
Book: *Seeds of Deception* (Sept 1 2003), Author: Jeffrey M Smith

Health Benefits of Broccoli: pg 22

Condensed from World's Healthiest Foods: http://www.whfoods.com/
Condensed from Dr. Mercola: http://articles.mercola.com/sites/articles/archive/2013/11/09/broccoli-benefits.aspx
Beauty Benefits of Broccoli: pg 22
The JHU Gazette: *Broccoli Sprout Extract Protects Against UV Rays*, Author: Nick Zagorski
Journal of Agricultural and Food Chemistry: *Broccoli (Brassica Oleracea Var. Italica) Sprouts and Extracts*

Health Benefits of Onions: pg 23
Condensed from World's Healthiest Foods: http://www.whfoods.com
Vegetarianism & Vegetarian Nutrition: *Onions are Beneficial for Your Health*, Author: Winston Craig, MPH, PhD, RD.
Beauty Benefits of Onions pg 23
National Center for Biotechnological Information: *Onion Juice (Allium cepa L.) A New Topical Treatment for Alopecia Areata* (Jun 29 2002) , Department of Dermatology and Venereology, Baghdad Teaching Hospital, Iraq, Authors: Sharquie KE, Al-Obaidi HK

Why Miso should not be boiled: pg 23
Dr. Weil on Anti-Aging, Author: Dr. Andrew Weil, MD.

Pressure Cooking is a healthier form of cooking: pg 24
Q&A Library-*Is Pressure Cooking Healthy* (Aug 28 2011), Author: Dr. Andrew Weil, MD.

Health & Beauty Benefits of Potatoes: pg 24
USDA National Nutrient Database for Standard Reference: *Potatoes, Flesh and Skin, Baked*
Harvard Medical School: Listing of Vitamins

Health Benefits of Tomatoes: pg 25
Tomatoes condensed and retrieved from World's Healthiest Foods http://www.whfoods.com
Scientific Journal of the National Cancer Institute (January 2002): *A Prospective Study of Tomato Products, Lycopene, and Prostate Cancer Risk*, Author: E Giovannucci

Beauty Benefits of Tomatoes: pg 25
Website: http://www.dailyglow.com/articles/46/tomato-very-useful-for-skin-care.html by Dr. Wu

Health & Beauty Benefits of Turmeric: pg 26
Book: *Healing Herbs: The Ultimate Guide to the Curative Power of Nature's Medicines* (1995), Author: Michael Castleman (reviewed by Medical Reviewer: Sheldon Saul Hendler, M.D., PhD., Biochemist, Researcher and Assistant Clinical Professor at the University of California, San Diego.

The benefits of Raw: pg 27
Book: *The Beauty Detox Solution* (2011), Author: Kimberly Snyder, C.N.

Health Benefits of Beets: pg 28
What's New & Beneficial about Beets condensed and retrieved from World's Healthiest Foods Website: http://www.whfoods.com
Scientific Journal of the Academy of Nutrition and Dietetics: *Whole Beetroot Consumption Acutely Improves Running Performance* (April 11 2012), Authors: Murphy M, Eliot K, Heuertz RM, Weiss E

Beauty Benefits of Red Wine Vinegar: pg 28
The Vinegar Institute Research News
Website: http://www.versatilevinegar.org/researchnews.html

Health & Beauty Benefits of Miso: pg 29
Dr. Weil on Anti-Aging, Author: Dr. Andrew Weil, MD.
University of Illinois – McKinley Health Center: *Vitamin B12: What Vegans Need to Know*

Health Benefits of Kelp: pg 30
Scientific Brochure: American Thyroid Association *Iodine Deficiency* (Jun 4, 2012), Website: http://www.thyroid.org

Beauty Benefits of Kelp: pg 30
University of Southern California Sea Grant Program: *Help with Kelp*
Book: *Healing Herbs: The Ultimate Guide to the Curative Power of Nature's Medicines* (1995), Author: Michael Castleman (reviewed by Medical Reviewer: Sheldon Saul Hendler, M.D., PhD., Biochemist, Researcher and Assistant Clinical Professor at the University of California, San Diego.

Health & Beauty Benefits of Eggplants: pg 32
Eggplants condensed and retrieved from World's Healthiest Foods Website:
http://ww.whfoods.com
ARS Magazine: *Scientists get under eggplant's skin* (January 2004), Author: Bliss RM, Elstein D.

Health & Beauty Benefits of Basil: pg 33
Basil condensed and retrieved from World's Healthiest Foods Website: http://www.whfoods.com
Book: *Healing Herbs: The Ultimate Guide to the Curative Power of Nature's Medicines* (1995), Author: Michael Castleman (reviewed by Medical Reviewer: Sheldon Saul Hendler, M.D., PhD., Biochemist, Researcher and Assistant Clinical Professor at the University of California, San Diego.

Health & Beauty Benefits of Tofu: pg 35
Scientific Publication Number FS792 by Rutgers New Jersey Agricultural Experimental Station Cooperative Extension: *Tofu: Nutritious and Versatile* (Aug 29 2003), Author: Dr. Debbie Zigun

Health & Beauty Benefits of Refried Beans: pg 36
USDA National Nutrient Database: *Refried Beans, Canned, Traditional Style 1 Cup*
Harvard School of Public Health Study: *Protein,* Website: http://www.hsph.harvard.edu/nutritionsource/what-should-you-eat/protein/

Health & Beauty Benefits of Lentils: pg 37
Lentils condensed and retrieved from World's Healthiest Foods Website: http://www.whfoods.com
Book: *The World's Healthiest Food* (1996), Authors: Anne Marshall, Carolyn Kelly

Health & Beauty Benefits of Avocados: pg 39
Avocados condensed and retrieved from World's Healthiest Foods Website: http://www.whfoods.com
Book: *The World's Healthiest Food* (1996), Authors: Anne Marshall, Carolyn Kelly

Health & Beauty Benefits of Kale: pg 41
What's New & Beneficial about Kale condensed and retrieved from World's Healthiest Foods Website: http://www.whfoods.com
Book: *The World's Healthiest Food* (1996), Authors: Anne Marshall, Carolyn Kelly

Reasons for eating more raw food: pg 42
Article in Zen Habits: *10 Reasons Eating Raw is Healthier For You and the Planet* (Jan 29 2009), Author: Jonathan Mead (Editor of Illuminated Minds Magazine)

The History of Kati Roll: pg 43
Website: http://thekatihouse.com/history-of-kati-roll/

Why skins of almonds should be removed before eating: pg 45
Book: *The Body Ecology Diet Book* (June 15 2011), Author: Donna Gates

Health & Beauty Benefits of Chickpea Flour/Gram Flour/Besan: pg 46
Website: http://www.stylecraze.com/articles/benefits-of-besangram-flour-for-skin-and-hair/#
10 Best Benefits Of Besan/ Gram Flour For Skin And Hair (Dec 24 2013), Author: Ankita

Why potato peels are alkaline forming: pg 47
Book: *Alkalize or Die* (December 1, 1991), Author: Dr. Theodore A. Baroody

Health & Beauty Benefits of Salsa: pg 48
Alabama Cooperative Extension; *Health Benefits of Tomatoes* (June 28, 2006), Author: Researcher Cheryl Vasse
USDA National Nutrient Database for Standard Reference: *Tomatoes, Cilantro and Peppers*
Book: *Healing Herbs: The Ultimate Guide to the Curative Power of Nature's Medicines* (1995), Author: Michael Castleman (reviewed by Medical Reviewer: Sheldon Saul Hendler, M.D., PhD., Biochemist, Researcher and Assistant Clinical Professor at the University of California, San Diego.

Health & Beauty Benefits of Spinach: pg 50
What's New & Beneficial about Spinach condensed and retrieved from World's Healthiest Foods Website: http://www.whfoods.com
Book: *The World's Healthiest Food* (1996), Authors: Anne Marshall, Carolyn Kelly

Oil Sprayer instead of store-bought PAM®: pg 51
Misto® Stainless Steel Oil Sprayer available at Bed Bath and Beyond or http://www.amazon.com

Health & Beauty Benefits of Carrots & Cabbages: pg 53
Website: http://foodfacts.mercola.com/carrot.html *What are Carrots Good For*
Website: http://foodfacts.mercola.com/cabbage.html *What is Cabbage Good For*
Book: *The World's Healthiest Food* (1996), Authors: Anne Marshall, Carolyn Kelly

Health & Beauty Benefits of Sushi: pg 56
Sea Vegetables retrieved from World's Healthiest Foods http://www.whfoods.com
The History of Sushi: pg 56

Website: http://www.pbs.org/food/the-history-kitchen/history-of-sushi/ *Discover the History of Sushi* (September 5, 2012), Author: Tori Avey

Health & Beauty Benefits of Beets: pg 58
What's New & Beneficial about Beets condensed and retrieved from World's Healthiest Foods Website: http://www.whfoods.com
Book: *The World's Healthiest Food* (1996), Authors: Anne Marshall, Carolyn Kelly

Health & Beauty Benefits of Millet: pg 59
Indian Journal of Biochemistry and Biophysics: *Antioxidant Activity of Commonly Consumed Cereals, Millet* (Feb 2009), Authors: Sreeramulu D, Reddy CV, Raghunath M.
Millet condensed and retrieved from World's Healthiest Foods Website: http://www.whfoods.com

Health & Beauty Benefits of Pineapple: pg 60
University of Maryland Medical Center: *Bromelain* (March 14, 2009), Author: Dr. Steven D. Ehrlich, NMD
Pineapple condensed and retrieved from World's Healthiest Foods Website: http://www.whfoods.com
History of Pineapple: pg 60
Website: History of the Pineapple by Dole Plantation: http://www.dole-plantation.com/History-of-the-Pineapple

Potatoes & Sweet Potatoes don't come from the same family: pg 61
Potatoes: United States Department of Agriculture, Germplasm Resources Information Network: *Solanum L* (Jan 9 2009)
Sweet Potatoes: United States Department of Agriculture, Germplasm Resources Information Network: *Convolvulaceae tribe Cuscuteae* (April 13 2009)

The benefits of Probiotics: pg 62
Book: *The Beauty Detox Solution* (2011), Author: Kimberly Snyder, C.N.

Difference between Mirin & Rice Wine Vinegar: pg 63
Cooks Thesaurus: http://www.foodsubs.com
Eden Foods: http://www.edenfoods.com

Health & Beauty Benefits of Wakame – pg 63
Sea Vegetables retrieved from World's Healthiest Foods http://www.whfoods.com
Comparison between TVP and Ground Beef – pg 65
Results from website: http://www.calorieking.com

Health & Beauty Benefits of Cumin, Caraway and Anise Seeds – pg 67
Book: *Healing Herbs: The Ultimate Guide to the Curative Power of Nature's Medicines* (1995), Author: Michael Castleman (reviewed by Medical Reviewer: Sheldon Saul Hendler, M.D., PhD., Biochemist, Researcher and Assistant Clinical Professor at the University of California, San Diego.

Health & Beauty Benefits of Tulsi (Holy Basil) – pg 68
Book: *Healing Herbs: The Ultimate Guide to the Curative Power of Nature's Medicines* (1995), Author: Michael Castleman (reviewed by Medical Reviewer: Sheldon Saul Hendler, M.D., PhD., Biochemist, Researcher and Assistant Clinical Professor at the University of California, San Diego.

Health Benefits of Collard Greens – pg 69
USDA National Nutrient Database
Collard Greens are the Food of the Week condensed and retrieved from World's Healthiest Foods Website:
http://www.whfoods.com
Beauty Benefits of Collard Greens – pg 69
Book: *The Beauty Detox Solution* (2011), Author: Kimberly Snyder, C.N.

Health & Beauty Benefits of Dulse – pg 70
Sea Vegetables retrieved from World's Healthiest Foods http://www.whfoods.com

Health & Beauty Benefits of Sprouts – pg 71
Book: *The Sprouting Book* (1986), Author: Ann Wigmore

Where does the fishy taste come from in Vegan Fish Filets – pg 72
http://store.veganessentials.com/meat-alternatives-c67.aspx
http://store.veganessentials.com/oceans-delight-vegan-fish-patties-by-ecovegan-p3148.asp

History of Pita Bread – pg 74
Shamsane Pita Bakery in Canada website: http://www.shamsane.com/history.html

Health & Beauty Benefits of Pita Bread – pg 74

USDA National Nutrient Database
Article: Fitness Magazine *Power Up Your Diet "Whole Wheat Pitas"* (Aug 2013), Author: Camille Noe Pagan

Health & Beauty Benefits of Seitan – pg 75
Website: http://www.bobsredmill.com/vital-wheat-gluten.html
Book: *Healthwise for Life* (1992), Authors: Molly Mettler, MSW and Donald Kemper, MPH

Why too much soy should be avoided – pg 76
Article: *Soy Bad, Soy Good: The Pluses of Fermented Soy* (Aug 4 2004)
Website: http://articles.mercola.com/sites/articles/archive/2004/08/04/fermented-soy.aspx
Well Being Journal Vol. 11, No.6
Contra Costa Times July 14, 2004

Health & Beauty Benefits of Tempeh – pg 77
Journal of Food Science, Vol. 35, issue 5, 25: *Studies on the Nutritional Value of Tempeh* (Aug 2006), Authors: Kiku Murata, Hideo Ikehata, Teijiro Miyamata
Journal of Food Science, Vol. 28, issue 4, 10: *The pytate and phytase of soybean tempeh* (May 2006)
Authors: Slamet Sudarmadji, Pericles Markakis
Journal of Food Science, Vol 50, issue 1: *Reduction in phytic acid levels in soybeans during tempeh production, storage, and frying* (25 Aug 2006), Author: Sutari K.A. Buckle

Names of Adzuki Beans – pg 80
Health & Beauty Benefits of Adzuki Beans – pg 80
Book: *The World's Healthiest Food* (1996), Authors: Anne Marshall, Carolyn Kelly

Why we retain the cooked asparagus water – pg 81
Cooking and Nutrient Loss retrieved from World's Healthiest Foods http://www.whfoods.com
Health & Beauty Benefits of Asparagus – pg 81
Book: *The World's Healthiest Food* (1996), Authors: Anne Marshall, Carolyn Kelly
Asparagus condensed and retrieved from World's Healthiest Foods Website: http://www.whfoods.com

Rendang voted No. 1 dish on CNN Online Poll – pg 83
Website: http://travel.cnn.com/explorations/eat/readers-choice-worlds-50-most-delicious-foods-012321 *Your pick: World's 50 best foods* (Sept 7 2012), Author: Tim Cheung

Brown Rice Pasta has lower cholesterol than Regular Pasta – pg 84
Scientific Report – University of Massachusetts Medical School: *Healthy Heart – What you can do to LOWER your TRIGLYCERIDES?*
Website: http://www.umassmed.edu/healthyheart/tipsheets/triglycerides.aspx

Health & Beauty Benefits of Black Eyed Peas – pg 85
Article *Health Benefits of Black Eyed Peas* – condensed and retrieved from
Website: http://www.livestrong.com/article/414892-health-benefits-of-black-eyed-peas/

Health & Beauty Benefits of Celery – pg 87
What's New & Beneficial about Celery condensed and retrieved from World's Healthiest Foods Website: http://www.whfoods.com
Book: *Healing Herbs: The Ultimate Guide to the Curative Power of Nature's Medicines* (1995), Author: Michael Castleman (reviewed by Medical Reviewer: Sheldon Saul Hendler, M.D., PhD., Biochemist, Researcher and Assistant Clinical Professor at the University of California, San Diego.

What is the difference between mai fun (rice noodles) and sai fun (cellophane noodles) – pg 89
Book: *The World's Healthiest Food* (1996), Authors: Anne Marshall, Carolyn Kelly

Health & Beauty Benefits of Curry – pg 89
Book: *Healing Herbs: The Ultimate Guide to the Curative Power of Nature's Medicines* (1995), Author: Michael Castleman (reviewed by Medical Reviewer: Sheldon Saul Hendler, M.D., PhD., Biochemist, Researcher and Assistant Clinical Professor at the University of California, San Diego.

History of the Pie – pg 90
Book: *A child`s history of England (1851)* Author: Charles Dickens
Book: *An Anonymous Andalusian Cookbook of the Thirteenth Century* Author: Charles Perry
Translation, published in *A Collection of Medieval and Renaissance Cookbooks* (1987), Author: Duke Sir Cariadoc of the Bow

Eggplant genus – pg 91
Eggplants: United States Department of Agriculture, Germplasm Resources Information Network: *Solanum melongena* (Dec 2 2010)

Facts about Szechuan Cooking – pg 92

Book: *Land of Plenty: A Treasury of Authentic Sichuan Cooking* (June 2003), Author: Fuchsia Dunlop

Why we should buy canned foods that are BPA-free – pg 98
FDA Report: Bisphenol A (BPA): Use in Food Contact Application (March 2013),
Website: http://www.fda.gov/newsevents/publichealthfocus/ucm064437.htm
Book: *The Staying Healthy Shopper's Guide,* USA (1999), Author: Dr. Elson M. Haas, MD
Scientific Report by European Food Safety Authority: *Toxicokinetics of Bisphenol A, Scientific Opinion of the Panel on Food additives, Flavourings, Processing aids and Materials in Contact with Food* (9 July 2008)

Halloween Facts – pg 100
History Channel Website: http://www.history.com/topics/halloween
Health & Beauty Benefits of Corn – pg 100
Corn condensed and retrieved from World's Healthiest Foods http://www.whfoods.com

Health & Beauty Benefits of Chilis – pg 102
Book: *Healing Herbs: The Ultimate Guide to the Curative Power of Nature's Medicines* (1995), Author: Michael Castleman (reviewed by Medical Reviewer: Sheldon Saul Hendler, M.D., PhD., Biochemist, Researcher and Assistant Clinical Professor at the University of California, San Diego.

The History of Macaroni & Cheese – pg 103
Original Manuscript of Ancient English Cookery: *The Forme of Cury* (1390 AD), Compiled by the Master-Cooks of King Richard II, Presented afterwards to Queen Elizabeth by Edward Lord Stafford, and now in the Possession of Gustavus Brander, Esq.

The Health & Beauty Benefits of Vegan Cheese: pg 103
Vegetarian Journal: *Guide to Vegan Cheese, Yogurt, and Other Non-Dairy Product Alternatives* (Nov/Dec 2000, Author: Reed Mangels, PhD, RD

Scallion genus – pg 105
Scallions: United States Department of Agriculture, Germplasm Resources Information Network: *Allium chinense G. Don* (Jun 3 2009)
Health & Beauty Benefits of Rice – pg 105
Scientific Paper from the School of Medical Sciences "Edith Cowan University, Western Australia" – : *Rice as a Source of Fibre* (Nov 21 2013), Author: Binosha Fernando

Pad Thai voted No. 5 dish on CNN Online Poll – pg 106
Website: http://travel.cnn.com/explorations/eat/readers-choice-worlds-50-most-delicious-foods-012321 *Your pick: World's 50 best foods* (Sept 7 2012), Author: Tim Cheung
History of Pad Thai – pg 106
Magazine Article in Gastronomica The Journal of Food Studies: *Finding Pad Thai* (Winter 2009 issue), Author: Alexandra Greeley

Health & Beauty Benefits of Tamarind – pg 107
Scientific Paper from Purdue University, Horticulture and Landscape Architecture: *Tamarind Fruits of warm climates* (1987, Miami, FL), Author: Julia F. Morton, PhD
Scientific Paper from Department of Nutrition and Dietetics, Concordia College, Moorhead, MN: *Exploring the Nutritional Benefits of the Tamarind Pod* (2011) by Kate Monger PhD

History of Palak Paneer – pg 108
Book: *Curry: A Tale of Cooks and Conquerors* (May 1 2007), Author: Lizzie Collingham

Health & Beauty Benefits of Pine Nuts – pg 109
Book: *The World's Healthiest Food* (1996), Authors: Anne Marshall, Carolyn Kelly

History of Pineapple Fried Rice – pg 111
Thesis from the National University of Singapore: *What is Thai cuisine? Thai culinary identity construction from the rise of the Bangkok dynasty to its revival* (July 2 2009), Author: Panu Wongcha-Um

Potatoes are happy food – pg 112
Scientific Paper: *Brain serotonin: Increase following ingestion of carbohydrate diet* (Dec 3 1971), Authors: Fernstrom, J.D. and R.J. Wurtman

Why potatoes are so popular in Irish food – pg 113
Book: *The Great Irish Famine* (Feb 2002), Author: Christine Kinealy

History of Ratatouille – pg 114
Book: *The Oxford Companion to Food* (Oct 15 2006), Author: Alan Davidson

Health & Beauty Benefits of Zucchini – pg 115

Book: *The World's Healthiest Food* (1996), Authors: Anne Marshall, Carolyn Kelly
Squash, Summer condensed and retrieved from World's Healthiest Foods http://www.whfoods.com

Red bells have the most nutrients – pg 122
Book: *The Beauty Detox Solution* (2011), Author: Kimberly Snyder, C.N.
Health & Beauty Benefits of Bell Peppers – pg 122
Bell Peppers condensed and retrieved from World's Healthiest Foods http://www.whfoods.com
University of Illinois Extension: *Watch Your Garden Grow Peppers*
Different names for Stuffed Peppers – pg 122
Book: *Miss Parloa's Kitchen Companion* – 19th edition (1887), Author: Maria Parloa
Health & Beauty Benefits of Raw Apple Cider Vinegar – pg 123
Book: *The Beauty Detox Solution* (2011), Author: Kimberly Snyder, C.N.

History of Biryani – pg 125
Magazine Article in India Currents Magazine: *Tracing the History of Biryani* (May 26 2011), Author: Malar Gandhi

How chilies were used to preserve before refrigeration – pg 126
Scientific Paper: *Why some like it hot: Spices are nature's meds* (Nov 11 2005), Author: Roach, J. retrievef from website:
http://news.nationalgeographic.com/news/2005/11/1111_051111_spicy_medicine.html

Health Benefits of Bananas – pg 134
Bananas condensed and retrieved from World's Healthiest Foods http://www.whfoods.com
Book: *The World's Healthiest Food* (1996), Authors: Anne Marshall, Carolyn Kelly
Ripe Bananas are alkaline forming – pg 134
Book: *The Beauty Detox Solution* (2011), Author: Kimberly Snyder, C.N.

Health Benefits of Chocolate (Dark) – pg 136
Study presented at the 247th National Meeting & Exposition of the American Chemical Society (ACS)
Published March 19, 2014, in Medicine Net March 18, 2014, in TIME March 17, 2014
 J Cereb Blood Flow Metab. 2010 Dec;30(12):1951-61.
GreenMedInfo.com, Chocolate Research

Using a Non-Stick Skillet – pg 139
Dangers of PFOA: Article: EPA *EPA Seeking PFOA Reductions*, (Jan 25 2006), Author: Enesta Jones
Website:
http://yosemite.epa.gov/opa/admpress.nsf/68b5f2d54f3eefd28525701500517fbf/fd1cb3a075697aa485257101006afbb9!OpenDocument
Product Ecolution® non-stick skillet – available online at http://www.amazon.com

Health Benefits of Mangoes – pg 140
Scientific Research published in ScienceDaily:. *Mango effective in preventing, stopping certain colon, breast cancer cells, food scientists find* (January 12 2010) Author: Kathleen Philips PhD Website:
http://www.sciencedaily.com/releases/2010/01/100111154926.htm
Beauty Benefits of Mangoes – pg 140
Book: *The World's Healthiest Food* (1996), Authors: Anne Marshall, Carolyn Kelly

Health & Beauty Benefits of Morning Must Have Bars – pg 142
"Low in fat" results derived from Website: http://www.calorieking.com
"Beautify you" information condensed from Book: *The Beauty Detox Solution* (2011), Author: Kimberly Snyder, C.N.
"Happy Foods" information condensed from Book: *The Happy Food: Mood Lifting Recipes* (Dec 15 2013), Author: Donna E. Pickels
"Improves Your Immune System" condensed and retrieved from World's Healthiest Foods http://www.whfoods.com
"Benefits Of Consuming Raw Seeds And Nuts" – British Medical Journal Scientific Paper: *Frequent Nut Consumption And Risk Of Coronary Heart Disease In Women: Prospective Cohort Study* (Nov 14 1998), Authors: Frank B Hu, RA, Meir J Stampfer, professor and Walter C Willett PhD, professor
"Prevent Constipation with Psyllium Husk and Flax Seeds" – Book: *YOU: On A Diet Revised Edition: The Owner's Manual for Waist Management* (2009), Authors: Dr. Michael F. Roizen and Dr. Mehmet C. Oz.
"High in Protein" – condensed and retrieved from World's Healthiest Foods http://www.whfoods.com
"Detox you Everyday" information condensed from Book: *The Beauty Detox Solution* (2011), Author: Kimberly Snyder, C.N.
"Benefits of Coconut Oil" – Book: *Alzheimer's Disease: What If There Was a Cure?* (Oct 31 2011), Author: Mary T. Newport

Orange is a berry – pg 143
Merriam Webster Dictionary definition of *hesperidium – a berry (as an orange or lime) having a leathery rind*
Health & Beauty Benefits of Oranges – pg 143
Oranges condensed and retrieved from World's Healthiest Foods http://www.whfoods.com

Healthy Juice Elixirs & Their Benefits – my Mother's Wisdom – pg 152

These come from my great grandmother who passed them down to my grandmother who passed the recipes down to my mother but I double checked them with an Ayurvedic manual and they checked out!
Book: *Ayurveda, The Science of Self-Healing* (1984), Author: Dr. Vasant Lad

Health & Beauty Benefits of Cilantro – pg 156
Book: *Healing Herbs: The Ultimate Guide to the Curative Power of Nature's Medicines* (1995), Author: Michael Castleman (reviewed by Medical Reviewer: Sheldon Saul Hendler, M.D., PhD., Biochemist, Researcher and Assistant Clinical Professor at the University of California, San Diego.

Health & Beauty Benefits of Sauerkraut – pg 157
Website: http://www.mercola.org
Book: *The Beauty Detox Solution* (2011), Author: Kimberly Snyder, C.N.
Book: *Wild Fermentation Book* (2003) Author: Sandor Katz
Scientific Paper: Green Med Info: *Probiotics-February 24, 2011*
Scientific Journal: The British Journal of Nutrition *July 2010;104(2):227-32*

A Simple Detox Protocol using Cilantro – pg 160
Adapted this from Dr. Klinghardt's Neurotoxin protocol which has all the details Website:
http://www.klinghardtacademy.com/images/stories/neurotoxin/NeurotoxinProtocol_Jan06.pdf

Health & Beauty Benefits of TVP – pg 161
Scientific Paper by Agriculture and Consumer Protection: *Isolated Soy Protein in New Protein Foods* (1985), Authors: Kolar C.W., S.H. Richert, C.D. Decker, F.H. Steinke and R.J. Van der Zanden, A.M. Altschul and H.L. Wilke eds.
Soybeans condensed and retrieved from World's Healthiest Foods http://www.whfoods.com

Let's Talk About Ayurveda – pg 171
Book: *Ayurveda, The Science of Self-Healing* (1984), Author: Dr. Vasant Lad
Book: *Ayurvedic Yoga Therapy" (2007),* Author: Mukunda Stiles
Book: *Ayurvedic Manual – Ancient Hindu Medicine For Better Health* (1999), Author: Dr. Jose Maria Gomez, M.D.

Chakra Eating – pg 183
Article: *Eating for Your Chakras*, Author: Dr. Chaudhary, Director of Neurology at Wellspring Health in Scripps Memorial Hospital
Book: *Chakra Foods for Optimum Health: A Guide to the Foods that can Improve Your Energy, Inspire Creative Changes, Open Your Heart, and Heal Body, Mind, and Spirit* (Mar 1 2009), Author: Deanna Minich, PhD, CN
Article: *Healing From The Heart*, Author: Timothy Pope
Website: http://www.healingfromtheheart.co.uk

Other Products by Neeta Sanders and Soul2Soul Educare

Books

Create Divine Magic in Your Daily Life – Book and CD

What if you could find any lost object? What if you could clear all the traffic, just by singing a song? What if all your computer problems could be fixed, with a snap of a finger? Literally! What if you never had to go to the doctor again? What if you could cure insomnia without a sleeping aid? These are just some of the questions this book will address. There are myriads of different day to day problems which can be solved with "Create Divine Magic in your Daily Life". The knowledge in this book will help you lead a life filled with ease, happiness and perfection. The companion CD (sold separately) is full of helpful visualization techniques and powerful prayers, chants and songs which will guide you in creating magic for you and those around you.

Audio CDs

Journey to God – A Musical Tale of Creation, Karma, Cause & Consequence

- Great tool for developing right-brained creativity for all ages
- Helps children diagnosed with ADD & ADHD
- In this 1 hour narrated tale filled with uplifting songs, your children will learn to deal with life issues including racism, bullying, vegetarianism, death, reincarnation, desires, materialism, mental impressions, and the effect of violent T.V and video games. Adults can also benefit from this CD with valuable life lessons including unity, having a prosperous family, dealing with death, and attaining ultimate freedom from the life cycle. Come take this journey with your children, and enjoy exploring spirituality and character building in a fun and joyous way.

Meditation for Beginners

- Do you want to meditate? Are you unsure of where to start? This hour-long guided meditation will provide a simple step-by-step method in which to silence your mind and connect with your inner self. There is also a detailed explanation on "Why Meditation is important". The relaxation techniques taught in this CD can also help you to cope with the stresses of everyday life.

Visualization Adventure Meditations for Children

- These meditations will transport you to the far reaches of the earth, and beyond! You'll meet fairies, aliens, and other wonderful creatures as you traverse forests, deserts, mountains, space, and even take a deep-sea dive. These Visualizations can be anything you want them to be – a unique learning experience, a matchless way to travel, and even a fun right-brained activity for all ages.

Healing Meditations

- Do you feel tired all the time? Are you sick of going to the Doctor?
  Would you like to heal a particular illness?
  Are you ready to live a life of complete well-being?
  If you answered yes to any of the above questions, then this CD set is for you. This Healing Meditations 2-CD set can help you attain perfect wellness in body, mind and spirit. Whether you are looking for a specific healing, a general chakra cleansing, or even a sound healing, there is something here just for you.

Spiritual Nursery Rhymes

- This Audio CD revisits classic nursery rhymes with new uplifting and spiritual lyrics set to musical styles including polka, jungle beats, bluegrass, classical, blues, new age, rock, and pop.
- Fun for both kids and adults! Kids will enjoy dancing, playing and singing along to these popular tunes!
- Help your children form a strong connection with the Divine with these heartfelt nursery rhymes.

All of the above are available on www.amazon.com
or can be ordered by visiting:
Neeta Sanders' Website:
www.soul2souleducare.com or www.soul2souleducare.org

Index